April ... Nixon in th... d ever get o... es, the answer is, we only taped ... ecurity information. All other information is scrapped, never transcribed. Get the point? That's what I want you to remember. You never want to be in a position to say the President taped somebody.'

This conversation led to Erlichman's mention of impeachment. Nixon said, 'I slept a little on that and it's good for John to look at it that way, but, my God, what the hell have we done to be impeached?'

THE ENDS OF POWER

H. R. HALDEMAN
with
Joseph DiMona

STAR

A STAR BOOK

published by
the Paperback Division of
W. H. ALLEN & Co. Ltd

A Star Book
Published in 1978
by the Paperback Division of
W. H. Allen & Co. Ltd
A Howard and Wyndham Company
44 Hill Street, London W1X 8LB

First published in Great Britain by
Sidgwick and Jackson Limited, 1978

THE PHOTOGRAPHS
The first ten: Official White House photographs
The last three: H. R. Haldeman

Printed in Great Britain by
Hunt Barnard Printing Ltd.,
Aylesbury, Bucks

ISBN 0 352 30324 7

To Jo, who has, for over thirty years, and most especially for the last four, shown me the very real and wonderful meaning of the phrase 'truly whole'; to Dad, who missed the glory and was spared the agony; to Non, Susan, Hank, Peter and Ann; and to the rest who make up that 'whole' which is my beloved family.

AN APPRECIATION

To the millions of Americans who have 'kept the faith' through a long and difficult struggle; especially so many wonderful personal friends and family.

To the outstanding members of the White House Staff with whom I had the real privilege and pleasure of serving, most particularly to Larry Higby, my 'strong right arm' and devoted friend through it all.

To Joseph DiMona, whose literary skill brought the whole story together.

And to President Nixon, who made possible what was, despite its ending, the mountain-top experience of my life.

CONTENTS

AUTHOR'S NOTE

This is not the book I set out to write after leaving the White House and returning to California in 1973. In between the legal investigations; Grand Jury hearings; Congressional inquiries; civil suits; indictment, trial and appeals; I spent whatever time I could working on an overall effort to try to put together all of my memories of the Nixon White House years – good, bad, and otherwise – in a complete memoir of that exhilarating and tragic period of my life, and the life of the nation.

Many others were writing the Watergate story, albeit from the other side, and I felt that my greatest contribution would be in the area of telling the *rest* of the Nixon story rather than rehashing Watergate one more time. There was a gnawing concern, though, because as the various Watergate stories came out in print I saw they were not really covering the whole story. And certainly not with any insight or knowledge of what went on at my level and the President's in the White House.

I hoped, and assumed, that this void would be filled by the Nixon-Frost television interviews in the Spring of 1977 when President Nixon would finally have the opportunity to talk directly to the American people and the world. But after the Frost series was over, I realised that not only had my hopes been unrealised, but the net effect had been to distort and confuse the issue even further. I still don't know whether this was the result of the questions, the answers, or the cutting process. But it was the result.

I decided then and there to put aside my long-range effort and to turn specifically to the true story behind Watergate. I now believe that a clearer understanding of that tragedy is an essential prerequisite to any valid overall view of the Nixon Presidency.

I do this reluctantly because it necessitates concentrating on the one overwhelming failure of the Nixon Presidency, when I would much prefer to write about its many great accomplishments. Most of what is here I would like to ignore and forget. Almost all of what I would like to say is not here.

Because Watergate is the story of a disaster without parallel in Presidential history, it is essentially a negative story. Because Watergate was a result – and an expression – of the dark side of President Nixon, it is obvious that a book on Watergate will reflect this, rather than the far more numerous and substantively more significant expressions of the light side.

There is no excuse for Watergate. It is inexcusable in every phase and aspect. But I hope I can provide explanations that will clear up many of the continuing mysteries, and also to point out new facts about other mysteries that still remain.

This is by no means the whole story, even of Watergate. That would take volumes. The public record alone covers many thousands of pages and scores of books. It is, instead, my selection of the significant (often unknown, despite all that has already been published) portions that are needed to achieve an overall understanding of what lay behind Watergate, and what really happened. It is my best effort to bring together what I know at first-hand with what I have learned from others, and then to draw some conclusions.

In several areas, such as the Democratic Party Trap Theory or the Cienfuegos and Russo-Chinese confrontations, I had to rely upon expert sources for information I did not have at the time.

Writing this book has been very difficult for me. After more than four years of being the subject of investigation and criminal prosecution, my natural tendency is to present my own defence. And after even more years of the closest possible association with President Nixon, a greater tendency is to try to present him and his thoughts and actions in the best possible light. That was the essence of my job at the White House and it is still my strong personal inclination.

I have been accused of blind loyalty to President Nixon – both during and since my White House years. I plead guilty to the loyalty, but not to the blindness. My loyalty was, and is, based on a clear recognition of both great virtues and great faults in the man I served. On balance, there has never been any question in my mind as to the validity of that loyalty.

There are many others with a similar feeling who will be deeply disturbed by this book because it deals with so many of the 'bads' and so few of the 'goods'. They will argue, with good reason, that the bads have already been so thoroughly reviewed that no repetition or expansion can serve any useful purpose. And they will feel that by my approach I am falling into the trap of the 'enemy' and confirming what they have all been saying.

That is not my intent, and I trust it will not be the result. I believe that the honest and fair-minded reader of this book, regardless of his previous convictions or doubts about Watergate, and all of us that were drawn into it, will find some help here in trying to understand what really did happen, and why. There is no way to accomplish this without admitting and dealing with many grievous errors.

I feel as loyal today to the President I served as I ever have, and I honestly believe this book to be a valuable service to and demonstration of that loyalty.

I have been persuaded, however, that the cause of truth and the interests of history are best served by facing the negative and unpleasant factors that are also a part of the whole picture and in attempting to present them in context with the more positive side on which I have always concentrated.

To do this, I had to go through the mental exercise of developing what I called the 'devil's theory' of the Watergate case. I forced myself to look at the worst possible interpretation of every factor, instead of the best, and to try to piece the whole picture together from that viewpoint. In doing this, I did not accept any conclusion or assumption that was not consistent with what I knew to be true. I simply looked at all of those things in which there was any doubt in the worst possible way, and then worked back from there to a point of reasonable balance.

I will readily admit that this is exactly and totally the opposite approach from that which I had unwaveringly taken to this point. Since the story deals with many people whom I know well and have worked with closely, it is hard to accept this reverse approach, but I believe it has been a constructive enterprise.

One of the key functions of my collaborator, Joseph DiMona, in the preparation of this book has been to keep me on this track, to challenge all my assertions and prohibit me from sticking to self-satisfying but perhaps self-deluding conclusions.

Obviously, some of us did something wrong. In my view, all of us at the White House involved in Watergate did a lot of things wrong. Some criminal, some harmless, some wilful, some accidental, some shrewdly calculated, some stupidly blundered, but each wrong. By trying to review what happened from my vantage point, I hope I will make a contribution to the eventual understanding of one of the great mysteries of American history.

In trying to understand Watergate, it is essential to understand a very basic truth about the White House. By definition almost, only crises come to the White House. Only those things that cannot be handled at a lower level even reach the White House. The President and his staff deal not with both high and low matters, but with high and higher, and sometimes highest. Watergate was initially a low level problem and thus was not dealt with at the senior level of the White House until it escalated externally into a high concern.

One of the major distortions inevitable in this book, and highly regrettable to me, is the enormous attention given to the minute aspects of things related to Watergate, and the resultant almost ignoring of what we were really doing, and thinking, and worrying about in those days. Until March of 1973, when we really did focus in on Watergate and started spending an enormous amount of time and worry on that one subject for about six weeks, it was never at any time a principal subject of thought, discussion, or action.

I have tried to give some glimmer of some of the other things that were our very real concerns and interests. Foremost among them, and never mentioned, because it is routine, was our main job of simply the day-to-day running of the government – a more than full-time task in itself. The normal flow of business, problems, decisions, new initiatives went on with no decrease.

On top of that, Watergate took place in the period in which the most intensive and at many times most exasperating efforts were underway to bring the Vietnam War to an end. It was the right time after the spectacular and grueling trips to China and Russia had just been completed, and all the follow-up was underway. It was the time that the development of the far-reaching reorganisation of the Executive Branch was being conceived and fleshed out. It was the time that the basic policy and legislative initiatives of the second term were being planned, researched, revised, tested, and prepared for presentation and implementation.

In addition to all of this – the normal work flow, in itself overwhelming, and the tremendous extras of Vietnam peace, summit follow-ups, reorganisation, and second-term initiatives – we were in the midst of the campaign for re-election with the party conventions, the election campaign itself, and then the inaugural.

In its coverage of the Watergate action and activity prior to March 1973, this book is almost solely concerned with only about ten days out of a time period of more than 250 days, from June 1972 through February 1973. In other words, I have not covered anything we were doing or thinking on 96 per cent of the days in this time period. And even on those ten days in which I do tell about our Watergate activities, I am omitting at least 90 per cent of what we actually did throughout each day because it was not concerned with Watergate.

The reason for all these statistics is to try to make the point that Watergate is *not* the story of the Nixon Presidancy – even in the so-called Watergate period. I wish there were space to give at least a listing of all the other meetings, conversations, problems, trips, decisions, disasters and triumphs that took place during this period.

In my opening statement to the Ervin Committee I mentioned that the eye of a fly can appear terrifying when viewed through a powerful microscope. Unfortunately, this book is turning a very powerful microscope on to the eye of this particular fly, and it does indeed appear terrifying. In the long run, and to obtain a valid viewpoint, it must be properly weighed in its complete context. But for this book, we will concentrate instead on the microscope view.

A word of explanation about the direct quotations from the President, and others, as they appear here. They are derived from many sources. Some are from the transcripts (published and unpublished) of the White House tapes. Some are from the public record of speeches or other statements. Some are reconstructed from my notes made at the time. And many are simply my best effort to reconstruct what was said on the basis of my memory, review of related material and events, and the later reports of others. While I cannot, therefore, claim verbatim accuracy for these quotations, I do believe they are reasonably reconstructed reports of what was said.

I have not always identified, as such, those quotes that come directly from the tape transcripts because, in many cases, I believe them to be no more accurate representations of what was said than my reconstructions by other means. The transcripts are not flawless either.

In some cases during the course of the book, I have drawn on information that has come to my attention by various means – usually long after the action took place. It is, therefore, not first-hand knowledge, but I felt it was important to a complete understanding of the subject. I am deeply indebted to my collaborator, Joseph DiMona, for his extensive research work which was primarily responsible for producing this valuable additional material.

My report of certain events and my conclusions as to reasons for them will, of necessity, differ from those of others who were equally involved and close to the scene. Some of these variations will be enormous, some only matters of detail. If all the facts were clear and simple, there would be no Watergate mystery, and we would all agree exactly as to what happened and why. The final conclusions can only be drawn when all the views are in and can be weighed against each other, against the known facts, and against the best judgements of logic and reason. This time may never come, but I hope this book is a contribution towards that objective.

I am neither pleased nor proud to be leaving this particular literary heritage to my sons and daughters. I hope someday to have the ability and opportunity to tell the rest of the story of the Nixon Presidency as I saw it – the major part, the significant part, with the pluses and minuses in their real perspective instead of grossly distorted by the concentration on one totally negative area which this current effort has required.

I hope this study of Watergate and its insights into what lay behind it will enable you better to understand how it could have happened, and perhaps to forgive those of us who made some terrible mistakes.

H. R. Haldeman

FOREWORD

Four weeks after the first inaugural of Richard Nixon as President of the United States, I left Washington for a very special occasion. I had been on the road throughout the campaign of 1968, and then in New York for the transition period, and had seen very little of my family for nearly a year. They didn't move to Washington until later in 1969.

But February 19, 1969, was our twentieth wedding anniversary and I was on my way home to Los Angeles to celebrate with Jo and a few close friends.

Recognising the dual significance of that particular year, Jo had arranged a very thoughtful surprise for her anniversary gift to me. Unbeknownst to me, she had made arrangement through the Presidential Appointments Secretary, Dwight Chapin, to have the newly inaugurated President inscribe in his own hand a segment from his inaugural address that Jo knew was especially meaningful to me. This he had done on beautiful parchment-like paper embossed with the Presidential seal, and Jo had had it framed. It hangs today on the wall of my study.

This accompanied Jo's own contribution, a beautiful scrapbook she had made of the inaugural – stamped in gold on the cover with the words 'Truly Whole'. The sentence from the Nixon address which included that phrase was, 'Until he has been part of a cause larger than himself, no man is truly whole'. These words summed up the reason for my desire to serve President Nixon and my enormous satisfaction in having the opportunity to do so.

But what was the 'cause larger than himself' that I served? The automatic assumption of even those as close to me as my wife was that it was the President of the United States, and the programmes and policies he represented. I guess maybe that is what I would have said too, if I had been asked the question when I was at the White House. But if I really had thought it through, and I since have, I would have answered quite differently.

My 'cause' was neither the Presidency, as an institution, nor the man, Richard Nixon. It was the unique combination of the two: President Nixon. I doubt I would have ever served any other man in the office of the President. And I doubt I would have ever served Richard Nixon except in his quest for and service in that office. It was neither the office nor the man, but the two together that captured my loyalty, dedication and energy.

I am not a politician. I had no real interest in politics, and no participation, until I volunteered for a Nixon campaign. And I am no worshipper of Richard Nixon. I had no interest in working with him except in his political endeavours. Our paths parted completely when he was out of office and not seeking office.

While working with Richard Nixon on and off over the past twenty years, and intensely for a cumulative total of more than seven of those years, I gained a tremendous appreciation and respect for the greatness in him – and a strong sense of what he could accomplish for this country and for a stable world peace.

I strongly felt that whatever there was that I didn't like or didn't agree with was so overwhelmingly over-ridden by the potential for good that it was well worth the effort to work with both the good and the bad.

I did not become blinded to the dark spots – but I also did not just give up because of them. I know they were relatively unimportant even though they did create great problems for me and for others.

I saw my mission and my opportunity as unique. I felt I could play a very special role in what I firmly believed would be a drama of enormous success and accomplishment. And I was willing to accept the accompanying drawbacks as a necessary price to be paid.

I tried to submerge myself totally to the cause – and to work behind the scenes where I felt I could be most effective. I had no interest in power for myself – and gave no thought to the subject. I simply exercised the power which was an integral part of my position in the way and for the purpose which I felt I would do the most good for President Nixon.

My own satisfaction was gained not from any personal power or glory but from my secure knowledge of the vital part I played in the day-to-day development and exercise of the Presidential powers by President Nixon. I knew, and few others even suspected, that I was making a very real and constructive contribution. I was little concerned about the frequent misrepresentation or misinterpretation of my role or my contribution. What others thought didn't really matter so long as I knew the truth was positive, and I felt sure it was. I did not represent the Administration publicly and did not want to.

My effectiveness was dependent to a great degree on my ability to work with the President and within the Administration – to get things done, or prevent things from being done, accountable directly to the President, leaving public explanation to others. And that's how a Presidential aide should and must work. Once he becomes a public figure, or a public issue, in his own right, his real effectiveness is greatly reduced, if not eliminated.

Every President is different – and each Presidential staff should be different – to meet its own unique requirements. No one outside can adequately prescribe or control these requirements.

As we shall see, Watergate did not disprove this thesis, but was the exception that proved the rule.

Book I

THIS SIDE OF THE 'SMOKING GUN'

1

June 17, 1972, a Saturday afternoon in Key Biscayne, Florida. I stretched and yawned. Across the terrace of our villa at the Key Biscayne Hotel, Larry Higby, my young assistant, read a book, shielding his eyes with one hand from the glare of the sun.

It was the second day of a long lazy weekend in this Florida resort. Two weeks ago I had returned with President Richard Nixon from Moscow where he had worked out the beginnings of the first meaningful disarmament agreement with the Soviets in this century, and had begun a new policy, which was being described as 'détente', that could reverse twenty-seven years of cold war. But the conference in Moscow – despite the allure of détente – had been a nonstop round of tough negotiating sessions on every subject from wheat to missiles.

The President needed a rest and he flew south on June 16 with a few staff members.

It promised to be a unique weekend – the only one in recent memory in which I would have little real work to do. For the first time, Nixon had not gone directly to his Key Biscayne home from which he could – and did – telephone me constantly on matters large or small. Instead, Air Force One had dropped him off in the Bahamas where he went to Walker's Cay, owned by one of his friends, Robert Abplanalp, the aerosol-valve millionaire.

Nixon's critics would later point to the coincidence of that one date on which he chose to be out of the country for a weekend.

At 2.30 a.m., June 17, while Nixon slept in a luxurious private home in the Caribbean, three Cubans, one Italian-American who everyone thought was Cuban, and a man named James McCord, had been apprehended in the

Democratic National Committee Headquarters in the Watergate complex in Washington, outfitted with gloves, flashlights, sophisticated burglary tools, and electronic wiretapping equipment. Now, almost fifteen hours later, none of this was known to those of us who were enjoying our holiday in Florida, nor to Nixon at Walker's Cay.

Higby saw a familiar figure in bathing trunks walking towards us on the beach, trailing a long white paper in one hand. 'Hey, look,' said Higby, 'Old Whaleboat.'

The man approaching was Ron Ziegler, the President's Press Secretary, whose Signal Corps code name was 'Whaleboat', a name which drove the Californian up the wall. Almost his first act in the White House had been to call the Signal Corps and demand that he be issued a more suitable designation. To the delight of the White House staff, I had quietly instructed the Signal Corps to stand firm. It was a private joke we played on Ron, whose constant preoccupation with his 'image' always amused us.

Ziegler handed me the sheet of paper. I saw it was wire service copy. The news bulletin said that five men had been caught breaking into the Democratic National Committee Headquarters in Washington with electronic equipment.

The news item was jarring, almost comical, to me. Watergate historians have always supposed that the heavens fell when those in the President's party in Florida learned the break-in had been discovered. Quite the reverse was true. My immediate reaction was to smile. Wiretap the Democratic National Committee? For what? The idea was ludicrous.

Not that I was all that horrified at the idea of wiretapping or bugging in general. Ever since a conversation with J. Edgar Hoover in New York's Hotel Pierre in 1968, which revealed the extent of the political wiretapping by President Lyndon B. Johnson, I had felt no instinctive aversion to such bugging by Republicans. In fact, as I knew very well, President Richard Nixon had used wiretapping in his first term in his search for the identity of government employees – and others – who leaked security information. I had agreed with that action, and helped execute it.

Not only was I fully aware of the Nixon Administration's use of wire tapping, but I knew that practice had been much more extensively used in earlier administrations, particularly that of President Kennedy. Justice Department statistics confirm this. And even before entering the government, I was very much aware, through newspaper and magazine articles, of the widespread use of wiretapping and bugging in business espionage. I certainly did not regard the practice as an unheard-of evil.

But wiretappers invading the Democratic National Committee Headquarters? They couldn't be our people, because nothing was to be gained by bugging the D.N.C. Headquarters. This was June 17, 1972. Nixon was leading Senator George McGovern, his likely Democratic rival, by nineteen points in the Gallup Poll – an enormous, indeed unprecedented, lead at that stage of a Presidential campaign. McGovern was the darling of the militant antiwar youth who had engineered a series of primary victories for him, culminating in California. But he was by far the weakest nationwide candidate that the Democrats could nominate. So Nixon didn't need political information to defeat him.

And beyond that fact, every Washington insider knew that the D.N.C. was only a shell. Useful political information could be found only in a candidate's office, not in the office of a ceremonial 'front' organisation such as the D.N.C. So why?

I tried to visualise the scene: a darkened political office, burglars prowling, flashlights wavering. Whose operation did that sound like?

This led me to my second reaction: 'Good Lord,' I thought, 'they've caught Chuck Colson.'

It was a chilling thought. If Charles Colson was involved, he could very well have been on one of his projects for the President of the United States.

Chuck Colson had become the President's personal 'hit man'; his impresario of 'hard ball' politics. I had been caught in the middle of most of these, as complaints thundered in about 'Wildman' Colson either crashing arrogantly, or sneaking silently, through political empires supposedly controlled by top White House staffers such as Domestic Counselor John Ehrlichman or Cabinet Officers such as Attorney General John Mitchell. Colson cared not who complained. Nixon, he said, was his only boss. And Nixon was behind him all the way on projects ranging from his long-dreamed-of hope of catching Senator Teddy Kennedy in bed with a woman not his wife, to more serious struggles such as the I.T.T. anti-trust 'scandal'.

Colson had signed up an ex-C.I.A. agent named Howard Hunt to work for him and thereafter became very secretive about his exploits in the name of Nixon. Years later I heard of such wild schemes as the proposed fire bombing of a politically liberal foundation (Brookings) in order to retrieve a document Nixon wanted; feeding LSD to an anti-Nixon commentator (Jack Anderson) before he went on television; and breaking into the offices of a newspaperman (Hank Greenspun) who was supposed to have documents from Howard Hughes that revealed certain secrets about Nixon.

But Colson's 'black' projects were so widely rumoured around the White House that I believe almost every White House staffer thought of his name the minute they heard the news of Watergate. Beside me on the beach, Higby said it aloud. 'I'll bet they're Colson's gunners.'

'Hell,' said Ziegler. Then, 'Should I inform the President?'

I thought it over. John Ehrlichman was in Washington. The break-in had happened almost fifteen hours ago. If any real problem had surfaced he would have telephoned me by now. But still . . .

Ziegler was waiting, shuffling his feet in the sand. I saw behind him a boy in blue trunks throw a frisbee. It sailed, then skidded in the sky before plummeting into outstretched hands. I said, 'Ehrlichman's in Washington and he hasn't contacted me. So I don't think there's anything to worry the President about.'

Ziegler said O.K., and walked off with a promise to alert me if any more news came over the wires. None did. And the telephone didn't ring from Washington all that Saturday.

I went in to get dressed for dinner. But an hour later that item about the break-in still needled my mind. What on earth were those burglars up to? If they did turn out to be White House or C.R.P. (Committee to Re-elect the President) sponsored, we were in for some real problems, no matter what their motive.

I relaxed. Whatever the problems, if any, I felt I could handle them. Four years as Chief-of-Staff to a man like Nixon had toughened me, I believed, for anything. And if I somehow slipped, the most astute politician in the nation, Richard Nixon, would step into the breach.

At that point I believed Nixon could accomplish almost anything. In fact, this was Nixon's year. In the past six months he had not only begun the disarmament talks with the Soviet Union, he had dramatically reopened relations with China and – finally – he was about to end the crippling, suicidal Vietnam War.

On June 17, 1972, Richard Nixon was at the peak of his powers, a certain winner in the November election.

Nothing could hurt him now.

Larry Higby and I took my wife, Jo, to a restaurant that featured delicious stone crabs. Driving back to the hotel, the night air was soft. Last month I had been in Moscow, among the old spired battlements of the Kremlin. Now I was in Florida at a beautiful resort.

Working for Nixon, a complex and sometimes unfathomable President, had its unique problems, but the excitement and sense of accomplishment of the job made it all worthwhile.

No messages when I returned to the hotel. No telephone call from Ehrlichman.

Richard Nixon, sipping coffee, walked through his kitchen and saw a *New York Times* on the counter. Idly, he thumbed through it. It was Sunday, June 18, the day after the burglary. On page 30 of the *Times*, Nixon stopped. A news story about the break-in appeared there.

Nixon had decided to return to his Key Biscayne home that morning. He made his usual telephone call to me in order to catch up on any new developments – most particularly the news item.

I had awakened refreshed, realising happily that the whole night had passed without word from anyone in Washington. And now my suspicion of an involvement of Chuck Colson (and, therefore, Nixon) in Watergate was dissolved completely when I spoke to Nixon. The President wasn't concerned at all by the break-in. In fact, he was amused. 'What's the crazy item about the D.N.C., Bob?' I told him I hadn't heard anything from Washington yet. Nixon said, 'Damndest thing I ever heard of. Why would anyone break into a National Committee Headquarters? Nothing but crap in there. The real stuff is in the candidate's headquarter's, not the Committee's.' He paused. 'Track down Magruder and see what he knows about it.'

Jeb Magruder, a 38-year-old public relations specialist, was 'our man at the Committee to Re-elect the President'. At the White House, where he previously had been employed, I had found him eager but unreliable. Under constant pressure from me to produce, he would furnish massive memos designed to please the President's ever-present urge to mount a P.R. initiative to kick back at his enemies in the outside world. But on closer inspection, they generally turned out to be flights of fantasy without much possibility of Magruder carrying them out.

President Nixon clearly recognised his need for effective public relations, and constantly pushed me to get something going. I had brought Magruder into the White House specifically to help fill this need. When the Committee to Re-elect the President was first being staffed, I saw a chance to reassign him to a position that was less demanding and better suited to him. At the No. 2 post of C.R.P., he simply would be following the orders of a strong leader, John Mitchell, who would be moving over from Attorney General to Campaign Chairman.

Then towards the end of the confirmation hearings for Richard Kleindienst as Mitchell's successor as Attorney General, the I.T.T. scandal surfaced with its politically explosive charge that in exchange for a $400,000 political contribution to the Republican Party, John Mitchell's Justice Department had made a favourable settlement of an anti-trust case against the multi-national corporation, Kleindienst demanded the hearings be reopened so he could deny the charges.

In 1977, Richard Nixon said that the secret story of Watergate is that it would never have happened if not for Martha Mitchell's illness – and the resultant diversion of John Mitchell's attention.

This is only partly true because those Kleindienst Hearings also took up much of Mitchell's time and attention. There was no doubt that Mitchell was preoccupied by Martha's problems in those days. He was actually afraid she might jump off the balcony and would not allow her to be left alone. I have been at meetings where Mitchell would receive a call that whoever was then with Martha had to leave, and Mitchell would quit the meeting – no matter how important – in order to rush home and be with his wife.

I don't know what her medical problem was, but I do know she was a character. I was among many on her list for personal calls. She was always, for example, angling for a seat on Air Force One. (She said she was afraid to fly on any other plane.) Nixon didn't want her aboard, and I would evade the issue in one way or another. But once in a while she would phrase her request in such a way and at such a time that I couldn't say no. And, most often, she would be the life of the party on the trip. Even though a 'life of the party' was hardly what was needed on Air Force One.

Between Martha and I.T.T., Mitchell was totally unable to concentrate on his duties as Chairman of the Committee to Re-elect the President. And that meant that Magruder, the smooth-talking but weak executive I had moved to C.R.P., had been making many of the command decisions with no Mitchell to deflate his fantasies.

Well before the break-in, I made my first Watergate mistake by leaving Magruder in charge at C.R.P. without the direct and continuing supervision of John Mitchell. By failing to perceive this rather obvious result of Mitchell's serious problems with the Kleindienst nomination and the resultant I.T.T. furor and the even greater personal problems with his wife, I left the campaign committee under the actual direction of a young man whom I would never have considered qualified for that level of responsibility. Because I just didn't want to be burdened with the additional responsibility for the campaign myself, I guess I conveniently overlooked the problem and hoped Mitchell would soon take actual charge.

We could have done in the Spring of 1972 what we were forced to do in the Summer of that year when John Mitchell had to leave his C.R.P. post. We could, and should, have moved a new campaign manager in, either temporarily or permanently, to run C.R.P. as it should have been run. I think I would have strongly urged the President to do this if I had adequately assessed the seriousness of the problem at the time. It would certainly have been possible. There were several qualified alternatives including Clark MacGregor, who did take over in the Summer.

A new campaign manager would never have permitted the break-in, and there would have been no Watergate.

The White House switchboard found Magruder at the Beverly Hills Hotel in California where he and other C.R.P. executives were on a combined fund-raising expedition and holiday. As soon as Magruder started to speak, I began to worry. He was nervous and his sentences faltered. His words, when they reached me, were disturbing.

The break-in was sponsored by the C.R.P. after all. But in a special way.

'Those guys were operating on their own, Bob. They just got carried away.'

'What guys?'

'McCord. He's our security man at C.R.P. He works for Gordon Liddy.'

I thought about those names. I didn't know McCord, but Liddy was a name I recognised. John Dean, the White House legal counsel, had recommended him for a job as legal counsel at C.R.P. with a second job as head of campaign intelligence.

I had never met Liddy and I haven't to this day, but I had approved his transfer to C.R.P. I also knew that C.R.P. was supposed to have an intelligence branch and that it had accomplished virtually nothing so far. I knew this because the President kept reminding me: 'When are they going to *do* something over there?' he would ask over and over again, drumming his fingers on the desk. And after I relayed his complaint, my young aide, Gordon Strachan, who handled liaison with C.R.P., would spring into furious action, spilling out memos urging them on, all to no avail. With Mitchell diverted and Magruder in charge, things didn't always get done right at C.R.P.

I asked Magruder whether Liddy was involved in the break-in too. 'Well, I told you . . . uh . . . he was working with McCord.'

Magruder has admitted that he didn't tell me all the real facts about the break-in (such as his own involvement) in that telephone call because, he said, he assumed I knew them already. This is vintage Magruder softening of the truth. Magruder didn't tell me all the facts because he was afraid to. It's that simple. His people had been caught, a terrible mess could develop as a result, and he couldn't face telling Nixon's ferocious Chief-of-Staff what he had done.

Instead he read me a press release he had prepared for Mitchell which said that McCord was a free-lance operator and C.R.P. had no involvement in the break-in.

It sounded O.K. to me. It was accurate as far as it went to my knowledge. And it sidestepped the Liddy problem, since his name had not yet surfaced in the news story.

I hung up as quickly as I could, and tracked down John Ehrlichman by telephone to find the real story. I trusted

John whom I had known since our college days. Now the Assistant to the President for Domestic Policy, John was known for three traits: a sarcastic wit, intelligence, and a love of intrigue. But he had never lied to me – and he didn't now.

'We're in a bit of a bind on this one, Bob,' he told me. 'One of those Cubans had a cheque on his person signed by Howard Hunt.'

Hunt's name alerted me. It was the link to Colson, the man I had first suspected. In fact, Hunt was Colson's boy. If Colson was involved through Hunt, this could involve the Oval Office, too. I asked worriedly, 'Have you talked to Colson?'

'Yes, and he raised the sound level in Washington 1000 decibels. He doesn't know *anything* about Watergate, and he hasn't seen Hunt in months.'

'What do you think, John?'

'I'm afraid to speculate. If brother Colson is involved in this little jamboree, we're in for a lot of problems.'

This made me very anxious to talk to Mr Colson. I reached him and the familiar heavy voice boomed over the wires. I could see him: heavy black eyeglasses askew, powerful hand gripping the telephone as he sought to reassure me and, through me, Nixon, that he was not involved, despite the evidence pointing to Hunt. 'I used Hunt two months ago on I.T.T. – and that's it, Bob. Even then he was off my payroll.'

But Colson was worried. His voice lowered, he said, 'You gotta believe me, Bob. It wasn't me. Tell the President that. I know he'll be worried.'

'Well, what's Hunt doing in this?'

Colson told me Gordon Liddy was using Howard Hunt for projects at C.R.P., after Hunt left the White House. 'They're working together over there.'

But I persisted. 'He's not on your payroll? You're not working with him on anything? This is important, Chuck.' I was probing, hoping not to hit paydirt.

'Hell, I know it's important. More than you do,' he

said, his voice high. 'It's my life. They'll try to tie me into an absolutely idiotic break-in, and it's not right. Hunt left my office months ago, like I said . . . '

He frothed on until I hung up. I thought about the conversation. It was possible – even probable – that Colson was telling the truth. Magruder had said that Liddy at C.R.P. was the ring-leader of the break-in. He had not even mentioned Colson.

What a riddle. From Magruder I learned that Gordon Liddy and James McCord had been responsible for the break-in. From Ehrlichman I discovered that Howard Hunt was involved, and therefore Chuck Colson – and the White House – might be implicated. And from Colson I learned that Hunt was now working at C.R.P. for Liddy. Where was the truth?

But when I called the President, I relaxed again, because I found him as cool about the break-in as he had been before. Colson's name apparently never even occurred to Nixon even when I mentioned Hunt. 'It has to be some crazies over at C.R.P., Bob. That's what it was. And what does it matter? The American people will see it for what it was: a political prank. Hell, they can't take a break-in at the D.N.C. *seriously*. There's nothing there.' He paused. 'I've got some real business to go over with you. Why don't you come over tomorrow at noon?'

And that was it. I stopped worrying. Everything was under control; only my imagination had been raising spectres. And, in fact, there were no more calls from Nixon that day. The next day the President didn't even mention Watergate in our conference about campaign and other matters. On Air Force One that evening, heading north, sipping a beer in his armchair, he only smiled in boredom when I brought it up. 'Silly damn thing,' he said.

Calm, cool, even amused. What an effort that façade must have cost him. It wasn't until years later that I learned that the 'calm' Nixon had been frantically telephoning Chuck Colson himself about that 'unimportant' break-in. Calm? At one point he was so upset he threw an ashtray across the room, according to Colson. I had seen

Nixon blow up in towering rages, but never throw anything.

Why did he telephone Colson so angrily, yet hide that emotion from me and everyone else?

All I knew on Air Force One that night was that Nixon seemed relaxed. And I felt that was beneficial. Nixon had survived one of the roughest four-year terms in Presidential history before his triumphs in early 1972. Four years punctuated by Kent State, nationwide demonstrations, and mass hatreds caused by the Vietnam War. He had waded through them all to end the War.

Air Force One glided towards Washington. Nixon relaxed and gazed out of the window.

I wonder, now, what he was thinking.

I left the President's compartment and went back to my seat aft in the plane. My wife said, 'Look.' Ahead through the window could be seen the lights and monuments of Washington. The plane settled in towards Andrews Field as Jo said, 'I can't believe we had so much time together this trip. It was really great. I hope we can do it again sometime.'

June 20, 1972. A Chrysler sedan (we didn't have long sleek White House limousines, contrary to popular conception) pulled up to the kerb in front of my home in Kenwood, Maryland. Larry Higby was in the back. We drove to Chevy Chase, picked up Dwight Chapin, Presidential Appointment Secretary, and arrived at the White House, as usual, at 7.45 a.m.

On most days in the White House in the Nixon years the first man to stroll down the corridor to my office for our morning staff meeting would be Henry Kissinger. He always picked up my spirits with his humour. In deference to my 'Nazi' image he would start my day with a Teutonic welcome, 'Guten morgen, Herr Haldeman.' I'd smile and say, 'And a guten morgen to you, Heinz.'

After the routine staff conference, Ehrlichman gathered the people who would have to deal with Watergate in his office. John Mitchell arrived first, then John Dean, and eventually Richard Kleindienst, who had replaced Mitchell as Attorney General. Strangely, Mitchell looked better than I had seen him for days. He puffed on his pipe with that humorous glint in his eye that we all knew so well. I felt that was a good sign because Mitchell was now the Chairman at C.R.P., and should have been worried if there was a major crisis impending. Instead, he said, 'I don't know anything about that foolishness at the D.N.C. I do know I didn't approve the stupid thing.'

We believed him – and that lightened our mood considerably. The involvement of Mitchell, known as one of the President's closest advisers (and, by some, a father figure, even though Mitchell was younger than Nixon), would not only have made gamy press coverage, but might even endanger the election which seemed so secure.

And this was important because the Democrats were moving swiftly to exploit the opening. That very morning, only three days after the break-in, they launched a multimillion dollar law suit against C.R.P. (In later days, as the mystery of Watergate deepened, we would wonder about this swiftness. Seemingly, the Democrats had this lawsuit, with its complex legal briefs, all cranked up and ready to go.)

But if Mitchell wasn't implicated, the problem could be handled, even if some C.R.P. underlings were involved. We could always explain zealots. So when John Dean arrived he found us joking about suntans and other trivia instead of worrying about Watergate. Dean later said he was surprised.

But when I returned to my office I found a nervous aide, Gordon Strachan. Strachan told me he had combed our files and removed 'embarrassing' material. With the Democrats launching a lawsuit with the legal right of discovery of all documents, Strachan thought these materials should be hidden from them. I later learned that he had an additional and earlier motive, too. Jeb Magruder had told him over the weekend that he should destroy all 'damaging material' in his files – as they were busily doing at C.R.P.

Watergate became a climactic tragedy for me personally, but in the middle of the deepest tragedies, as we all know, there are sometimes events or circumstances which have an ironic, and even comical, quality. Such was the case with the materials Strachan showed me. Total confusion. He thought they were wiretap transcripts from Watergate. This would be dynamite indeed. But he handed me the papers and I saw something labelled 'SEDAN CHAIR II'. It was a written report from 'confidential sources' that had nothing to do with D.N.C. telephone conversations. Later we would learn that the report was from a chauffeur we had planted in Muskie's camp, not wiretap transcripts. The material had nothing to do with Watergate. Even so, I didn't want the Democrats to see it when they went through our files. I handed it back to Strachan and told him it looked 'interesting', that I was sorry I hadn't read it before, and to keep it away from the Democrats.

Strachan did that in spades. He shredded the material and that shredding was to have dramatic consequences for me. John Dean would tell the President the following spring that I was 'tied into' the break-in from the beginning because I had received Watergate wiretap transcripts from C.R.P. – and I didn't have the evidence to refute it.

(It was only after I resigned that Magruder testified that the wiretap transcripts never left the C.R.P. offices.)

After Strachan left, the buzzer rang. It was the President summoning me. We were about to begin one of the most fateful conversations in Watergate history. For this was to be the June 20 meeting in which 18½ minutes of taped conversation was mysteriously erased.

Ironically, while I had been talking with Strachan in my office, the President had been meeting with John Ehrlichman in the Oval Office. In fact, Ehrlichman had gone straight from our 'Watergate group' meeting in his office (with Kleindienst, Mitchell and Dean), to his meeting with the President. And this was the first meeting Nixon had after Watergate with anyone except me – with anyone who had been in Washington – and with anyone who had met with Mitchell and Dean.

Therefore the impeachment staff was later to assume great significance for this Nixon-Ehrlichman meeting because it constituted Nixon's first chance to get a report on what had happened. This was a very important tape on the list of those they needed in order to get to the bottom of the whole affair. So, as the staff attempted to review the tapes in response to the subpoena to deliver them, this was the first one they listened to.

But – wonder of wonders – there was no mention of the D.N.C. break-in at all, despite the fact that Ehrlichman had just come from a special meeting of senior officials which had been concerned solely with that subject.

I would not be so lucky.

I stepped into Nixon's office and found the President sitting before slightly garish gold draperies – Pat Nixon liked 'cheerful' colours), leaning back, feet on his desk in a relaxed posture sipping the usual cup of coffee.

We spent the first part of the conversation on government and campaign business of no great importance or urgency. Then, with seemingly no increase in interest, we turned to the D.N.C. break-in. The D.N.C. discussion occupied only about 18½ minutes – after which we turned to other mundane and routine matters. The whole meeting lasted about an hour and a half.

Nevertheless, because that particular 18½ minutes was subsequently erased from the tape of that meeting – and only that particular 18½ minutes – a great deal of interest naturally has arisen as to how we spent that short period and what we said to each other. Court hearings and legal investigation, technical analyses, and all sorts of efforts have since been made to try to find the answer. To no avail.

In 1977, Nixon, in the David Frost interviews on television, discussed that famous 18½-minute gap. He said that I always took thorough notes of our meetings for the files, and the fact that my notes only mentioned P.R. tactics proved the talk about Watergate during that missing 18½ minutes was innocuous.

At least part of what he said was not true.

By the nature of my job – and the character and personality of *this* President – I often had to sit through long periods of general conversation, rambling discussion, and recitations of gripes, major and minor. I never bothered to take notes of these, as Nixon very well knew. Even in substantive meetings, I only made notes of specific actions he ordered me to execute, or assign.

Since I have no clear recollection of anything else, it could be that the discussion *was* limited to the P.R. area covered in my notes – and the reason for erasing this relatively harmless subject matter was simply that it happened to be the *first* mention of the Watergate matter on the White House tapes, and the erasure was the first step in a plan to eliminate all such mention – a plan that was not pursued further. But this is only one theory.

It's just as possible that there was something in that conversation which Nixon believed was so uniquely damaging that it had to be erased. Since the discovery of that gap, I've racked my brain trying to remember what was said on that June 20 morning. And then years later evidence started to come in that I hadn't heard before, such as Nixon's telephone calls to Colson from Key Biscayne the weekend before.

I checked the President's log and remembered how often in the first week after the break-in Nixon had called Colson into his office. And revolving in my mind were Presidential conversations, whose dates I couldn't pin down, concerning Colson. Now, looking back, taking all the new evidence of what was really going on that week, I wonder if one of my conversations with Nixon about Colson didn't take place June 20. With that thought in mind I've reconstructed the way the conversation might have gone:

NIXON: On that D.N.C. break-in, have you heard that anyone in the White House is involved?

HALDEMAN: No one. Magruder says Liddy at C.R.P. did it on his own. And Hunt's been gone from here for months.

NIXON: Well, I'm worried about Colson.

HALDEMAN: Why?

NIXON: The F.B.I.'s starting their investigation, and I know one thing, I can't stand an F.B.I. interrogation of Colson.

HALDEMAN: Chuck tells me he's clean. Hunt hasn't been on his payroll in months. Colson hasn't even *seen* him.

NIXON: *Colson can talk about the President, if he cracks. You know I was on Colson's tail for months to nail Larry O'Brien on the Hughes deal. Colson told me he was going to get the information I wanted one way or the other. And that was O'Brien's office they were bugging, wasn't it? And who's behind it? Colson's boy, Hunt. Christ.*

HALDEMAN: Still, Magruder didn't even mention Colson . . .

NIXON: He will.

HALDEMAN: Why?

NIXON: *Colson called him and got the whole operation started. Right from the Goddamn White House. With Hunt and Liddy sitting in his lap. I just hope the F.B.I. doesn't check the office log and put it together with that Hunt and Liddy meeting in Colson's office.*

HALDEMAN: I'd better get Colson in here.

NIXON: No need for that. I talked to Chuck myself. He says he's innocent. Colson tells me he never mentioned O'Brien when Hunt and Liddy were in his office. [laughs] Never mentioned it. Just talked generalities about getting their intelligence plan approved.

HALDEMAN: I'm still not convinced . . .

NIXON: So I go along with it, saying I wonder who was so crazy to go into the Democratic National Committee. You think there's a chance Colson's telling the truth?

HALDEMAN: Yes. I think Magruder would be dumping on Colson . . .

NIXON: Not if Colson used *my* name in the call. I hate

> things like this. We're not in control. We don't know who's lying . . . Well, we'll just have to hang tough, no matter what. In fact, we'd better go on the attack.

And with those words, he began the discussion of public relations approaches to combat the Democratic National Committee efforts to capitalise on the break-in, on which I made the notes that survive.

2

For years Nixon had been trying to track down proof that Larry O'Brien was on Howard Hughes's payroll as a lobbyist at the same time that he was Chairman of the Democratic National Committee. This could be hot ammunition to discredit O'Brien, Nixon believed. What had O'Brien done in exchange for Hughes's money (reportedly, a huge $180,000-a-year retainer)? A wiretap on O'Brien's telephone and a bug in his office could obtain the proof Nixon wanted.

To take such a risk as that burglary to gain that information was absurd, I thought. But on matters pertaining to Hughes, Nixon sometimes seemed to lose touch with reality. His indirect association with this mystery man may have caused him, in his view, to lose two elections.

His brother Don had been granted a $205,000 loan from Hughes in the 1950s when Nixon was Vice-President. Jack Anderson had broken that story shortly before the 1960 election, and Nixon felt his razor-thin defeat by John Kennedy was partially due to that story.

Then, in the 1962 California gubernatorial race the loan had surfaced again, this time in a *Reporter* magazine article by James Phelan – and Governor Pat Brown could have credited his surprise victory over Nixon to the repercussions of that story.

And yet, even with this background, at that very moment, unknown to me at the time, $100,000 of Hughes's cash was resting in a safe deposit box in Florida leased by Charles 'Bebe' Rebozo, Nixon's closest personal friend.

Years later, in 1976, I asked Nixon about that $100,000, which by then had been the subject of vigorous investigation for years. The investigation had finally petered out with no results. Rebozo explained that the $100,000 was a campaign contribution, and the reason it never reached the Campaign Committee was that an internecine war had broken out in the Hughes empire. Rebozo said he was afraid the President would be embarrassed by one side or another in the Hughes war if the campaign contribution was revealed.

The investigators couldn't find the evidence to refute this. But I had questions in 1976 – based on a personal experience.

In 1973 when Nixon 'requested' Ehrlichman and me to resign, he softened the blow by offering us money for our legal fees. The amount he cited was $200,000 on one occasion, $300,000 on another. We had refused it. But I had always wondered about that offer. In 1976 I asked Nixon where that money would have come from.

We were sitting in the den of his San Clemente residence. Nixon had his feet on a hassock, piles of paper on either side of him. He said, 'Bebe had it.'

But I reminded him that Bebe had only $100,000 of the Hughes money. Where would the rest of the two or three hundred thousand have come from? Nixon told me this interesting news. There was much more money in Bebe's 'tin box' than the Hughes $100,000. For example, Dwayne Andreas, a Minnesota financier, who had also been inadvertently and unknowingly connected to the Watergate money, had contributed another $100,000. That, Nixon said, made the $200,000.

But then I remembered another reference to J. Paul Getty, the oil billionaire. In that case Nixon had ordered

Ehrlichman to set up Getty's money in a separate fund administered by Bebe Rebozo. That was in 1969, only months after Nixon took office. As far as I knew, the Getty money never materialised.

I asked Nixon about the testimony of his lawyer, Herbert Kalmbach. The background of my question was painful to Nixon. Kalmbach had testified that Bebe Rebozo told him on April 30, 1973, that he had given portions of the Hughes money to Rose Mary Woods, Nixon's secretary, and to his two brothers, Donald and Edward.

When Kalmbach told Rebozo he should ask the I.R.S. for advice on how to handle the expenditures for tax purposes, the Cuban recoiled. 'This touches the President, Herb.'

(The idea of consulting the I.R.S. on this subject is not as odd as it sounds. Money from campaign contributions can be spent by a candidate for personal use if he declares the amounts as income. But Nixon hadn't done this.)

Rose Mary Woods and the President's brothers denied they had received money from Rebozo. And the investigators who probed Bebe's finances never found any such payments, although they did find that Bebe had paid for such items as personal gifts for Pat Nixon as well as improvements to Nixon's Key Biscayne home. But there was no evidence that this came from the Hughes money.

In fact, Bebe Rebozo told F.B.I. investigators that the $100,000 from Hughes had been kept untouched in the safe deposit box for years. But when an agent opened the box to count the 'untouched' $100,000, he found it had at least been nudged. There was an extra $100 bill.

Now in San Clemente, Nixon told me the full story for the first time.

He said that Bebe also kept his *own* money in that box, mingled with the 'campaign contributions', and that's where the extra $100 came from. The $100,000 was apparently only part of a much larger cash kitty kept in a safe deposit box.

How much money was really in that box, or other bank accounts, for the President's use? Dwayne Andreas'

$100,000, made the kitty at least $200,000. Bebe Rebozo, in effect, maintained a private fund for Nixon to use as he wished.

Nevertheless, despite all the rumours, I can say that in all my years with Nixon, I never knew him to do any special favours for Hughes. Quite the contrary, when Hughes objected violently to the nuclear testing in Nevada, Nixon ordered the testing to go forward, even though Hughes was enraged.

3

June 20, 1972. Sometime before noon. I bumped into Colson in the hall of the West Wing of the White House, 'I'm going to talk to Walters at the *Star*, Bob, and fill him in on the fact that the White House was not involved in the D.N.C. break-in.'

'Why?'

'I'm going to get the blame for this thing if I don't.

But Nixon went off like a rocket when I told him what Colson planned to do. 'That's all we need,' he said. 'Colson talking to the newspapers. You tell him he's not to say anything, anywhere.'

Strange, their relationship. When I left Nixon's office I reflected once again on the situation. My job was to protect the President, but I didn't know where to turn. Was Colson guilty or not of initiating the break-in? If he was, Colson surely wasn't confirming it. I left the room, went back to my office, and called Colson. I told him to hold up on the Walters idea, or any newspaper story. Colson grumpily said O.K. Then I saw Ehrlichman who cheered me tremendously when he said, 'Brother Dean has finished touching all the bases and it's C.R.P. all the way.'

'No Colson?'

Ehrlichman scratched his chin. 'Believe it or not, according to Mr Dean, on this one Colson is clean. How do you like that?'

'And Dean *knows* this? It isn't speculation?'

'Sure. He talked to Liddy himself, yesterday.'

I thought, well, great. The President was in there trying to stem a fast-beating heart for nothing. According to everybody who should know – Magruder, Liddy, and Dean – Colson, the White House Chief of Dirty Tricks, had by a miracle managed to miss the one trick that exploded.

And if that was so, the D.N.C. break-in became simply a matter of containment. Contain it to C.R.P. where it belonged; don't let it slop over into the White House. Hold it to as low a level as possible. Furnish the Democrats as little political ammunition as possible out of the idiotic incident.

To me, it sounded very simple at the time.

4

The complications began that night, when I received a telephone call which is unknown to anyone but the President and me to this day. I believe a tape does not exist because the call was probably made from a telephone in the White House Residence which was not covered by the taping system.

But my notes on the call add important new information on Nixon's role in the cover-up. For in this telephone conversation, on our very first evening back in Washington, Nixon, himself, initiated the idea of raising funds for the Watergate burglars in an indirect manner. Even more surprising, he indirectly suggested the idea of involving the C.I.A. in the Watergate problem three days before the famous 'smoking gun' conversation, in which the same idea was consummated.

The telephone call was curious to me from the beginning because Nixon sounded so relieved. He must have found out from Ehrlichman or someone else, that Colson's story of innocence would hold, and might even be valid. To make things seem even better, the television news that day had emphasised the Cuban connection – concentrating on the fact that anti-Castro Cubans were involved (the *New York Times* even assigned an expert on Cuban affairs as their first Watergate reporter). Now Nixon said to me on the telephone, 'This thing may be under control because of the Cubans who went in there. A lot of people think the break-in was done by anti-Castro Cubans.'

I said, 'Well, I've never understood, myself, what Cubans were doing there.'

The President warmed to the notion even more. 'Right. I'm going to talk to Bebe and have him round up some anti-McGovern Cubans in Miami. You know, those Cubans down there hate McGovern.'

And it was then the President made his suggestion about payments to the defendants. He said, 'Those people who got caught are going to need money. I've been thinking about how to do it.'

At that point I hadn't even thought of the problem of the defendants in human terms. What consideration I had given to the whole subject had been concentrated so much on the question of who sent them in, that I'd forgotten those were real people in jail and we were, one way or the other, responsible for them. I said I didn't know how; that maybe they had lawyers. Nixon said he had a better idea. 'I'm going to have Bebe start a fund for them in Miami. Call it an anti-Castro Fund, and publicise the hell out of the Cuban angle. That way we kill two birds with one stone. Get money to the boys to help them, and maybe pick up some points against McGovern on the Cuban angle.'

Nixon never missed a chance to counterattack when he felt he was in trouble. This time his approach sounded O.K. to me. Unfortunately it was to have reverberations to this day. Because when John Dean approached me later and asked if he could use Nixon's lawyer and fundraiser Herb Kalmbach to raise money for the defendants, it never even occurred to me to question the basic concept. The pattern had been set by the President, beginning with that telephone call to me on June 20, and I saw no reason why Kalmbach should not lend a hand in the effort.

Incidentally, Nixon was to refer to this 'Cuban Defense Fund' in his later meetings with John Dean in instant reaction to Dean's mention of the efforts to raise money for the defendants. He remembered it clearly then, although he later denied on television all knowledge of money-raising efforts.

But then in this call Nixon veered sharply off the money angle into completely unknown terrain, as far as I was concerned. In fact, I was puzzled when he told me, 'Tell Ehrlichman this whole group of Cubans is tied to the Bay of Pigs.'

After a pause I said, 'The Bay of Pigs? What does that have to do with this?'

But Nixon merely said, 'Ehrlichman will know what I mean,' and dropped the subject.

After our staff meeting the next morning I accompanied Ehrlichman to his office and gave him the President's message. Ehrlichman's eyebrows arched, and he smiled. 'Our brothers from Langley? He's suggesting I twist or break a few arms?'

'I don't know. All he told me was "Tell Ehrlichman this whole group of Cubans is tied to the Bay of Pigs".'

Ehrlichman leaned back in his chair, tapping a pencil on the edge of his desk. 'All right,' he said, 'message accepted.'

'What are you going to do about it?'

'Zero,' said Ehrlichman. 'I want to stay out of this one.'

He was referring to an unspoken feud between C.I.A. Director Richard Helms and Nixon. The two were polar opposites in background: Helms, the aloof, aristocratic, Eastern elitist; Nixon the poor boy (he never let you forget it) from a small California town. Ehrlichman had found himself in the middle of this feud as far back as 1969, immediately after Nixon assumed office. Nixon had called Ehrlichman into his office and said he wanted all the facts and documents the C.I.A. had on the Bay of Pigs, a complete report on the whole project.

About six months after that 1969 conversation, Ehrlichman had stopped in my office. 'Those bastards in Langley are holding back something. They just dig in their heels and say the President can't have it. Period. Imagine that! The Commander-in-Chief wants to see a document relating to a military operation, and the spooks say he can't have it.'

'What is it?'

'I don't know, but from the way they're protecting it, it must be pure dynamite.'

I was angry at the idea that Helms would tell the President he couldn't see something. I said, 'Well, you remind Helms who's President. He's not. In fact, Helms can damn well find himself out of a job in a hurry.'

That's what I thought! Helms was never fired, at least for four years. But then Ehrlichman had said, 'Rest assured. The point will be made. In fact, Helms is on his way over here right now. The President is going to give him a direct order to turn over that document to me.'

Helms did show up that afternoon and saw the President for a long secret conversation. When Helms left, Ehrlichman returned to the Oval Office. The next thing I knew Ehrlichman appeared in my office, dropped into a chair, and just stared at me. He was more furious than I had ever seen him; absolutely speechless, a rare phenomenon for our White House phrase-makers. I said, 'What happened?'

'This is what happened,' Ehrlichman said. 'The Mad Monk has just told me I am now to *forget* all about that C.I.A. document. In fact, I am to cease and desist from trying to obtain it.'

(Ehrlichman wouldn't forget it. Years later he would recreate his Oval Office session with 'The Mad Monk' – his favourite nickname for Nixon – in his novel, *The Com-*

pany, whose fictional president was, not surprisingly, Monckton.)

When Senator Howard Baker of the Evrin Committee later looked into the Nixon-Helms relationship, he summed it up. 'Nixon and Helms have so much on each other, neither of them can breathe.'

Apparently Nixon knew more about the genesis of the Cuban invasion that led to the Bay of Pigs than almost anyone. Recently, the man who was President of Costa Rica at the time – dealing with Nixon while the invasion was being prepared – stated that Nixon was the man who *originated* the Cuban invasion. If this was true, Nixon never told it to me.

In 1972 I did know that Nixon disliked the C.I.A. Allen Dulles, the C.I.A. Director in 1960, had briefed Jack Kennedy about the forthcoming Cuban invasion before a Kennedy-Nixon debate. Kennedy used this top secret information in the debate, thereby placing Nixon on the spot. Nixon felt he had to lie and even deny such an invasion was in the works to protect the men who were training in secret. Dulles later denied briefing Kennedy. This betrayal, added to Nixon's long-held feeling that the agency was not adequately competent, led to his distrust and dislike.

And now that antipathy was to emerge again on June 23, 1972, when Nixon would once again confront and pressure the C.I.A.

This time the C.I.A. was ready. In fact, it was more than ready. It was ahead of the game by months. Nixon would walk into what I now believe was a trap.

5

The trap, if it was one, started to spring when John Dean called me at 8.15 on that fateful morning of June 23, 1972.

The call from Dean was a surprise because I had believed

Ehrlichman was the 'project manager' on the Watergate problem. But in ways no one has ever made clear, my crafty friend, Ehrlichman, had almost abruptly faded from the investigation to be replaced by young, bright, eager John Dean.

It's interesting to see how our two major White House staffers who were involved in surreptitious projects acted in the Watergate crisis, beginning with that first week. Chuck Colson, in personal command of almost every so-called White House dirty trick in the first term, vanished almost immediately from this one. John Ehrlichman, who had commanded the Plumbers which included Howard Hunt, moved gratefully back into the shadows after the first two days. Almost by osmosis, it seemed, John Dean took over.

And that move for Dean was, as everyone will admit, including Dean himself, a disaster.

To begin with, Dean *hid* much of what he was doing, creating giant problems later. In those early days, for example, he told me nothing about the original meetings in Mitchell's office to discuss Liddy's plans for intelligence. Later, as the pressure increased, a strange phenomenon took place. Dean kept reminding me that I had joined him in 'turning the Liddy plan off' after the second of two meetings in Mitchell's office. He had come to my office, he told me, and said he had turned it off, and we both agreed he should have nothing further to do with it. This made sense to me because – as any of my former associates know – if Dean had come to my office and said he had approved a sex-oriented plan involving kidnapping, prostitutes, and houseboats as whorehouses, his lifeless body would have been found in the hallway after the explosion. The only problem with Dean's 'reminder' that I had rejected the plan was that I couldn't, for the life of me, ever remember even hearing about it.

But Dean, as the months passed, 'reminded' me so many times of that meeting in my office I eventually believed it. Therefore I was surprised years later when I checked the visitors' log kept by my secretary and discovered no such meeting with Dean took place. It just didn't happen.

At other times he *did* check with me, just as he testified, and as *I* testified. (Special Prosecutor Richard Ben-Veniste was later to say that I was the only defendant in Watergate to voluntarily confess on the witness stand to a charge that wasn't even in my indictment. The charge was misuse of a Federal Agency and involved my June 23 'smoking gun' conversation with Nixon.)

From time to time, Ehrlichman and I would be called in, but only when it was absolutely necessary. Dean was for a long time, as he admits, having fun. He was becoming recognised.

And what we saw was a young man, unquestionably intelligent, unfailingly courteous, doing his job efficiently – including his call to me the morning of June 23, 1972, which precipitated the 'smoking gun' conversation.

6

June 23, 1972. A dried frog looked at me, unblinkingly, from my desktop. I used the end of a pencil to turn him towards the door. The frog was a symbol of the Nixon advance men I had once headed. They called themselves the 'Frogmen' because of the leapfrog nature of their assignments, jumping from one place to another.

I was waiting for the President's buzzer to sound, summoning me to our regular early morning conference that always began the President's day. The telephone was silent. I looked out of my window at the tops of the trees along the south drive. A gardener was repotting the geraniums in the window box.

The telephone rang, startling me. But it wasn't the President's buzzer. I picked up my telephone and was told John Dean was on the line. In an instant my serenity was shattered, as the young voice spoke urgently, beginning with these upsetting words:

'Bob, the D.N.C. break-in is becoming a real problem. They're out of control over at the Bureau. [Patrick] Gray doesn't know what the hell to do, as usual.'

'What have they found so far?'

'They traced one cheque to a contributor named Ken Dahlberg. And apparently the money was laundered out of a Mexican bank, and the F.B.I. has found the bank. If that's true, they'll know who the depositors are today.'

'Great news,' I said sarcastically. 'What else has the F.B.I. found?'

'Those guys were really brilliant,' Dean said. 'They took the photographs of the documents they made in the D.N.C. to a *commercial* photographer in Miami, and the photographer's already told the F.B.I.'

I made notes as Dean ploughed ahead.

'But our problem now is to stop the F.B.I. from opening up a whole lot of other things. I don't know where that money trail is going to lead from that Mexican bank if they start checking. Who knows what contributors' names are going to pop up if they start down that track. Mitchell and Stans [C.R.P. Finance Chairman] are really worried about that.' He paused. 'They say we have to turn off that investigation of the Mexican bank fast, before they open up everything and spread this mess a lot wider than it is.'

I instantly understood the basis for the concern about the revelation of contributors' names. Although it doesn't seem to be very important now – after all that has transpired since – at that time this was a big issue. The C.R.P. had collected an enormous precampaign war chest during the period when the law did not require the disclosure of the names of campaign donors. Much of the money had come from sources who, for various reasons, did not want their contribution known. Some were strong Democratic contributors who were either playing both sides or abandoning their own party; some were concerned for business reasons; some just didn't want to get on the 'sucker lists'.

The Democrats had made a major political issue in

April out of the fact that C.R.P. started the campaign reporting period with some $10,000,000 cash on hand, and refused to reveal the names of the donors of this money. This was perfectly legal, but politically damaging. But C.R.P. had stood firm on the grounds that the contributions were legally made with the assurance that they would not be identified.

Now I said: 'Fine, just tell me the bottom line and keep it brief. Who does the F.B.I. think did the break-in? Have they got a theory?'

Dean said, 'Well, that's the good news. The F.B.I. is convinced it's the C.I.A. McCord and the Cubans are all ex-C.I.A. people. Practically everyone who went in there was connected to the agency. And now the F.B.I. finds a *Mexican* bank involved which also sounds like the C.I.A.'

Dean told me other welcome news. The F.B.I. had cleared Colson on the basis of his F.B.I. interrogation. Then returned to the C.I.A. angle. 'Gray [the acting F.B.I. Director] has been looking for a way out of this mess. I spoke to Mitchell, and he and I agree the thing to do is for you to tell Walters [Deputy Director of C.I.A.] that we don't know where that Mexican investigation is going to lead. Have him talk to Gray – and maybe the C.I.A. can turn off the F.B.I. down there in Mexico.'

I hung up, wondering at a coincidence. Three nights ago, Nixon had called me, suggesting I tell Ehrlichman that the Cubans were in the Bay of Pigs. The implication was that there was some sort of connection between that C.I.A. operation and Watergate. Now the F.B.I. also thought there was a connection. But this prior conversation with Nixon has another significance. It led me to make a crucial – even historical – error.

I did something I shouldn't have done. Dean had suggested that I call Walters at the C.I.A. I knew Walters well. Normally, I would have simply called him over to my office at the White House and asked him if he would help us out. Whether he would have turned me down or not doesn't matter. The fact is there never would have been the 'smoking gun' conversation in the Oval Office that resulted in Nixon's resignation, if I had just called Walters, myself, as I usually would have.

Ironically, it was one remark that Nixon had made earlier in his telephone call on June 20 that caused me to change my routine. His surprising reference to the Bay of Pigs had puzzled me. Nixon obviously knew something about the C.I.A. that was unknown to me, and I felt I should check with him before asking Walters to help.

And so I walked into the Oval Office and as it turned out sealed Nixon's doom, as soon as I closed the door.

7

June 23, 10.05 a.m. After going over several other matters Nixon listened silently as I read from my notes about Dean's report on the Mexican bank connection. 'Mitchell came up with yesterday – and John Dean analysed very carefully last night and concurs now with Mitchell's recommendation – that the only way to solve this . . . is for us to have Walters call Pat Gray and just say "Stay the hell out of this – this is business we don't want you to go any further on." That's not an unusual development and that would take care of it.'

Nixon wanted to know if they had traced the money to the contributors.

'I said, 'They've traced to a name, but they haven't gotten to the guy yet, Ken Dahlberg. He gave $25,000 in Minnesota and the cheque went directly to this guy Barker' (one of the Cuban burglars).

In the next colloquy I realised Nixon was thinking in deeper political terms than I. He asked me if the money was traceable from C.R.P., and I said yes. He said, 'I'm just thinking, if the contributors don't co-operate, what do they say? That they were approached by the Cubans?

That's what Dahlberk has to say, the Texans, too.'

With that remark, I realised Nixon thought the connection of the Watergate burglars to C.R.P. might be avoided. I didn't think there was much chance of that with McCord under arrest, so I steered Nixon off that course, and back to the C.I.A. Nixon mused about my approach to the C.I.A., beginning by grumbling, 'Well, we protected Helms from one hell of a lot of things.'

How to make certain the C.I.A. would co-operate? Nixon suggested the involvement of Hunt as a lever. 'Hunt . . . will uncover a lot of things. You open that scab there's a hell of a lot of things . . . tell them we just feel that it would be very detrimental to have this thing go any further. This involves these Cubans, Hunt, and a lot of hanky-panky that we have nothing to do with ourselves.'

I didn't know what hanky-panky he was talking about, but Nixon wasn't finished. He gazed out of the window, then turned to me. 'When you get the C.I.A. people in say, "Look, the problem is that *this will open up the whole Bay of Pigs thing again.* So they should call the F.B.I. in and for the good of the country don't go any further into this case. Period." '

Later in a one-o'clock meeting just before I saw Helms and Walters, Nixon expanded on this theme: 'Tell them that if it gets out, it's going to make the C.I.A. look bad, it's going to make Hunt look bad, and it's likely to blow the whole Bay of Pigs which we think would be very unfortunate for the C.I.A.'

Dean had suggested a blatant political move by calling in the C.I.A. – now Nixon showed how much more astute he was by throwing a national security blanket over the same suggestion.

Two years later before Nixon's dramatic and touching meeting with key Republican congressional leaders on the eve of his resignation, he chatted briefly with speechwriter Ray Price who was working on the draft of the resignation speech. Ray tells in his book, *With Nixon*, that he had worked out something that he thought made the point of the resignation being the equivalent of impeachment without 'admitting' guilt.

'And that's right!' Nixon said. 'That six-minute conversation – Haldeman ran that C.I.A. thing by me – it went by so fast I didn't even pay attention. It was a stupid damn thing, but wrong.'

His reference, of course, was to the fact that our original discussion on June 23 of Dean's proposal to use the C.I.A. had occupied only about six minutes of a meeting that lasted more than an hour and a half. But his self-deluding contention that he 'didn't even pay attention' is hard to accept in the light of what he actually said to me at the time. He certainly was paying attention then. And he went on paying attention long after I left the office because when I met him later in the day, before my meeting with the C.I.A., he had even further thoughts on how I should handle the C.I.A. meeting.

This failure to face the irrefutable facts, even when it was absolutely clear that they were irrefutable, was one of our fatal flaws in handling Watergate at every stage.

John Ehrlichman and I were to meet the C.I.A. officials. I went to John's office to await their arrival. 'Guess what,' I said to John. 'It's Bay of Pigs time again.'

'The man will never quit,' Ehrlichman said.

He thought about it and added, 'Well, the President has a point. It will put pressure on Helms. But this time you're going to push the red button, not me. I've had it on that route.'

Helms and Walters entered Ehrlichman's office at 1.30. I laid out the situation. Helms surprised me by revealing he had already talked to the F.B.I. director about Watergate on the previous day. He said he had made it plain to Gray that the C.I.A. was *not* connected to Watergate in any way, and none of the suspects had worked for the agency in the last two years.

Elegantly put, with just the right tone of injured innocence. Of course, the Ervin Committee would later discover that pious statement was three-fourths baloney. The

C.I.A. was connected to the Watergate matter in innumerable ways; indeed, *at least* one of the burglars, Martinez, was still on the C.I.A. payroll on June 17, 1972 – and almost certainly was reporting to his C.I.A. case officer about the proposed break-in *even before it happened.* The first lawyer in the police precinct when the burglars were brought in the night of June 17 was reportedly a C.I.A.-connected attorney, there to represent men who had allegedly retired from the agency and had no connection with it.

In 1974, the Special Prosecutors would experience what they termed a 'nasty surprise' because of Helms' mysterious actions and motivations in the Watergate crisis. According to prosecutors Richard Ben-Veniste and George Frampton in their book *Stonewall,* Helms first appeared before them as an extremely co-operative witness, smoothly reassuring the prosecutors that the idea of the F.B.I. investigation actually endangering any C.I.A. agents in Mexico was, of course, a fabrication by Nixon's men. Unfortunately for Helms, after he departed, a C.I.A. memo surfaced which had been written by Helms five days after my June 23, 1972, interview. According to the book, it said,

> The C.I.A. will 'adhere to' its request to the F.B.I. 'to desist from expanding the investigation into other areas *which may well, eventually, run afoul of our operations.*'

The prosecutors were dismayed because 'the memo expressed an opinion that was 180 degrees apart from the opinion Helms told us he actually held at the time [of the White House meeting].

'Ben-Veniste and Frampton quizzed Helms about the news, pointing out that it seemed to say just the opposite of what he had claimed he was thinking at the time. Helms was sorry, but he just couldn't explain it.'

The Prosecutor's book didn't mention what could be the greatest irony of the 'smoking gun' tape. If the Mexican Bank connection was actually a C.I.A. operation all along, unknown to Nixon; and Nixon was destroyed for asking the F.B.I. to stop investigating the bank because it might uncover a C.I.A. operation (which the Helms memo seems to indicate it actually was after all) the multiple levels of deception by the C.I.A. are astounding.

At that time I knew nothing of this serpentine intrigue. What I did know was that the C.I.A. was an agency hostile to Nixon, who returned the hostility with fervor. And as I sat there, listening to Helms stonewall me, I remembered my only direct experience with the C.I.A. early in Nixon's term, when I also had drawn a blank trying to deal with them.

8

In early 1969, John Ehrlichman, C.I.A. Deputy Director General Robert Cushman and I sat on the patio outside of my office. I had constructed the patio in an attempt to recreate at least one facet of my old life-style in California. (Recently, I was pleased to see in a photo two non-Californians enjoying lunch on that same terrace: President Jimmy Carter and Vice-President Walter Mondale.)

Earlier, Ehrlichman had told me of a somewhat unnerving conversation with the President. John had described it in this fashion:

Nixon said, 'You've got to do something about Don.'

Ehrlichman said he groaned inwardly. Not Nixon's brother again! 'What's the problem now?'

'He's getting himself into some more business deals. People keep coming to him with their great ideas. Now it involves a lot of foreign contacts.'

'Well, that sounds innocent enough on the surface.'

'Yeah,' the President replied unenthusiastically, but

went on: 'Look, I want a complete surveillance on Don. Keep tabs on him and all the contacts he makes. I don't want people taking advantage of him.'

Ehrlichman was surprised. 'You mean like the F.B.I., or something?'

Nixon said, 'I don't care how you do it – just keep him covered.'

John asked my advice as to how to handle this one. I suggested checking with Nixon's former Vice-Presidential military aide, General Robert Cushman, who was now Deputy Director of the C.I.A. I figured Bob could be trusted, and could advise us on how to go about this. Since it involved foreign contacts with the President's brother, I thought it might be a natural for the C.I.A.

Now we sat with Cushman on the terrace, and Ehrlichman relayed the President's request. Cushman's eyes widened. 'My God,' he said. 'Is he serious? You want the *C.I.A.* to put a tail on his own brother?'

'Yes, because it's ultra-confidential, as you can imagine, and we figured it would come under your bailiwick.'

Cushman didn't like it and kept shaking his head. 'This is way outside the agency's charter.' Then he said, 'Can't the President just *talk* to his goddamn brother? Isn't this surveillance going a bit far?'

I said, 'He's not concerned about Don, but some shady characters that may try to use him.'

After thinking it over, Cushman said, 'Domestic operations of any sort are precluded from the C.I.A. by its charter.' (What the C.I.A. Director *didn't* point out was that the agency, unknown to us, was *at that very moment* actively carrying on domestic operations of all kinds including break-ins and wiretapping, *despite* their charter.)

Cushman suggested we ask the Secret Service to handle the President's request. Ehrlichman spoke to the head of the Secret Service and they said 'no problem.' Anything to protect the President and his family even in this indirect fashion. And so they wiretapped his brother's telephone and tailed him, too.

When this was revealed years later Nixon claimed his brother had known about the surveillance all along. Could be. But I know I never told Don Nixon and Ehrlichman has never said that he did.

9

So we had failed in our one previous attempt to obtain C.I.A. co-operation, and now in Ehrlichman's office on June 23, 1972, the C.I.A. was stonewalling me again: 'Not connected.' 'No way.' Then I played Nixon's trump card. 'The President asked me to tell you this entire affair may be connected to the Bay of Pigs, and if it opens up, the Bay of Pigs may be blown . . . '

Turmoil in the room. Helms gripping the arms of his chair leaning forward and shouting, 'The Bay of Pigs had nothing to do with this. I have no concern about the Bay of Pigs.'

Silence. I just sat there. I was absolutely shocked by Helms' violent reaction. Again I wondered, *what was such dynamite* in the Bay of Pigs story? Finally, I said, 'I'm just following my instructions, Dick. This is what the President told me to relay to you.'

Helms was settling back. 'All right,' he said.

But the atmosphere had changed. Now surprisingly, the two C.I.A. officials expressed no concern about the request that Walters go to see Gray. And Walters later testified that when he and Helms went downstairs they talked briefly and Helms said, 'You must remind Mr Gray of the agreement between the F.B.I. and the C.I.A. that if they run into or expose one another's "assets" [a C.I.A. term for "agents"] they will not interfere with each other.' Meaning: 'F.B.I., stop the investigation.' Just what Nixon wanted.

I went back to see the President and told him his strategy

had worked. I had told Helms that the Watergate investigation 'tracks back to the Bay of Pigs. So at that point . . . he said we'll be very happy to be helpful.'

And so the 'smoking gun' conversations were created . . . to rest, stored on a reel, in a closet gathering dust until August, 1974.

Years later, former C.B.S. correspondent Dan Schorr called me. He was seeking information concerning the F.B.I. investigation Nixon had mounted against him in August, 1971.

Schorr later sent me his fascinating book *Clearing the Air*. In it I was interested to find that evidence he had gleaned while investigating the C.I.A. finally cleared up for me the mystery of the Bay of Pigs connection in those dealings between Nixon and Helms.

It's intriguing when I put Schorr's facts together with mine. It seems that in all of those Nixon references to the Bay of Pigs, he was actually referring to the Kennedy assassination.

(Interestingly, an investigation of the Kennedy assassination was a project I suggested when I first entered the White House. I had always been intrigued with the conflicting theories of the assassination. Now I felt we would be in a position to get all the facts. But Nixon turned me down.)

According to Schorr, as an outgrowth of the Bay of Pigs, the C.I.A. made several attempts on Fidel Castro's life. The Deputy Director of Plans at the C.I.A. at the time was a man named Richard Helms.

Unfortunately, Castro knew of the assassination attempts all the time. On September 7, 1963, a few months before John Kennedy was assassinated, Castro made a speech in which he was quoted, 'Let Kennedy and his brother Robert take care of themselves, since they, too, can be the victims of an attempt which will cause their death.'

After Kennedy was killed, the C.I.A. launched a fantastic cover-up. Many of the facts about Oswald unavoidably pointed to a Cuban connection.

1. Oswald had been arrested in New Orleans in August, 1963, while distributing pro-Castro pamphlets.

2. On a New Orleans radio programme he extolled Cuba and defended Castro.

3. Less than two months before the assassination Oswald visited the Cuban consulate in Mexico City and tried to obtain a visa.

In a chilling parallel to their cover-up at Watergate, the C.I.A. literally erased any connection between Kennedy's assassination and the C.I.A. No mention of the Castro assassination attempt was made to the Warren Commission by C.I.A. representatives. In fact, Counter-intelligence Chief James Angleton of the C.I.A. called Bill Sullivan of the F.B.I. and rehearsed the questions and answers they would give to the Warren Commission investigators, such as these samples:

Q. Was Oswald an agent of the C.I.A?

A. No.

Q. Does the C.I.A. have any evidence showing that a conspiracy existed to assassinate Kennedy?

A. No.

And here's what I find most interesting: Bill Sullivan, the F.B.I. man that the C.I.A. called at the time, was Nixon's highest-ranking loyal friend at the F.B.I. (in the Watergate crisis, he would risk J. Edgar Hoover's anger by taking the 1969 F.B.I. wiretap transcripts ordered by Nixon and delivering them to Robert Mardian, a Mitchell crony, for safekeeping).

It's possible that Nixon learned from Sullivan something about the earlier C.I.A. cover-up by Helms. And when Nixon said, 'It's likely to blow the whole Bay of Pigs' he might have been reminding Helms, not so gently, of the cover-up of the C.I.A. assassination attempts on the hero of the Bay of Pigs, Fidel Castro – a C.I.A. operation that may have triggered the Kennedy tragedy and which Helms desperately wanted to hide.

10

But Friday, June 23, wasn't over. That day ended on a note of high irony that no one has ever mentioned.

The 'smoking gun' conversations would one day be greeted with cries of outrage by the press and Congress – not only because of the order to use the C.I.A. to impede an F.B.I. investigation, but because of extraneous conversation on the tape of which the most famous is Nixon's remark when I told him the Italians were devaluating their currency: 'I don't give a shit about the lira.'

This is the President? cried the critics. The man in charge of our economic policy?

The ironic aftermath of the 'smoking gun' conversations is that as I left the Oval Office the doors opened and a motion picture camera crew entered. This was the day they chose to show Nixon functioning at his finest as President. It was a film to be screened on television at the Republican Convention. The theme of this particular sequence was the President at work in the Oval Office on a typically glorious day, discussing great problems of state in a Presidential manner – and never once turning to the camera to say, 'I don't give a shit about the lira.'

The film went over well on television.

It's easy now to laugh at this historical irony. Of all the days to photograph Nixon for public relations as a brilliant President – the very day he had the 'smoking gun' conference that would force him to resign in disgrace amid jeers at his language.

There are some other interesting points about that day. A small point, the lira remark: Nixon was preoccupied with my meeting with the C.I.A. directors, and what he meant was that right now he didn't even want to talk about the lira.

On profanity in general: I need not even guess what expletives clouded the air when the earthy Lyndon B. Johnson was in the Oval Office.

And *Washington Post* editor Ben Bradlee, as well as former White House associates, have given us many examples of John F. Kennedy's profanity. A classic is the Cuban Missile crisis. At an N.S.C. meeting at the height of the tension, an aide handed Kennedy a C.I.A. message which indicated that now, of all times, a U-2 aircraft had strayed over the Russian borders. Kennedy's response was to the point: 'Fucked again,' he said. It is obvious that Presidents, like many men in all walks of life, sometimes use earthy language in private conversation with other men.

What hurt Nixon in that regard was that for the first time in all the history of their country the American people had heard what really goes on in the Oval Office. The profanity on the tapes seemed to bother them almost more than any cover-up crimes that might be indicated, especially because Nixon's pious attitude made the earthy talk that much harder to accept. So this was an added burden that Nixon had to bear when the crunch came. And, ironically, it was greatly intensified by whoever decided to issue the transcripts with all profanity replaced by the tantalising phrase 'expletive deleted', thus making the usually mild oaths seem worse than they were.

What may be called a more significant irony is that after the filming of the documentary, Nixon saw Henry Kissinger and Secretary of State Bill Rogers for an extremely important hour-long conference on the S.A.L.T. negotiations. Earlier that day he had seen congressional leaders at breakfast to discuss his meeting with Leonid Brezhnev, the Soviet leader. And in midday, he met with no less than nine top economic aides on moves to strengthen the nation's economy.

All of this on June 23, a day which to me is a microcosm of the real Watergate tragedy. It showed that Nixon was on top of his job at that time. And the people, according to all the polls, decidedly felt he was performing well in office. But in the midst of his most successful year as President a monster, unseen, was rising.

Book II

THE HALDEMAN APPROACH

1

Before grey-coloured draperies in a San Francisco hotel room, Dick Nixon stood among a group of Republican delegates. This was the first time I had seen Nixon close up. I moved closer and listened in dismay. My first thought was that he had been drinking. His sentences were almost incoherent; his monologue rambled on circuitously while everyone around him looked at each other, wonderingly.

This was in 1956 at the Republican Convention, where a segment of the party led by Harold Stassen was trying to unseat Nixon as Eisenhower's Vice-President. I had come north from Los Angeles to sign on as an advance man.

I discovered later that these slurred late-at-night monologues were a feature of Nixon's evenings on the campaign trail. They were caused not by alcohol, but by the utter fatigue of long days of campaigning. The fact is Nixon *couldn't* drink when he was tired. One beer would transform his normal speech into the rambling elocution of a Bowery wino. What was even more bizarre was that when he was merely fatigued, not drinking at all, the same phenomenon would occur. John Ehrlichman, who at the time was more of a 'puritan' than I, was concerned because Nixon imbibed any liquor at all. I've no reason to defend Nixon on drinking, but I must speak the truth, and that truth is: in all my years with him as candidate or as President, I never saw him intoxicated.

The problem was he didn't *need* to drink to excess to start losing his faculties and appear foolish. Not knowing this, I was embarrassed when I first saw him, but the next day I heard him speak, looking fit and contained, and I signed on as an advance man for the re-election campaign.

What brought me to Nixon in the first place instead of to another political candidate?

Most reporters believe it was ideology; rabid anti-Communism was in my blood. And Nixon, at the time, was one of the most aggressive anti-Communists in the land. These reporters unfailingly point out that my paternal grandfather was a founder of the Better American Federation, and early anti-Communist organisation.

True, but neither I nor my family were anti-Communist zealots. I didn't grow up in an atmosphere of intense discussions about the 'Communist menace'. In fact, in school I was not only apolitical, but had gone completely the other route. I was a rah-rah college type, a Homecoming Chairman, no less, and a campus leader.

This was not a reaction to politics of any kind, but to the simple fact that my first two years in college were spent in the Navy V-12 programme at the University of Redlands at the end of World War II. On that campus, my university life was a round of military drills and discipline. When the war ended, and I transferred to U.C.L.A. as a civilian, I was determined to enjoy myself in a traditionally collegiate manner for my last two years.

Ironically, the one political campaign I did manage in college was not that of John Ehrlichman's wife-to-be, as is always reported in my biographies, but for an ultraliberal. In fact, Jane Wilder went on to become one of the national leaders of the Students for Democratic Action, the student branch of the A.D.A., an organisation far from conservative.

Frank Mankiewicz, later Bobby Kennedy's press secretary, and later still, a campaign director for George McGovern, was editor of the U.C.L.A. newspaper, the *Daily Bruin*, at the time. For reasons which are obscure to me, he had constantly represented me as a militant anti-Communist on campus. It's even more obscure when you realise that the one candidate for whom I did campaign, Jane Wilder, was Mankiewicz's steady romance.

A truer description of me in those years comes from another fellow student who couldn't be further removed from me ideologically. Clancy Sigal, now a Marxist English author, was then on the staff of the *Bruin*. Recently he came to visit me on research for a book about his U.C.L.A. class and said, 'I can't understand all the talk about your being a great anti-Communist leader in those days, and leading a campaign to get rid of Communist control of the *Bruin*' (Mankiewicz had charged me with that also). 'I don't remember that at all. I recall you running around in saddle shoes and a cashmere sweater, ushering at pep rallies, and silly stuff like that.' And Clancy added, 'I was a campus radical myself at the time – and I'd remember it if you had been an enemy in those years.'

Incidentally, when Sigal returned to U.C.L.A. and asked to speak to some present-day students in order to contrast their views with those of his generation, a professor suggested that he talk to a student named Hank Haldeman. I believe Clancy must have been surprised and perhaps delighted when he found that my son Hank wore shoulder-length hair, and intended to make his career in rock music. Or maybe he wasn't surprised, knowing the true story of Hank's father at the same college.

My opinion of politics in my college days is best summed up by my comment to a classmate of mine at Redlands. He was a political science major and was distressed that I took no interest in politics. I remember his complaining to me about it, and my reply, 'Well, what does it matter who you vote for? You just have one vote – and it really doesn't make any difference anyway.'

I didn't begin my career in politics. I chose advertising as a profession. I reasoned that advertising was a field that cut across all areas of the business world, and if I wasn't happy with it later as a career I could easily use it as a springboard into another field.

After I graduated I found a job at J. Walter Thompson Co. in New York for $35 a week, and transferred later to San Francisco before returning to Los Angeles, where I was eventually promoted to vice-president and manager.

As a part of my responsibilities as J.W.T. Manager in

Los Angeles, I became involved in a number of both business and community activities. Before long, the tail was wagging the dog. I found that I got much more personal satisfaction and sense of accomplishment from this kind of activity than I did from running the business.

I was particularly interested in several things involving young people, Junior Achievement and the Coro Foundation, and I became a trustee of both these fine organisations. I was also greatly intrigued with the dynamic growth in both size and stature of my alma mater, U.C.L.A. After serving as General Scholarship Chairman for the Alumni Association, and heading the fund-raising drive to build Pauley Pavilion, I was elected President of the U.C.L.A. Alumni Association for a two-year term. This also made me an ex-officio Regent of the University of California.

My time on the Board of Regents, both ex-officio, and later as an appointed Regent for a 16-year term (from which I resigned upon going to the White House because I felt there was a conflict of interest in the fact that the University derived about one-third of its operating revenue from the Federal government – a nicety which did not seem to concern several of my fellow Regents who kept their seats on the Board while serving in the Kennedy and Johnson administrations), was the most enjoyable and productive experience I had had up to that time. One of my very real regrets on leaving California for Washington was the resignation from the Regents.

I also served on the Board, and for a short time as Chairman of the Board, of Trustees of the California Institute of the Arts during its formative years.

Incidentally, the turning point of my career as an advertising man was my success in launching a television show called *I Search for Adventure.*

In a way it was my own search for adventure that led me away from advertising. I wanted action beyond the routine of the advertising career I had entered. And Richard Nixon in 1952 was the centre of action – and one I could reach because Nixon was a Californian.

What attracted me to Nixon? As I've said I wasn't a

rabid conservative. (And, of course, neither was Nixon, as the *real* conservatives discovered when Nixon became President and introduced economic proposals that made them shudder, and a reopening of relations with China that inspired absolute fury.)

What appealed to me first about Nixon was that he was a fighter. I became aware of him in the Alger Hiss case and was impressed. Everyone else on the Congressional Committee fell apart when the elegant Hiss appeared and issued his eloquent denial. Nixon refused to be cowed.

Of course, as I write this, I have to laugh. I can almost hear my own groans during so many Oval Office conferences when Nixon would launch into a recreation of the Hiss case. How he loved that case! He was able, somehow, to compare every tough situation we ever encountered, even Watergate, to his handling of the Hiss case.

Nixon would sometimes switch the subject – to his book, *Six Crises*, and off he would go exhorting you to 'read that book again, really, a hell of a book, great stuff in there, everything you need to know is in it,' etc., etc., etc.

In 1952 Nixon was nominated to be Vice-President by the Republican party. As a fellow Californian, I was proud of him – and sympathetic when a scandal about a financial fund hit the press. (It would later turn out that Nixon's opponent, Adlai Stevenson, had an almost identical fund, but as usual, no headlines there.) It appeared that Nixon's career was finished almost before it began. I joined other Californians in a show of support; stood outside the television studio the night he made his famous Checkers speech and sent a note volunteering to work in the campaign. My offer was not accepted.

I'm well aware that I'm recalling two events which set Democrats' teeth chattering with disgust: the Hiss case and the Checkers speech. But I, a young Californian, viewed those two events differently: as two incidents which revealed Nixon fighting against odds, and the establishment, and winning.

Again in 1956 I made my pitch to be an advance man for the Nixon re-election campaign. This time I succeeded.

Bob Finch, who was to be Nixon's campaign manager in 1960, was impressed with my work in 1956 and again in the Congressional campaign of 1958, and in 1960, persuaded me to take a leave of absence from J. Walter Thompson Co. to become Nixon's chief advance man in his drive for the Presidency.

From that point on I was very close to Nixon during the political campaigns. It turned out, somewhat to my surprise, that I was a born advance man. This is one of the most demanding jobs in politics. It needs organisational ability (I'm not modest about my credentials as an advance man), a passion for precision and punctuality, and a strong enough character to counterbalance the demands of different political groups and personalities.

I worked in five political campaigns with Nixon, none of them easy. In fact two, in 1960 against Kennedy, and in 1962 against Pat Brown for Governor of California, were crushing disappointments for Nixon. Always he recovered, to the dismay of the growing legion of Nixon-haters in the land.

The legions kept expanding partly because Nixon was an aggressive campaigner; his theme was always attack, attack, and attack again.

Nixon rarely spared the rod or the knife in his speeches and, to put it mildly, he wasn't averse to using all possible means to try to defeat his opponents. I believed in tough campaigning too, but even from my hard-line standpoint, Nixon went too far at times. But political strategy wasn't my province, only the mechanics. For political advice Nixon consulted experts such as John Mitchell, Robert Finch, Len Hall, Bill Rogers, or Murray Chotiner, Nixon's first guru in politics.

Therefore I was surprised and pleased when, after his 1968 victory, Nixon informed me that I was going to be his Chief-of-Staff in the White House. It's fair to say that Nixon's confidence in me for that high position added to my sense of loyalty to him.

Having served Nixon in the Chief-of-Staff role during the campaign, I had a good idea of what the job would involve. I gave it a lot of thought during the transition period, as we were setting up our White House staff structure and procedures. I studied everything I could get my hands on regarding the operations of earlier White House staffs, but I recognised from the outset that we had to develop our own approach, adapted to the particular needs and demands of this particular President.

The Assistant to the President, or Chief-of-Staff, or whatever it may be called, is a unique post, which varies to fit each Chief Executive. We developed our original senior staff as a group of five general assistants to the President, with no specific areas of responsibility. Each would be available for whatever the President needed.

But this approach inevitably changed substantially to adjust to day-to-day experience, and we found that my position evolved as the one general assistant; while each of the others took on specific areas such as domestic policy, foreign policy, congressional relations.

My primary responsibility was simply to enable the President to function most effectively. This meant he could rely on the staff for handling details, referring all possible matters to others for preliminary handling, assuring that when a problem did come to the President all sides were adequately represented. Contrary to the popular belief, the President always saw *both* sides to every question because he insisted that this be done, and I saw it as one of my major assignments.

I also planned the President's schedule, following his guide-lines as to how he needed to spend his time. We used the President's day most efficiently, giving him sufficient periods for both preparation and consideration of decisions, as well as the time he needed for meeting with people. This process involved very complete preparation for each meeting the President had, to make the conference most useful.

As part of my scheduling responsibility, I also planned and executed the many Presidential trips, both in this country and to foreign countries.

I was the focal point for the whole range of problems

that concerned the staff and the President. I knew at all times exactly what the President was doing, what his current priorities were, what he was expecting others to accomplish. I had no independent schedule of my own. I operated totally at the President's beck and call, working my own projects in between his demands. I based my plans for each day completely on the President's. I travelled with him on all trips, including holiday and vacation weekends. I was rarely more than a few feet away from him during the working day, and never out of immediate touch by telephone at any hour of the day or night.

In order to assure adequate staff work and to eliminate duplication, I reviewed all paperwork before it went to the President and most of what came from him for action.

And I was generally responsible for the overall administration of the White House office and the many support facilities.

I saw few people during a regular working day other than the staff and the President. I was very definitely an 'inside man'. And I was very frequently the President's sounding board for whatever was on his mind. He particularly called on me for discussion of political matters and – at very great length – questions of public relations.

I found it a very demanding job in terms of both time and energy. It had its high and low points, as every job does, but I was fascinated by every minute of it. It was the greatest challenge I had ever faced. A rare opportunity to work hard at something that really could make a difference.

I was always at least generally conversant with whatever the President was involved in. So, instead of having to figure out who to contact on each particular item, he could simply call me in and cover everything on his mind, leaving it to me to follow up with the appropriate people.

I had an excellent junior staff of my own to help me handle the demands of this job. I even had my own 'Haldeman', a remarkable young man named Larry Higby, whom

I had brought with me from J. Walter Thompson Co., where he also had worked as my assistant.

I took my job very seriously – perhaps, in retrospect, too much so. I pushed for a 'zero defects' operation, for which I have been soundly ridiculed in the press. But I felt that there was no margin for error in the operation of the Office of the President of the United States. And that there was no reason why we should tolerate anything less than top performance from everyone at every level. And we usually got it.

We had a group of very capable young men on the staff. I rode them hard; made heavy demands on them for flawless work with no mistakes or excuses. I drummed into them the concept that anything can be done if you just figure out how to do it and don't give up. I wouldn't take 'no' for an answer. They knew they were expected to deliver.

I can see now that I substantially over-reached in this approach. I put on too much pressure, and in the process laid the groundwork for the mental attitude that 'the job must be done' which badly disserved the cause when Watergate struck. By then, our whole crew was so strongly indoctrinated in the principle that there were to be results, not alibis, that they simply once again swung into action – doing what they felt was expected of them.

Because I approached my own job totally impersonally, and handled the criticism I received from the President in that way, I just assumed others did likewise. But they didn't. I rode some of them too hard. And because they knew I wouldn't tolerate failure, they used their presumed power in my name to go too far. In many cases, I now realise, the 'Haldeman wants this done' line was used as a major threat – often in some matter that I knew nothing about.

My wife, getting glimpses of my operation and relationships with the staff, especially the junior men, very perceptively has since observed that it wasn't *Nixon*'s character or moods that allowed Watergate to happen. She points out that *my* character and demands pushed people to become 'little generals', which was out of character for them. What was natural for me (and worked effectively for me) was emulated by them, but their actions were artificial and created resentment. I had too much on my mind to realise how far-reaching this was – or how damaging it could be.

My demands always were expectant of results. Ideas weren't an answer, nor was a review of the problem. It was push, push, push for concrete action. In that setting the action got more and more out-of-hand as wilder schemes were proposed to get more answers and satisfy what they thought were my expectations.

During the transition period, Nixon told me a story that explained his decision to choose me for this job. In 1960, before running for President, Nixon had visited Eisenhower in the Oval Office. Eisenhower had told him that every President has to have 'his S.O.B.' Nixon had looked over everyone in his entourage and decided that Haldeman was a pluperfect S.O.B. And because of that somewhat unflattering appraisal, my career took a rise.

Nixon also liked to tell about other advice from Eisenhower. When Nixon was Vice-President, he visited Eisenhower in the Oval Office one day and found him signing letters. Eisenhower told Nixon, 'The mark of a good executive is when you're handed letters which you know you could have written better yourself and you sign them anyway.'

In any event, I certainly filled my role as the President's S.O.B. with gusto – according to the press which covered the White House. In fact, despite my desire for anonymity, I eventually fascinated reporters. These are some of their reactions which give a picture of my public image in those White House years:

From *Newsweek*:

> Harry Robbins Haldeman is, as he once put it, Richard Nixon's son-of-a-bitch. He sits 100 gold-carpeted feet down the hall from the Oval Office,

> glowering out at the world from under a crewcut that would flatter a drill instructor, with a gaze that would freeze Medusa. He is neither quite so forbidding as he looks nor quite so fierce as his reputation as the keystone of a Berlin Wall around Mr Nixon; he even has a sense of humour, about subjects other than his boss. But he is the man who says No for the President of the United States, a mission he executes with a singleness of purpose and an authority that are respected – and feared – thoughout official Washington. 'Bob Haldeman is probably the most powerful man in the country next to the President,' says one ex-colleague – and he got that way because he spends more time next to the President than anybody else in government.

And from *Time*:

> Spiky and glaring, he . . . personifies the Nixon Administration: the Prussian guard who keeps Mr Nixon's door, the 'zero-defects' man who bosses the White House staff, the all-knowing assistant president of legendary arrogance, efficiency and power.

My image bothered reporters, no doubt about it. Bad enough that Nixon was President, did he have to have a 'Nazi' as his Chief-of-Staff?

That German name. Those eyes 'that would freeze Medusa'!

In early 1977, I was taken to lunch by a friend at the Cafe Swiss in Beverly Hills. A movie producer approached me, looking tentative. 'Mr Haldeman, I hate to bother you, but I have a picture opening Monday and it's about Watergate. A satire.'

'Oh,' was all I could think to say. The producer, who identified himself as Robert Enders, plunged on. 'It takes place in a convent.'

'A convent? Who plays Haldeman?'

'Geraldine Page.'

I never saw his movie, *Nasty Habits*, but I sympathise with Miss Page, or any performer, including Robert Vaughn in television's *Washington – Behind Closed Doors,* who has to play my role.

Of course I realise that what fostered the 'Nazi' image wasn't merely a German name and a crewcut. It was both my personality and my approach to my job.

I'm naturally reclusive. I'm content to enjoy the company of my family, and don't enjoy going out at night to dinners and parties.

Also, I envisioned my job at the White House as that of a manager, and was determined to be the best manager a President ever had. That meant I had to be tough. I was tough.

Add to that a reputation for 'puritanism' and you're nearing the Nazi image. I'll admit I didn't swing with the likes of John Dean, Alex Butterfield, Ron Ziegler, or some of the other more lively members of the White House staff. I did smoke a pipe, and enjoy an occasional vodka-and-tonic during my first two years in the White House, but then I quit basically for religious reasons. As for pursuit of women other than my wife, I gladly plead guilty to being square in that regard. In fact, I was always all-business-and-no-play on trips. One of my hard-pressed assistants, Dwight Chapin, finally made the ultimate comment about his tyrannical boss which made me laugh when I heard it. Chapin and others were sitting around the White House one day discussing their chief, and Chapin remarked, 'I've finally figured out Haldeman's secret.'

'What is it?'

'He keeps an inflatable woman in his briefcase.'

My style at work was exactly opposite to Nixon's. I was brusque, direct, I 'chewed people out'. I would come straight on at a problem or person, hammering culprits over the head, verbally. Nixon would attack the same problem or person by coming in at the side, often through subordinates when the victim wasn't looking, and trying to strike his blow unseen. Interestingly, Nixon never worried about his own deviousness; instead he was concerned that his Chief-of-Staff was *too* direct.

In fact, Nixon once sent Bebe Rebozo to lecture me on this subject. Over coffee at the Key Biscayne Hotel, Bebe got down to business. The President felt I would do better in my job if I were more circuitous, more diplomatic, less straight-ahead. The swarthy Cuban ordered more coffee, snapping his fingers so loudly a busboy jumped. Then he considerately offered me a whole string of Dale Carnegie homilies. Nixon obviously wanted me to become more like Nixon. The description Nixon gave of himself was 'diplomatic' – others seemed to have termed it 'tricky', or worse. I, of course, couldn't have changed my character any more than Nixon could his, and so Bebe's mission was a failure.

A remarkable young artist named Garry Trudeau creates a comic strip 'Doonesbury'. This happens to be my children's favourite strip, and when they introduced it to me, I saw why. I imagine young Mr Trudeau must have been a bit shocked when I, a monster in the 'Watergate Alumni Club', which was featured in his strip, sent word to him that I liked two of his strips about me which were hardly flattering. I said that I hoped he would give me the originals to frame. Trudeau said he didn't usually do this, but in my case he would make an exception – and they're framed on the wall of my den today.

In one of them, two characters are talking. 'Did you hear Mark's profile of Haldeman?' one asks. The other replies, 'Yes, it sounds like he was unfit for office. How could the second most powerful man in the world come from an advertising agency?' The other character remarks, 'Well, he could have done a lot of reading on his own.'

The fact that I enjoy Trudeau's humour – even at my own expense – is an admittedly round-about way of saying that I wasn't born an Iron Chancellor. In my advertising days that Trudeau has fun with I was known as an easy-going executive. Larry Higby, who worked for me both at J. Walter Thompson Co. and the White House, was the first to realise I had changed one hundred per cent in my latter capacity.

Much has been made of the 'Berlin Wall' that I am supposed to have constructed around Nixon – either to keep him in or the world out, or both. This is usually raised in making the point that Nixon was 'isolated' by his staff, didn't have any communication with the outside world, was a loner who made all his decisions in a complete vacuum.

I have strongly denied these charges because they are completely off the mark. My comment has always been that Nixon was really the most *un*isolated President in history. And I based this opinion on the concept that our staffing system gave him the opportunity to control his time and his access to the advisers he knew would be most useful. The system was designed neither to keep him in or others out, but to provide the means for making sure that he had ready access to all those who could be helpful to him.

In another sense, however, I realised that many problems in our administration arose not solely from the outside, but from inside the Oval Office – and even deeper, from inside the character of Richard Nixon. And to deal with these problems I realised I would have to turn myself into the man you know and don't love.

And start to build a wall.

2

Why did I think – rightly or wrongly – that Nixon needed a wall of any kind? There were two reasons, only the first of which Nixon knew about, the 'official' reason.

Nixon was able to halt, through me, the unending flow of government officials who 'just had to see the President'. Time and again these 'urgent' meetings would turn out to be either meaningless ego trips ('I saw the President today') or, worse: long, time-wasting discussions of some minor departmental gripe.

Nixon wanted these officials to submit their problems in writing or to deal with someone on the staff better able to handle their concerns than the President *before* they were granted precious Presidential time. And this infuriated them, because the man who said 'no' to them was a staffer, me. I'm afraid that all too often the 'no' was delivered without a velvet glove that would have made it more diplomatic. They vented their fury on me, but every White House insider knew that I was doing this at the President's direct order. And so did most of the outsiders, though they didn't want to admit it.

The other reason for the wall was my secret. I soon realised that *this* President had to be protected from himself. Time and again I would receive petty vindictive orders. 'Hugh Sidey is to be kept off Air Force One.' (Sidey was *Time*'s man.) Or even, once or twice, '*All* the press is barred from Air Force One.' (Pool representatives of the press accompanied the President on every trip.) Or, after a Senator made an anti-Vietnam War speech: 'Put a 24-hour surveillance on that bastard.' And on and on and on. If I took no action, I would pay for it. The President never let up. He'd be on the intercom buzzing me ten minutes after such an order. 'What have you done about Sidey?' I'd say, 'I'm working on it,' and delay and delay until Nixon would one day comment, with a sort of half-smile on his face, 'I guess you never took action on that, did you?'

'No.'

'Well, I guess it was the best thing.'

And so I had constructed this wall for a double purpose until another character entered the White House, Charles 'Chuck' Colson. Unfortunately, Colson encouraged the dark impulses in Nixon's mind, and *acted* on those impulses instead of ignoring them and letting them die. By 1971 Colson was one of the few on the small list of people who saw the President frequently. As a White House aide once put it, 'Haldeman built a wall, but Colson was jumping over the wall.' I must admit he was jumping over with my full knowledge and agreement.

Colson came to us as a political liaison man with labour and other outside groups. He achieved some excellent successes in that area, cementing the Teamsters Union behind Nixon in the 1972 election, for example. And in the 1972 election in general, Colson did well bringing ethnic groups into the Nixon camp.

But he was leading a double life. In between his official projects, he was inside the Oval Office listening enthusiastically to Nixon's outraged pleas for action against various persons or organisations and promising, 'Yes sir, I'll do that for you by tomorrow morning.'

What made it worse was that Colson in those years had an abrasive, boastful, and overbearing personality. Very soon he had enraged most of the White House staff, as well as John Mitchell, who once arrived in my office imploring me to fire Colson. 'He's bad news,' Mitchell said. 'He'll get the President in trouble.' But I told him my hands were tied. By then the President thought Colson was great.

And why not? One of Colson's first successes was very dear to the President's heart. It stuck a knife into a Kennedy. One hundred points on the Oval Office chart. Somehow Colson obtained a picture of Teddy Kennedy leaving a night club in Paris with a beautiful woman not his wife in the small hours of the morning. He then arranged for the picture to be published in a gossip-type newspaper. The President loved that picture. From then on, as far as the President was concerned, Colson was Mr Can-Do.

In battle, Nixon always wanted 'to go for the jugular'. The one jugular that fascinated him even more than Larry O'Brien's was Teddy Kennedy's. And some of my own orders, which might later be characterised as 'seamy', revolved around Kennedy. I was to place a 24-hour surveillance on him. I was to 'catch him in the sack with one of his babes'.

Nixon was particularly intrigued to see what Kennedy would do to get himself out of the Chappaquiddick mess.

And even more so when it appeared that the Senator had decided to adopt the 'Checkers speech' approach, first introduced by Richard Nixon himself in 1952. It so happened, however, that this major TV event was to take place at a time when the President of the United States was in Guam on his way to an historic event: the splashdown of the astronauts who had been the first men on the moon. And there was neither TV nor radio coverage of the speech on Guam, so Nixon had no way of knowing what Kennedy said. This was very frustrating – until we figured out a way.

Nixon's aides had been called 'gadget happy' with our walkie-talkies, beepers, and even my movie camera. In this case, I employed much simpler gadgetry to find out what Kennedy was saying in his TV address and to give the President the satisfaction of an immediate report.

I telephoned a staff member at the White House on our ever-available worldwide signal telephone network, and had him place his telephone next to his television set. I sat in my room at the B.O.Q. and listened to the speech over the telephone, making extensive notes. And gave Nixon an instant report. It was an odd feeling to sit in the house overlooking the Pacific from which Admiral Nimitz had directed much of the U.S. operations in World War II and run through my notes on this rather bizarre subject on the eve of welcoming the first men back from the moon.

By 1971 Nixon was using three subordinates – Haldeman, Ehrlichman, and Colson – for three different approaches to some projects. I was the man for the straight, hit-them-over-the-head strategy. Ehrlichman, who loved intrigue, was given the more devious approach. And Colson was assigned the real underground routes.

Of course, if there were no Nixon, there would have been no Colson in the White House. Colson only fed off Nixon; Nixon provided the output which all of us, including Colson, Ehrlichman, and myself, were ordered to put into action.

There can be no real insight into Watergate without

some glimpses into the character of the protagonist, Richard Nixon. I'm not a psychologist – but I know that much of what I've read about Nixon by psychologists is pure fantasy. By 1968 when Nixon entered office, I had learned a lot about my boss, both his strengths and his weaknesses – and by 1973 when I left, I had learned a lot more.

I believe it was my job to emphasise his strengths and protect his weaknesses against exploitation by his political rivals.

Some job. It hurt my marriage – or at least it temporarily cost me the understanding of my wife, Jo. It wasn't until years later, after I resigned and was back in California that Jo revealed what was bothering her. 'I thought you were blind about Nixon, that you couldn't see his faults. I'd hear you on the telephone, coddling and flattering him. It just wasn't like you.'

I told her I saw his weaknesses better than anyone – but I viewed it as my job, purely professionally, to emphasise his strengths. I believed he was a great President, and I didn't want those flaws to impede him.

Two men who knew Richard Nixon almost as well and almost as long as I did have undertaken to give their explanations of this mysterious man. I think both of them have some valid points, but both fail to hit the nail on the head. Certainly their views are far more valid than those of the pseudo-psychologists who, with no first-hand knowledge of the man whatsoever, have nonetheless launched themselves bravely on the waters of analysing Nixon – only to float so far off course as to be ludicrous in their attempts.

Bill Safire, former White House speechwriter, and now *New York Times* columnist, uses the analogy of a layer cake to try to explain the various levels of Nixon's personality. And he concludes that this cake, with its icing and its many light and dark layers, must be sliced vertically, not horizontally, in order to get its true flavour – and all the layers must be included.

Ray Price, also a former White House speechwriter, and now a Fellow at the Kennedy Institute of Politics at Harvard, inclines towards a simpler concept of light and dark sides – at constant war with one another.

I prefer the analogy described by a lady in Boston who has been in frequent correspondence with me over the past years. She, and I, see Nixon as a multifaceted quartz crystal. Some facets bright and shining, others dark and mysterious. And all of them constantly changing as the external light rays strike the crystal. Some of them very deep and impenetrable, others completely on the surface. Some smooth and polished, others crude, rough and sharp.

But the significant point is that each of us sees Nixon as a complex combination of lights and darks. I think to a greater degree than we see most people.

Although I never discussed the subject with Nixon, either directly or indirectly, I think that he clearly understood the role I assigned myself in the conspiracy to keep his dark side down, and his light side up.

I'm sorry now that I didn't discuss it with him because I think we might have made some real progress by getting the matter on the table before us instead of operating on unspoken assumptions.

I am also sorry, in retrospect, that I took the route of building up the light side in every possible way, to the exclusion of restraining positively the dark side. I tried to win the battle between the two by aiding the good guy instead of also fighting the bad guy. If I had it to do over, I would do so differently. I would take the bad guy in Nixon on frontally, at least some of the time.

I must confess that I gave this some thought at the time, but rationalised that if I was to have any effect at all, I must have Nixon's complete trust and confidence, and his willingness to rely on me. And I feared that this might well be destroyed by too many confrontations with his bad side. Clearly, Nixon did identify with the good, and like anyone else, had little interest in a critique of the bad. Those of his good friends like Bob Finch and Herb Klein who tried that route over the years didn't seem to last long. And lesser officials were simply allowed to fade into political oblivion. I remember one day, furious with what he felt to be a disastrous blunder on the part of his staff by putting him into the highly charged atmosphere of a college newspapers editors' press conference, and then compounding the error by exposing the whole thing on national TV, Vice-President Nixon lashed out at the staff. 'How could anyone have been so stupid as to get me into this kind of a no-win situation? Doesn't anyone think these things through – or are you all so enchanted by the great myth that we have to cater constantly to the "youth" that you just can't see straight?'

Ironically, the telecast had been a great success – originating from a college editors' conference at Cornell. But it had been a rigorous ordeal for the candidate under extremely hostile conditions, and he didn't like it. It was all over now; and there was no real purpose in beating a dead horse. But Nixon wouldn't let up. Blowing off steam, he went on and on.

The chief advance man during that campaign of 1956 was an old personal friend of Nixon's from California, rancher Ray Arbuthnot. Tall, bluff, rugged and completely unafraid of Nixon's tirades, Ray decided it had gone far enough, and undertook to calm things down. He knew that the overworked and dead-tired staff could only take so much before they would cut loose themselves.

Ray was one of those old friends who didn't hesitate to tell Nixon what he thought, even when he knew that his words might not be favourably received. He, as did all the rest of us close to Nixon, recognised the 'dark' side when it appeared. But, unlike most of us, he was willing to take it on frontally and challenge it. And this time he proceeded to do so. He ended up, along with the few others who did confront the 'dark' Nixon, fading into the background – where Nixon wouldn't have to face his unwelcome views.

And I felt that the first essential for me – to be of any effect at all – was to survive in the job. I honestly don't think this was a selfish route of self-preservation for my own interest, but an attitude that best served Nixon's interest. I feel content today that I at least did not attain and maintain my relationship with Nixon by the simplest route of playing to his bad side. But I am sorry I didn't directly fight it much either – I just tried to replace it with the good by whatever means I could in the circumstances.

I pursued a policy of active encouragement of the good and 'benign neglect' of the bad.

I completely agree with the Price view that the light side is by far the larger part, and is the side that Nixon himself identifies with. And I also agree that the dark side grew mainly not out of Nixon's nature but of his reaction to experience in public life.

My crystal analogy also permits me to join Price's concept of a third area, which he puts neither the light nor the dark side. That is the coldly calculating, devious, craftily manipulative side. Ray Price sees these, I think rightly, as necessary tools of statecraft. He states that Richard Nixon was both the statesman extraordinaire who reshaped the world in the pattern of his own architecture of peace and Tricky Dick, the shifty political con man, who was essential to bring the dreams of the statesman to reality.

Price explains this rather jarring contention by pointing out that it took a consummate politician to put together the electoral majorities that gave the statesman his opportunity. It took a devious manipulator to engineer public consent for national policies that often went against the grain of the voters' private interests, and to line up other nations of the world behind policies that their leaders had vowed never to accept. It required a politician with a keen sense of the possible, with a cynical sense of political reality with the drive and the ambition and the cunning to pull it off.

I was never a social friend of Nixon's. Only once, in my entire relationship with him over many years, were my wife and I invited to an informal personal dinner at his home, and that was in 1962. But that doesn't mean I wasn't close to him; indeed, closer than anyone else professionally. (As Alex Butterfield would later testify: Haldeman was 'an extension of Nixon, his alter ego'.) And from that proximate viewpoint I saw both greatness and meanness in Nixon in such a bewildering combination that, years later, peering out of a hotel window at the White House which I had been forced to leave, I muttered out loud: 'Nixon was the weirdest man ever to live in the White House.'

Mike Wallace of C.B.S. overheard that remark, put me on a special television show in 1975 at a great cost, and then was outraged when I stonewalled him. I was still determined to discuss only the positives and to refuse to dwell on the negatives. But then in 1977 I watched, in growing dismay, the performance of Richard Nixon on television in the David Frost interviews in which – in a flow of emotional doubletalk – he 'revealed' that his only guilt in Watergate was not firing Ehrlichman and me, the real villains soon enough.

I guess I shouldn't have been surprised. This part of his performance was vintage 'dark' Richard Nixon, fighting for survival, now trying to rehabilitate himself over the prostrate bodies of his aides: 'splendid fellows' who unfortunately ran the cover-up without telling Nixon anything.

The fact is Watergate was too great a drama to be determined by any one man; me, Ehrlichman, or even Nixon. But of all of us, and perhaps of all Presidents of the past century, Richard Nixon is by far the most fascinating individual.

3

Richard Nixon used to disappear in the middle of the night during campaign trips. I would call for him at his hotel room in a small Midwestern city in the morning and find that he was missing. Some time in the early dawn he had gotten out of bed and slipped away, with a nervous Secret Service man tailing him. We'd search all over town until we found the candidate looking haggard and wan in a flea-bitten coffeeshop.

Even after he became President, there was an occasion when Nixon made the same kind of strange excursion before the eyes of the world.

That was in 1970 during a massive antiwar protest demonstration in Washington, when he arose in the middle of the night and went to the Lincoln Memorial at four in the morning, where he talked with a group of young demonstrators. This event has been reported in many different ways; as a touching gesture by Nixon to reach out to the young; as a disastrous failure to communicate with youth; and various stages in between.

I was awakened after he got to the Memorial by a phone call from Ehrlichman who had been alerted by Bud Krogh, who was 'on duty' that night. I rushed to the Capitol where he had gone after leaving the Memorial. From there we went to the Mayflower Hotel coffeeshop where we all had breakfast and I tried to figure out exactly what had happened, and how to handle it.

To clear up some of the misconceptions, let me say first of all that I am certain that Nixon did not leave the White House in the early morning hours for the purpose of going out to talk with the demonstrators. It had been one of Nixon's most trying days in office. He was restless after a particularly difficult TV press conference and couldn't sleep. Some time in the small hours of the morning, he asked Manolo, his valet, to join him in a trip into the night, similar to those he had made on the campaign trail. When they reached the Lincoln Memorial, they found some students there.

Incidentally, the popular media concept that Nixon's ensuing conversation with the students was a 'dialogue of the deaf' and that Nixon was totally unable to communicate with the protestors is far from the mark.

But our efforts to have this rather odd junket portrayed

in its true light, were, as usual, not very effective. Realising the probability of misinterpretation, Nixon met with Jack Horner of the *Washington Star* on his return to the White House to brief him. But this failed to counter the devastating effect of a TV interview with one of the students who dismissed the Nixon conversation as a talk about football and surfing.

This situation set in motion a prime example of our rather heavy-handed but nonetheless well-meaning efforts at improving our public relations.

I am indebted to Ray Price's outstanding book, *With Nixon* for a reprint of a memo I sent Ray several days later in the attempt to correct the media distortion. Ray presents it as written by me as a covering memo transmitting a detailed recount of Nixon's own recollections. But my memo – reprinted here – was not written by me but by Nixon. Following our usual practice, I had simply paraphrased a memorandum from Nixon to me insisting that something be done about the problem. Reading it in that light makes it far more interesting as an insight into Nixon's very direct concerns with such matters.

MEMORANDUM FOR: MR RAY PRICE

Attached is a memorandum of what actually took place at the Lincoln Memorial on Saturday morning.

After you read it I think you will probably have some feelings as to how our coverage of this activity could have been better and perhaps some ideas on steps that might be taken now to follow up on this.

It gives us a unique opportunity to communicate on matters that may in the long run be infinitely more important than the material specifics – that is the qualities of spirit and emotion which the President's visit to the memorial was really about.

The President has since made the point that he realises that it would have made more news from the standpoint of the students for him to engage with a spirited dialogue with them about why we were in Cambodia – why we haven't ended the war sooner –

the morality of the war, etc. This kind of conversation would have been infinitely more easy for him, it would have made more news, but as he evaluated the situation he had the feeling that this was the one time this group of students most of whom appeared to him to be middle class or lower middle class – that this was the only time they would ever talk to a President of the United States. He felt they would see him many times in TV, etc., discussing the heated, angry subjects that they would hear later at the rally and that they hear in their classrooms. He felt that perhaps the major contribution he could make to them was 'to try to lift them a bit out of the miserable intellectual wasteland in which they now wander aimlessly around.'

I think that this urge – even need – to make these occasional post-midnight excursions was Nixon's unique way of letting off steam when things were very tense or he was very tired.

Another factor that I very soon became aware of was Nixon's insecurity about his truly humble background. He never let us forget that his mother had to scrub bedpans, for example. I remember the first time I realised how this attitude was reflected in his perception of me. We were preparing a campaign event in Houston, and I had gone on ahead to work on it with Oveta Culp Hobby, the publisher of the Houston *Post* and a social leader in the community.

She and I got along very well and I had a good time working with her on all the arrangements. The event was a great success. At the airport departure, Mrs Hobby said something to Nixon, conventional but kind, such as, 'Your assistant is a very bright young man.' To my surprise and Mrs Hobby's, Nixon replied, 'Well, I thought you knew, Bob comes from one of the finest families in Los Angeles.'

Nixon's statement had a note of grandeur above my family's limits, but beyond that fact, it was the first time

I realised Nixon was aware of *anyone*'s background – let alone mine. Ironically, I was the one awed by *his* background; a man who was Vice-President and knew world-famous statesmen on a first-name basis. And yet there was a defensiveness in that remark which I didn't miss, and I don't believe Mrs Hobby did either. She glanced at me with a humorous expression for an instant and then changed the subject.

Later, I was to see this Nixon attitude surface again even more markedly with one or another of his rich and 'well-bred' new associates. I believe that's why he hated the Eastern elite so much ('None of them in the Cabinet, do you understand? None of those Harvard bastards!' when we were reorganising the government for the second term). Nixon wanted to surround himself with self-made men from west of the Mississippi or south of the Mason-Dixon line, and I noticed on the Frost television interviews in 1977, he still took time to lambast the 'rich who have nothing to do but party' (i.e., the Eastern elite).

Nixon was more complex than the 'classic case of insecurity – poor boy, thrust among the rich and powerful, – therefore vulnerable.' There was an insecurity factor, but the interesting and perhaps unique ingredient in Nixon's make-up, as far as I was concerned, was the way he tried to *overcome* that insecurity. He accomplished it by imposing a rigid self-discipline to shield him from mistakes. That self-discipline was so tight it was *unnatural*. And when it burst, the effects were devastating.

The nation saw this happen only a few times. Once, when he exploded against the press after losing the 1962 gubernatorial race in California, and again in 1974 when he angrily shoved his press aide, Ron Ziegler, at an airport arrival ceremony, shouting that he wanted Ziegler to keep the press away from him. This was when Watergate was white-hot, and he was apparently losing his iron control.

I had seen such outbursts often enough before in private not to be surprised that he shoved Ziegler; what startled me was that he did it in public. Nixon was a man obsessed with maintaining what he perceived to be a correct public image (leading him, for example, to wear street shoes while walking along the beach for a publicity picture that Ziegler insisted on. The resulting laughter surprised Nixon). This obsession led to his fascination for – and enduring envy of – the Kennedy's. Nixon took pains with his public image; he dressed neatly and conservatively, handled himself calmly in public, made all of his ceremonial appearances in good style and humour – and yet, no matter what he did, he seemed to come across as flat, unattractive, unappealing. Jack Kennedy had only to stand up to project a charismatic image of 'class'. And, of course, to a lesser extent, this was also true of Kennedy's brothers.

It's difficult for me to account for another characteristic of Nixon, this one a classic as far as the White House staff was concerned. His bewildering combination of great grace and amazing awkwardness in dealing with people face-to-face on a personal basis. Some of those staffers, like Dean, have made fun of the fact that Nixon was mechanically clumsy, which he was. There are, however, a great many urbane sophisticates who can deal beautifully with people, but can't replace a light bulb without breaking it.

Nixon simply could not relax with people other than his family. (A unique exception is Bebe Rebozo, with whom he had a sort of spiritual affinity. I don't know Bebe well enough to be aware of what chords in him were attuned to Nixon's, but I know he played a valuable role, because Nixon needed someone with whom to talk and relax.) But in a personal, as contrasted to an official, context he was stiff, artificial, sometimes even embarrassing with individuals. Oddly, with groups, he could be superb.

(One White House staffer used to do a wicked impersonation of Nixon greeting a guest in the Oval Office. The President kept in his desk a drawer filled with mementoes of the White House – cufflinks, tie pins, things like that. Nixon would abruptly turn away, take one out of the drawer and – without looking back – thrust it towards his surprised guest, like an N.B.A. guard handing off a ball behind his back. Then he would turn to the man and tell his standard Nixon joke that never, in my memory, drew a laugh: 'Give this to your wife *or* your secretary, whichever you prefer.')

This awkwardness was sometimes also a problem for the President in the conduct of his official duties. Contrast, for example, his relations with Congress with those of his predecessor, Lyndon Johnson. L.B.J. was rough-tongued, but at the same time he could charm or bluster you into anything. He was an absolute master at Congressional persuasion. Nixon was not at his best at this vital art. Johnson could envelop a Congressman in charm, make him come out doing what Johnson wanted and at the same time lay in a very tough threat of what would happen if the Congressman *didn't* do it. Nixon tried the same approach, but the charm wasn't there – and the threat would be left hanging bald, bare, and glaring.

Unfortunately, this wasn't just the case with Congressmen. Nixon was often awkward in dealing, one-on-one, with government officials, business leaders, press tycoons, union officials, or anyone he needed to work with on purely personal or social terms. Oddly, when it was straight business, he was usually excellent. And this of course goes back to my reason for building a 'wall' around him. He hated to see people who needed either to be personally persuaded or forced to take action. He preferred to pass that job to others.

That awkwardness with people was an off-shoot of his rigidly imposed self-discipline that hid such strong emotions. He was conscious every minute of self-discipline; therefore he couldn't relax with most people.

This is one side of the man who had become President: insecure because of his humble background, personally awkward with people ('I'm an introvert in an extrovert's profession,' he said), trying to shield strong emotions behind an iron self-discipline. Such a man, in the pressures of the political world, would see enemies (most of them real) everywhere; would be unable to defeat those enemies by a normal 'easy' attitude that inspires popularity, would despair at his lack of natural charisma, and realise that if he was to win he would have to attack and destroy the enemy.

Why did Nixon go as far as he did? From my long relationship with him, I saw up-close this tendency to strike too hard – remarked by other observers – as a major flaw. It reflected a belief in, and too great a willingness to accept, the concept that the end justifies the means. In other words, 'It's good for the country if I'm elected, therefore, *whatever I do to get elected is good for the country.*' By that process, he rationalised as acceptable acts that by tighter standards would be judged not acceptable – in terms of statements to be made, actions to be taken, the methodology of fighting back, of counterattacking. A willingness perhaps to say that 'they're doing it to me, so I've got to do it to them.'

It's a natural human reaction, but as one arrives at the gateways of greatness, he's expected to rise above that sort of reaction and be able to do *better* than most men, rather than being excused for having the same failings that most men have.

All of this was what I once described in a note to myself as 'the dirty, mean, base side of Nixon'. (And I worried about that side.)

But if that were the sum of Nixon, he would not be so fascinating, and I would never have gone to work for him – or stayed so long. Nixon had many strong, positive characteristics which are generally conceded even by his detractors: intelligence, analytical ability, judgement, shrewdness, courage, decisiveness, and strength. And, believe it or not, he had a 'heart'.

He was considerate of those who worked for him, even though rarely close to them on a personal basis. (To this day he doesn't know how many children I have nor anything else about my private life; he never asked – and I was his closest professional associate.) But I always felt in those days, before the walls began closing in and he started to panic, that he cared for my welfare and the welfare of the other staffers who worked for him.

I realise, of course, that he now says and may very well feel that it was his very concern for his subordinates that brought about his downfall. This was not true. But at the same time, I know he did feel very emotional when I resigned.

And I can attest to his 'heart' with other less personal examples. One of the most difficult Presidential responsibilities, because it was always so poignant and sad, was the presentation of posthumous Congressional Medals of Honour to the families of men who had been killed in Vietnam. Strangely, Nixon, the 'awkward' man, had an amazing ability to relate to these people. I knew the incredible agony he went through before and after these ceremonies – they would tear him up – but his compassion always was real for these bereaved people, and he communicated it to them simply and beautifully. I'm aware that every President in time of war has acted the same way and felt the same emotions because of the knowledge of his responsibility for the loss of husbands or fathers. Nixon was no less deeply touched than Lincoln or Roosevelt – an indication that he is not such a cold-hearted, calculating human – compared to those famous wartime Presidents – as many might like to think.

There were lighter moments, too, in my association with Nixon. He absolutely hated the large formal dinners that he constantly had to host. Nevertheless he would throw himself headlong into the preparations, driving everyone, from the chef to the household staff, to his own wife, crazy. He'd check every item of the menu and each facet of the evening programme, adjusting this or that detail until he got it right.

I remember the humorous aftermath of our first formal state banquet at the White House. The next day Nixon critiqued the dinner as if it had been a major military battle. Every detail was commented upon. But one item more than any other drew his attention: the soup course. As he put it, 'We've got to speed up these dinners. They take forever. So why don't we just leave out the soup course?'

'Well – '

Nixon ploughed on: 'Men don't really like soup.'

That afternoon I met Manolo Sanchez, Nixon's valet, in the hall. I asked, 'Was there anything wrong with the President's suit after that dinner last night?'

Manolo said yes. 'He spilled the soup down his vest.'

I smiled. Just what I expected. And that's why soup was never again served at a state banquet in the Nixon years.

But more often he was irritated because he found those dinners so long and dull. 'Why do they have to wait until every single guest has finished a course before removing the dishes?' he said. 'The guest of honour and I are served first, so as soon as we finish they could remove our dishes, and then keep going right down the table.' He was excited as a child by the idea. 'Look, let's try that next time and put a stopwatch on it. I'll bet we can finish dinner in under an hour.'

So we had our memorable 'stopwatch dinner' – and Nixon was right. We finished in 58 minutes, but the waiters were breathing hard – not to mention the guests.

The fact that I wasn't a social friend was another reason I, instead of a Herb Klein or a Bob Finch, ended up with my job. In fact, Nixon actually shunted long-time personal friends as far away as possible during his Administration. (Despite the portrayal of me in television's *Washington – Behind Closed Doors* as a bitter enemy of Herb Klein's, I was a good friend of his. In fact, when Nixon got into deep trouble during the latter days of Watergate, I urged him to replace Ziegler with Klein as Press Secretary because I knew Herb would be much better in the job during that strained period. He had a natural rapport with newsmen.)

Nixon viewed Klein and Finch in human terms, as people, which meant he would have had trouble dealing with them on an official basis.

He didn't see me as a person or even, I believe, as a human being. I was a machine. A robot. Shortly after it came out I saw the movie *Star Wars*: there is a robot, a metal machine clanking along doing what it's told by a computer-like mind. From Nixon's viewpoint, that's what

I was. And I was a good machine. I was efficient, I didn't require a lot of 'oiling' – and he wasn't good at 'oiling'; or what L.B.J. called 'schmoozing'.

Nixon also had a terrible temper, but almost always succeeded in keeping it under control in public. In private, with one of us who worked closely with him, he could really blow.

I remember a campaign trip through Iowa in 1960. A new advance man (whose name was John Ehrlichman) had planned a full day's drive across the state, stopping at small towns in the midst of wheat fields where Nixon would step out of the car and make a speech. We soon realised that the planners had erred: while there were good crowds at the towns, it was obvious we had wasted a good part of a precious day of campaigning by driving the long distances between stops. Nixon seethed with anger. He was riding in an open convertible and Air Force Major Don Hughes, Nixon's military aide, was in the seat directly in front of Nixon's. Suddenly – incredibly – Nixon began to kick the back of Hughes's seat with both feet. And he wouldn't stop! Thump! Thump! Thump! The seat and the hapless Hughes jolted forward jaggedly as Nixon vented his rage. When the car stopped at a small town in the middle of nowhere, Hughes, white-faced, silently got out of the car and started walking straight ahead, and down the road and out of town. He wanted to get as far away as he could from the Vice-President. I believe he would have walked clear across the state if I hadn't set out after him and apologised for Nixon and finally talked him into rejoining us.

Nixon's most celebrated outburst took place after he lost the 1962 gubernatorial election. But this event has an ending unknown to anyone. To begin with, I had left Nixon in his hotel suite with some friends after the defeat became certain and had gone to Bob Finch's room in the hotel to have some breakfast. It had been decided that Herb Klein would make the concession statement for Nixon.

Then someone burst in and shouted, 'Nixon's going down there himself. And he's boiling.'

I ran to the elevator and down to the press room. Herb Klein, unaware of what was happening, was making the statement. Because he was on camera, I couldn't break in and stop him. I looked around for Nixon. Nowhere to be seen. He must have taken a different route from mine. Desperately I waved to Klein to alert him, but he couldn't see me behind the crowd of reporters. Too late: Nixon abruptly walked on to the podium. Klein was startled. What was this? Awkwardly he turned the floor over to Nixon and stood aside, worriedly.

Nixon gave him – and me – something to worry about with his statement 'you won't have Nixon to kick around any more.'

The unknown twist is this. Most reporters and editorial pundits quickly – and rather gleefully – reported that Nixon had finally 'flipped his lid' in public and by showing his paranoia' had destroyed himself as a viable political candidate. They pictured Nixon dumbstruck at what he had done, bitterly ruing the moment he let his fury show.

What they didn't know was that Nixon was delighted. 'I finally told those bastards off,' he told us, 'and every Goddamned thing I said was true.' And even after the editorial artillery rolled into line and lambasted him from almost every corner of the country, Nixon never wavered in his personal satisfaction with that incident.

Should he have been embarrassed as most other men would have been? Yes – although, in fairness, few political candidates had more provocation from the press than Nixon during that and earlier campaigns. But the bitterness that would drive a man to make such a spectacle of himself on camera boded ill for him, and for the country, after he became President.

What is sad from an historical viewpoint is that this man, with this deep-seated bitterness, was determined after he became President to really bring the country together – including the press. And for a while he succeeded.

Powerful political columnists such as Scotty Reston of the *New York Times* and Joe Kraft of the *Washington Post* hailed the 'new' Nixon who seemed so reasonable and calm, a welcome relief from the tumultuous L.B.J.

But there was a war raging, a conflict that had destroyed Nixon's predecessor. The tensions of that war had ripped the country apart, and sent L.B.J. into premature retirement.

For a few months the 'new' Nixon held sway in an unprecedented aura of serenity and praise. But the far-off guns never ceased firing; in Indochina, young American boys stepped on land mines, fell in machine gun fire, died in jungle ambushes.

Book III

THE WAR – AND THE WIRES

1

I firmly believe that without the Vietnam War there would have been no Watergate. Without the Vietnam War, Richard Nixon might have had the most successful Presidency since Harry Truman's. With Henry Kissinger as his point man he would have achieved his stunning diplomatic successes in China, the Soviet Union, and the Middle East – and be a President who is revered today.

But the Vietnam War destroyed Nixon as completely as it shattered President Johnson. What is little known is that the war drove L.B.J. to the same sort of wiretapping that was later to help drive Nixon from office. L.B.J. managed to exit before he was found out.

By 1968, L.B.J. was a besieged President. He could not go on the street without risking bodily injury. The emotions inspired by the War had flamed into ugly and frightening demonstrations and reached their peak at the 1968 Democratic Convention in Chicago (which L.B.J. could not visit for fear of his life). More and more, in his last months, L.B.J. had retreated into isolation in the White House, a bitter man who felt he had been misled by 'the best and the brightest' – the aides he had inherited from the Kennedy Administration.

But, typically, he went out fighting to the end. When he told the nation that he wasn't going to run for office again he called for a peace conference in Paris. Then, timing the announcement beautifully, he announced a few days before the election that he was halting the bombing of North Vietnam and expected a return to the peace table.

The only problem was he hadn't bothered to touch base with President Nguyen Van Thieu of South Vietnam. Or if he had, he touched it so lightly it didn't register because

Thieu angrily said he wouldn't agree to the terms, and L.B.J.'s 'big play' foundered.

He blamed that failure on Nixon and one of Nixon's backers, the so-called Dragon Lady, Anna Chennault. He believed that Nixon and Madame Chennault had conspired to sabotage the 'peace' negotiations by Mme Chennault's contacting President Thieu and advising him to hold off until after the elections, because those negotiations would help Senator Hubert Humphrey, Nixon's rival in the Presidential race.

In November of that year, after Nixon had won the Presidency, almost the first government official invited to visit the President-elect was F.B.I. Director J. Edgar Hoover.

Nixon and his aides, including me, were at the transition headquarters at the Hotel Pierre in New York. The President-elect asked me to be present when Hoover paid his respects. Hoover, florid, rumpled, came into the suite and got quickly down to business. He said that L.B.J. had ordered the F.B.I. to wiretap Nixon during the campaign. In fact, he told Nixon, Johnson had directed the F.B.I. to 'bug' Nixon's campaign aeroplane, and this had been done. Johnson had based his request on national security.

Hoover also said that, at Johnson's orders, the F.B.I. had installed wiretaps on the telephone of Madame Anna Chennault.

This angered Nixon, but he remained still as Hoover poured out more information. 'When you get into the White House, don't make any calls through the switchboard. Johnson has it rigged, and little men you don't know will be listening.'

He told Nixon that Johnson had installed electronic facilities that enabled his people to secretly monitor telephone conversations made through the switchboard. Not only that, but he had taping facilities which recorded his Oval Office conversations – and allowed aides in nearby offices to monitor such conversations, live.

Was Hoover telling the truth about bugging Nixon and Chennault? I believe he was, because his information about electronic equipment in the White House turned out to be correct. In fact, when I moved into the White House to work, I first used the office next to the Oval Office. As any new tenant, I inspected the fittings. I opened the door of a closet in the wall connecting my office to the President's suite, and found myself staring at a mountain of gleaming electronic components jammed in that closet, obviously for the use of the previous tenant of this office to tape or monitor L.B.J.'s conversations.

Hoover, in this visit to New York was, in the old Washington saying, 'covering his ass'. And no one was more adept at sheltering that broad expanse than he. After he died – and Watergate happened – Nixon was determined to find some documentation of Hoover's orders from L.B.J. to bug Nixon's aeroplane and Madame Chennault to counter the revelations about his own wiretapping. But the evidence had mysteriously disappeared.

In 1968 after the door closed behind Hoover, Nixon said to me, 'We'll get that Goddamn bugging crap out of the White House in a hurry.'

It was one of our first actions when he took office. His own White House taping equipment wasn't installed until February 1971 – and then he made a decision of historic significance. Johnson's equipment was manually operated; by pressing a switch under his desk, L.B.J. could turn the recorder on or off, thereby omitting some very juicy conversations. Nixon's equipment was totally automatic, recording everything. As a White House staffer once said, 'For want of a toggle switch, the Presidency was lost.'

Now, at the Hotel Pierre, Nixon decided it was an opportune moment for a cup of coffee, while he thought over this new information. 'Want one?' he asked. I said no, and Nixon stared at the cup for a minute. I remember the moment clearly because his next words surprised me. Instead of remarking angrily on the bugging of his plane, Nixon said with some sympathy for Johnson, 'Well, I don't blame him. He's been under such pressure because of the damn war, he'd do anything.' He paused, holding the cup, then said, 'I'm not going to end up like L.B.J., Bob, holed up in the White House, afraid to show my face on the street. I'm going to stop that war. Fast. I mean it!'

2

Inauguration day, a cold morning in the capital, Nixon looked out over a country torn by wartime dissension. He told Americans it was time to 'lower our voices'. He said he would free politics 'from inflated rhetoric that promises more than it can deliver; from angry rhetoric that fans discontents into hatred; from bombastic rhetoric that postures instead of persuading'. Regarding the war in Vietnam, he said, 'The greatest honour history can bestow is the title of peacemaker . . . We have endured a long night of the American spirit . . . but let us not curse the remaining dark. Let us gather the light.'

When Nixon spoke of his desire to be a peacemaker, he was not just delivering words his listeners wanted to hear. Nixon not only *wanted* to end the Vietnam War, he was absolutely convinced he *would* end it in his first year. I remember during the campaign, walking along a beach, he once said, 'I'm the one man in this country who can do it, Bob.'

What he meant was that in 1968 the Communists feared Nixon above all other politicians in U.S. public life. And Nixon intended to manipulate that fear to bring an end to the War. The Communists regarded him as an uncompromising enemy whose hatred for their philosophy had been spelled out over and over again in two decades of public life. Nixon saw his advantage in that fact. 'They'll believe any threat of force that Nixon makes because it's Nixon,' he said.

He saw a parallel in the action President Eisenhower had taken to end another war. When Eisenhower arrived in the White House, the Korean War was stalemated. Eisenhower ended the impasse in a hurry. He secretly got word to the Chinese that he would drop nuclear bombs on North Korea unless a truce was signed immediately. In a few weeks, the Chinese called for a truce and the Korean War ended.

In the 1950s Eisenhower's military background had convinced the Communists that he was sincere in his threat. Nixon didn't have that background, but he believed his hardline anti-Communist rhetoric of twenty years would serve to convince the North Vietnamese equally as well that he really meant to do what he said. He expected to utilise the same principle of a threat of excessive force. He would combine that threat with more generous offers of financial aid to the North Vietnamese than they had ever received before. And with this combination of a strong warning plus unprecedented generosity, he was certain he could force the North Vietnamese – at long last – into legitimate peace negotiations.

The threat was the key, and Nixon coined a phrase for his theory which I'm sure will bring smiles of delight to Nixon-haters everywhere. We were walking along a foggy beach after a long day of speechwriting. He said, 'I call it the Madman Theory, Bob. I want the North Vietnamese to believe I've reached the point where I might do *anything* to stop the war. We'll just slip the word to them that "for God's sake, you know Nixon is obsessed about Communism. We can't restrain him when he's angry – and he has his hand on the nuclear button" – and Ho Chi Minh himself will be in Paris in two days begging for peace.'

As it turned out it wasn't Bill Rogers, the future Secretary of State, who slipped the word to the North Vietnamese, but a brilliant, impulsive, witty gentleman with an engaging German accent – Henry Kissinger.

Kissinger became a member of the White House team because Nixon, in common with almost every President in history, had no love for the U.S. State Department. Franklin D. Roosevelt once said that dealing with the State Department is like watching an elephant become pregnant. Everything's done on a very high level, there's a lot of commotion, and it takes twenty-two months for anything to happen.

Nixon, himself, intended to run foreign policy from the White House, as had Roosevelt. So he decided to install a Presidential assistant who would be chief of the National Security Council, and work directly under him in the White House.

Kissinger had caught Nixon's eye with an audacious book, *Nuclear Weapons – and Foreign Policy*, which advocated use of tactical nuclear weapons in limited wars. Since the publication of that book, the good doctor had drawn back from that nightmare thesis, but Nixon could be certain he was no dove, even though he worked for Nelson Rockefeller.

I remember those first days when Kissinger was in the White House – quiet, deferential, engaging. I liked him immediately and worked with him closely; a fact which will surprise those who have read that I 'hated' Kissinger and was 'constantly trying to get rid of him'. I attended countless meetings between Kissinger and Nixon and, from the first, realised that they, although in many ways as different as any two people could be, were in almost perfect communion on foreign policy philosophy and strategy.

I hope, among the tapes which will eventually be revealed, that some of the conversations between these two men survive. Americans have all read the transcripts of tapes in which Nixon raves, rants, and curses about Watergate. But the tapes of Nixon and Kissinger will disclose another side of the President. In foreign affairs he had a comprehensive, wide-ranging mind, and a precise grasp of the political realities involved in every situation. Kissinger was greatly impressed with Nixon's mind. And Kissinger himself was a brilliant theorist who could place every problem in perspective and use historical precedent to help evaluate suggested options.

And so a great team was born with Nixon the leader and strategist, and Kissinger the implementer. But in early 1969, none of us sensed that Kissinger would grow into an international phenomenon who would eventually overshadow Nixon and receive much of the credit of Nixon's diplomatic moves.

I remember how jealous Nixon was when Henry won the Nobel Peace Prize which Nixon believed, with some justification, should have gone to himself. And how he was close to white-lipped in anger when Henry squeezed him aside as *Time* magazine's Man of the Year. Nixon ended up as part of an unprecedented dual selection, both appropriately carved in stony images.

Nixon was wise enough to see that Henry was invaluable in his field. It is not known yet just how well Nixon and Henry worked together because two of their greatest triumphs are little known even now . . . and these triumphs involved two world crises as dangerous to the world – if not more so – as Kennedy's famous Missile Crisis.

(A third tense situation not revealed until years after Nixon and Kissinger left office was the North Korea 'flap'. The Koreans, on April 15, 1969, had shot down an unarmed EC-121 electronic surveillance plane with the loss of all thirty crew members. Nixon revealed this during his last Frost television interview. Nixon believes Kissinger overreacted on the hawkish side. Kissinger recommended retaliatory bombing of the North Korean air fields. It is my recollection that he went even further than Nixon revealed on television: conceding the possible necessity of nuclear bombs as a bottom line if the North Koreans counterattacked. But the crisis was resolved when Nixon took the dovish advice of Bill Rogers, the Secretary of State, and Mel Laird, Secretary of Defense, and made no move at all against North Korea.)

In the other two crises, Henry was magnificent.

3

September 1970. Henry Kissinger charged into my office with a thick file under his arm. He slammed the file down on my desk. 'Bob, look at this.'

He opened the file and spread 8-by-10 pictures on my desk. I saw at once they were air reconnaissance photos. Henry was looking at me. 'Well?' he asked. 'Well!'

'Well, what?'

'Well, these are aerial photos. You can see that, can't you?'

'Yes.'

'And the place is Cienfuegos, Cuba, isn't it?'

I hadn't noticed the small white letters on the bottom right corner of the photos identifying the location. They wouldn't have helped anyway. I'd never heard of Cienfuegos, and told Henry that. He was bent over the pictures, peering at them angrily. 'It's a Cuban seaport, Haldeman, and these pictures show the Cubans are building soccer fields.' He straightened up. 'I have to see the President now. Who's in there with him?'

I told him Ehrlichman was meeting with the President, but if it was that urgent, Henry could go right in. But for what reason? Was he going to burst into the Oval Office in the middle of an economic conference and shout, 'The Cubans are building *soccer fields*?' Had he consumed too much 'bubbly' the night before? I asked him.

Henry stuffed the pictures back in the file and said to me, as patiently as he could, 'Those soccer fields could mean war, Bob.'

'Why?'

'Cubans play *baseball*. Russians play *soccer*.'

And then I understood. The Soviets were back in Cuba. Soccer fields next to Cienfuegos meant one thing: the Soviets were constructing their own naval base in Cuba.

And later photos would show communications towers, anti-aircraft sites, and military barracks under construction. When a Soviet U.G.R.A.-class submarine tender arrived at Cienfuegos complete with barges equipped to handle radioactive waste, we knew the worst.

The Soviets were installing a nuclear naval base in Cuba.

This was a serious circumvention of the 1962 agreement between the Soviets and the United States, drawn up after the Cuban Missile Crisis, in which the Soviets agreed not to place nuclear missiles in Cuba.

The Russian desire for proximity was based on a flaw in their technology. The U.S. was at that time far ahead of Russia in targeting electronics – we could pinpoint I.C.B.M. landings from half a world away. To counter this, the Soviets primarily relied upon enormous nuclear warheads that didn't need to be precisely targeted. At the same time, they reached for proximity to the U.S. through nuclear submarines and surface ships so that the need for precision guidance would be reduced.

But ships so far from the Soviet homeland required a support base, and Cuba, a Communist satellite, would be that base – unless Nixon stopped it.

By a self-serving literal reading of the 1962 agreement, the Soviets concluded that while they were specifically forbidden to base missiles on Cuban soil they were not expressly forbidden to base missiles *from* Cuba. In any case the only way for them to find out how America would react was to go ahead and see and that's exactly what they did.

Using the S.T.I.X. missile system of rather cumbersome but extremely accurate surface-launched medium-range missiles somewhat similar to the now-obsolete American Regulus, the Soviets could reach their most important targets in preventing a maximally effective American retaliation.

Their strategy was as simple as it was brilliant. Across the Arctic reaches of North America the American Ballistic Missile Early Warning System (B.M.E.W.S.)

could catch any incoming missile attack early enough to allow enough time for a massive American retaliation. The consequences of the retaliation were unacceptable to the Russians and so the balance of terror was maintained. But like the 'impregnable' Singapore and Maginot defences, B.M.E.W.S. had a fatal flaw: it was only oriented to intercept an attack from the north. By maintaining the capability for the S.T.I.X. type attack resupplied from a Cuban base, the Soviets could reach up behind B.M.E.W.S. and within fifteen minutes might be able to destroy all twenty-one American nuclear command headquarters which had nuclear release authority before sending their main attack over the pole.

By electronic monitoring of American military exercises in which our bases were alerted to prepare to execute a nuclear strike, the Soviets had learned which U.S. bases had the authority to pull the nuclear trigger; command headquarters such as the White House, the Pentagon, N.O.R.A.D., (Colorado Springs), C.I.N.C.L.A.N.T. (Norfolk), S.A.C. (Omaha), and the like. If the S.T.I.X. system could knock out enough of them, the resulting confusion might sufficiently delay the American retaliation to greatly reduce its effectiveness. In this U.S. command chaos the Soviet polar attack might even catch a good portion of our nuclear force on the ground. With the S.T.I.X. capability, then, minimised retaliatory damage to the Soviet Union might well make a pre-emptive strike an acceptable possibility.

What to do? Henry and Nixon huddled with N.S.C., State Department, and military chiefs. The first option was to act exactly as Kennedy had: make a dramatic announcement on television and confront the Soviets with a crisis of war or peace.

But Nixon was determined to go the other way, towards peace with the Soviets. He was interested in a long-term solid structure of peace, not just a quick and flashy triumph. He and Kissinger wanted détente, not conflict. So Henry saw Soviet Ambassador Anatoly Dobrynin and quietly informed him that the sub base would not only destroy détente but spark an updated missile crisis. If the construction was halted, nothing more would be said.

A week passed. No word from the Russians. Kissinger made a veiled announcement in public which he knew the Soviets would understand, then got word to them again in private – and strongly – that the President would regard the construction of a nuclear submarine base in Cuba as a 'hostile act'.

The quiet pressure worked. On October 22, Andrei Gromyko told Nixon that the 1962 understanding would be upheld, and in November, construction of the sub base stopped completely.

In my first months at the White House, sensing that I would play a small role in historical events as the man closest to Nixon, I kept a log of some special events.

Entry No. 26, entitled Chinese in Warsaw, hints at what may have been the most dangerous of all the confrontations this nation has ever faced. The confrontation was between China and the Soviet Union. The real story, never revealed so far by Kissinger or Nixon, is chilling. It involves not only brilliant last-minute diplomatic moves by Kissinger, but an unofficial ploy by an Air Force intelligence officer that combined to stave off an incredible disaster: a Soviet nuclear 'surgical' strike on China's atomic plants, which alone would have caused hundreds of thousands, if not millions, of deaths from fallout to Chinese, Japanese and American troops and civilians in Korea and Japan. If China had reciprocated, a full-scale nuclear holocaust would have begun, with fallout extending around the world.

Insane. And yet the Soviets were ready to go. In fact, they insisted we join them.

This is my log entry, which begins with a note of the first breakthrough in U.S.-Chinese relations:

Log 26 – Chinese in Warsaw
On December 10th Kissinger burst into my office in

> a great state of excitement to report that we had just received word that the Chinese in Warsaw had come to our embassy indicating that they wanted to meet with us, and, more significantly, that they wanted to use the *front door*. This latter point is significant because any meetings with the Chinese before had been with utmost secrecy, whereas the use of the front door would indicate that the Chinese were prepared to have it *known* that they were meeting with us.
>
> Kissinger at the same time volunteered the personal opinion that the Russian/Chinese situation was very serious and that he expected that there was a very strong probability that the Russians would attack China by April 15th.

Kissinger's concern about a Russian attack on China was expressed many times. I used to tease him about his use of percentages. He would say there was a 60 per cent chance of a Soviet strike on China, for example, and I would say, 'Why 60, Henry? Couldn't it be 65 per cent or 58 per cent?'

But most of the details about the Soviet-Chinese crisis were kept so secret even I wasn't advised of some of the day to day developments. It wasn't until later that I heard many of the details.

The world has heard of the border skirmishes in 1969 along the Ussuri River, between the northeastern province of Heilung Kiang in Manchuria and the Soviet Far East maritime province.

What it doesn't know is that the Soviets (called by our intelligence experts in the area 'paranoiac about China') had moved nuclear-armed divisions within two miles of the border, according to intelligence sources.

I am told that U.S. aerial photos revealed this grim story: hundreds of Soviet nuclear warheads stacked in piles. Eighteen thousand tents for their armoured forces erected overnight in nine feet of snow.

For years, the Soviets had been buttonholing U.S. diplomatic and military leaders. The message was always China, China, China. The Chinese must not be allowed to build a nuclear capability.

As far back as 1962, Secretary of Defense Robert McNamara had thought seriously enough of the proposition to ask the Air Force to make a feasibility study of a surgical strike on Chinese nuclear plants.

The study was completed in great secrecy. What the U.S. commanders found was that at that time, they didn't have a nuclear weapon in the entire stockpile 'clean' enough for a surgical strike. Our smallest weapon would have ended up causing millions of fatalities from fallout. In effect, we had no surgical capability then.

What made U.S. leaders supremely nervous was, as far as we knew, the Soviets had no 'surgical' capability either – but that fact apparently would not stop them. None of their warheads had been miniaturised as much as ours; instead, they were massive blockbusters whose fallout would be fantastic.

In 1969 there were several overtures by the Soviets to the U.S. for a joint venture in the surgical strike. Nixon turned the Soviets down, but was then informed, to his horror, that the Soviets intended to go ahead on their own.

A short review of Richard Nixon's – and Kissinger's – background in Chinese relations will set the stage for the drama to come. Nixon for years had been this nation's foremost enemy of Communist China. In a 1950 Senate campaign, Nixon said, 'Look at the map and we can see that if Formosa falls, the next frontier is the coast of California.' As late as 1960, in a television debate with John F. Kennedy, Nixon said, 'Now what do the Chinese Communists want? They don't want just Quemoy and Matsu. They don't want just Formosa. They want the world.'

But Nixon was always shrewd. By 1967 he had decided that Communist China was a fact of life. In an article in the influential *Foreign Affairs*, in 1967, Nixon said, 'Any American policy towards Asia must come urgently to grips with the reality of China . . . we simply cannot afford to leave China forever outside the family of nations, there to nurture its fantasies, cherish its hates and threaten its neighbours . . .'

When Nixon took office, one of his first priorities was a reopening of relations with China. His foreign affairs adviser, Kissinger, was rather a reluctant passenger those first six months. Kissinger had no background in Chinese affairs; his interests lay in European and Soviet relations.

On Air Force One in the midst of Nixon's round-the-world trip in the late summer of 1969, I was meeting with the President in his private cabin. We had a long talk about a lot of things, but one comment he made really amazed me.

When I returned to the staff section, the seat next to Henry Kissinger at his table was empty. I slipped in, leaned over to Henry, and said, 'You know, he actually seriously intends to visit China before the end of the second term.'

Henry took his glasses off and polished them, a small smile on his face, then he turned to me and said, 'Fat chance.'

Then came the Soviet-Chinese border clashes, surprising the rest of the world, which had seen the two countries as one great Communist monolith. And finally word from the Soviets that they could wait no longer for U.S. participation in the attack. If no signal was received from us, they would go ahead on their own.

Kissinger, at first inclined to dismiss a Soviet nuclear attack on China as a fantasy, now realised as the border clashes escalated that war was a serious possibility and told me so.

He and Nixon huddled. They decided they would send a signal to the Soviets that the U.S. was determined to be a friend of that Eastern nation.

How to send that signal? The U.S. and China had once held a series of meetings in Warsaw, but those talks had broken off. Kissinger contacted Walter J. Stoessel, Jr, U.S. ambassador to Poland. His orders to Stoessel: find the highest ranking Chinese envoy to Poland at a social function and tell him the U.S. wants to resume the Warsaw talks.

In the atmosphere of the time, when China was a bitter enemy of the U.S., and their diplomats never uttered a word to each other, this approach at a party would be a seismic event. It ended up as high comedy: the Chargé d'Affaires at the Chinese embassy, Lei Yang, attending a Yugoslavian reception, was so startled by Stoessel's approach, he turned and walked out of the door.

Stoessel ran down the stairs after him. Later, Chou En-lai told Kissinger in China: 'If you want our diplomats to have heart attacks, approach them at parties and propose serious talks.'

On December 10, Kissinger's unorthodox approach worked, as my log entry showed. The request to resume the Warsaw talks carried two messages. One to Peking, that we were ready to reverse our policy of enmity to China and reopen relations. The second to Moscow, that the U.S. and China had common interests and a Soviet nuclear strike might bring the Russians into confrontation with the U.S.

Meanwhile, Air Force Intelligence studied the photos of Russian missiles and nuclear warheads along the border. No one could tell whether the Soviets would launch the attack, no matter what the U.S. attitude. And their fallout studies showed the immensity of the catastrophe in store for the world. For example, it was possible that without advance warning and precautionary measures every man, woman, and child in Japan would have died.

In addition to Japan, the fallout would spread across Korea and Pacific islands where more than 250,000 American troops were stationed.

Major General George Keegan, Air Force Chief of Intelligence, was in Honolulu assaying the situation. He remembered that during the Cuban Missile Crisis in 1962, his Air Force Commander-in-Chief, Thomas Power, had said, 'Make a little mistake. Send a message in the clear.'

Keegan went to the code room and told the clerks on duty he had a message so sensitive they had to leave the room while he transmitted it. He then sent a message to the Secretary of Defense 'in the clear' (uncoded) as if by accident. The message said the U.S. had 1300 nuclear weapons airborne – and named Soviet cities which were targeted for the bombs.

Keegan states there was a Middle Eastern army officer visiting Nikita Khrushchev at his Black Sea dacha when Khrushchev got that message a few hours after its transmission. The officer said Khrushchev turned pale. He had four telephones on his desk and tried to pick them all up at once, calling Moscow. And that day the Russian ships turned back.

Whether that uncoded message was as significant as the officer indicated, Keegan remembered it now – and decided to try another message 'in the clear' that the Soviets would intercept.

This time the objective was to ensure that the Soviets clearly understood that many thousands of Russian citizens in Siberia would also die as a consequence of nuclear fall-out generated by a Soviet strike against China.

Meanwhile, U.S. intelligence sources, reading all the Soviet and Chinese messages from all the embassies around the world, saw at the same time that the Nixon-Kissinger rapprochement with China, begun in Warsaw, was having an electric effect on the Kremlin.

And just in time. The Soviets were on the brink of war. They believed that if the Chinese nuclear plants were destroyed, China would not be a military threat to them for decades. They teetered on the edge for days watching the Chinese moving more and more under the U.S. security umbrella. Finally, the Soviets realised they no longer could take the chance. Intelligence photos showed their nuclear armed divisions were withdrawing from the Chinese border.

Because of the timely diplomatic initiative of Kissinger and Nixon – and perhaps also the good memory of an air force general – a Soviet-Chinese nuclear war that had been called 'probable' by Kissinger in 1969 did not erupt into a worldwide catastrophe.

And Chinese leaders invited their old enemy to visit their country and resume relations at a time just before Nixon's re-election campaign in 1972, when it would have the greatest political effect in his favour.

4

From the first, Henry demonstrated what a great diplomat he was in a fashion known only to those of us inside the White House. We knew Henry as the 'hawk of hawks' in the Oval Office. But in the evenings, a magical transformation took place. Touching glasses at a party with his liberal friends, the belligerent Kissinger would suddenly become a dove – according to the reports that reached Nixon.

And the press, beguiled by Henry's charm and humour, bought it. They just couldn't believe that the intellectual, smiling humorous 'Henry the K' was a hawk like 'that bastard' Nixon.

During the Christmas bombing of North Vietnam in 1972, Kissinger was strongly in favour of the bombing. The North Vietnamese, he raged, had gone back on their word. Just two months before Henry had said, 'Peace is at hand,' and been criticised for political manoeuvring before election day. But peace *had been* at hand, Kissinger said, and now the North Vietnamese were reneging again. So he urged the bombing.

It was therefore with some amazement we read a column by James Reston in the *New York Times* after the bombing started saying, 'Mr Kissinger . . . has said nothing in public about the bombing in North Vietnam, which he undoubtedly opposes.' The whole tenor of the column was that a split was developing between Kissinger and Nixon on Vietnam and Reston provided a lot of 'inside information' on Kissinger's current thinking that could only have come from Kissinger himself.

Nixon was furious and told me to 'find out what the hell Henry's doing'. I talked to Henry that day. He hotly denied that he had said anything about the bombing to *anyone*. In particular, he vehemently claimed he had never talked to the *Times* columnist. He said, 'I did *not* give Reston an interview.'

But Reston's story implied that he *had* spoken to Kissinger. So we did some checking and found out that Kissinger had, in fact, conversed with him. I confronted Henry: 'You told us you didn't give Reston an interview but in fact you *did* talk to him,' and he said, 'Yes, but that was only on the telephone.'

Only on the telephone! Any scholar who wants to know just how superb a diplomat Henry was should interview all those who worked with him in the White House.

My attitude towards Henry was great respect and affection tinged with amusement. His humour tickled me. It so happened that, because of protocol requirements, I stood next to Henry at all state ceremonies. Constantly, he would nudge me sharply in the ribs and make a funny remark about the visiting statesman that would crack me up. His all-time funniest was his comment on Golda Meir's clothing. I'll leave that to Henry to publish – if he dares.

I'd get out of the President's office almost every day around one o'clock and have lunch with Higby in my office. About that time, Henry would drop in to find out what was happening and report on his own activities. But he also tried to read everything of interest on my desk. He would take a ten-minute 'Great Circle' route around the office as he was talking, meanwhile reading everything he could on the desk and conference table. We used to have fun with him because we knew what he was doing. We'd deliberately place letters or documents that looked very interesting in an exposed area. Then, when Henry got there, Higby would take his lunch tray and set it on top of the paper, as if by accident, just as Henry started to read it. So Henry would move around, and we'd always stay one step ahead of him in covering things up. And everyone kept a straight face.

By 1972 he also was a national legend as a lover, to our great amusement. Nixon secretly got a kick out of Henry's love life, and so did the rest of us. Ehrlichman worked on a longtime project that took him hours, but the effort didn't seem to bother him. He was compiling nude photos of various starlets Henry had dated. He then would forge Presidential memos complete with Nixon's 'bizarre demands' for certain types of action. One by one at a variety of times and places – Air Force One, Key Biscayne, San Clemente, as well as his White House office – Ehrlichman would send the memos to Henry in envelopes that always looked official – until Henry opened them and saw the nudes.

Henry's popularity was a problem on the 1972 campaign trail. We'd arrive at an airport, and when Henry came out of the plane a roar from the crowd would go up. Everyone recognised him. This was fine except Henry would play to the crowds. He'd go right over to the fence and start shaking hands down the line of people just as if he were the candidate. By the time Nixon emerged from the plane all eyes were on Henry far down the line.

Nixon told me to stop it, so I told Henry it was all right to respond to the cheers, but to leave the handshaking to the President. Henry smiled. 'You're just jealous, Herr Haldeman.' But we would only make it through a few more airport ceremonies before he would forget and plunge happily into the crowd again.

Recognising his love for attention, the staff at the 1972 Republican convention played a trick on Henry. Normally he was seated in one of the two front rows of dignitaries where he easily could be reached by roving television reporters. On this occasion Henry was purposely placed in the middle of the third row, out of convenient camera range of the reporters in the aisles. Then the staff sat back and spent the better part of the convention watching Henry cleverly manoeuvre himself against all odds into the eyes of the cameras.

One way or the other, Henry always came out ahead. He had a natural affinity for newsmen and, of course, his humour delighted them as it did us. And, as far as reporters were concerned, his 'romances' with movie starlets were just too good to be true.

Nixon once called me into his office, laughing. He had a newspaper on his desk that reported one of Henry's dates and included a picture of our foreign affairs Don Juan emerging from a nightclub with a beautiful woman. 'Isn't he something?' Nixon said.

Henry wasn't exactly the dashing glamour-boy type and yet here he was with Jill St John, and such. Gloria Steinem once said that power is an aphrodisiac to women. And Henry was powerful. (Miss Steinem was the subject of one of Henry's great *bon mots.* Told at a press conference that Steinem had denied she had had a romance with him, Henry agreed it was true. 'But she did not say if elected, she would not serve.')

I had a chance to needle him when he came to me wrestling with the problem of whether he should return to Harvard, or risk losing his tenure when his sabbatical was up.

I reminded him of an important factor. If he went back to Harvard as an ordinary professor, it would be the end of his allure to the Hollywood beauties.

'Unless they have good memories,' he shot back.

Funny, emotional, brilliant in his job, Henry was a winner all the way. Yet he was strangely insecure, which led to his famous outbursts against Bill Rogers, a quiet man who was no match for Henry in any war of words.

And it always amused me that Henry, whose anger at leaks really started the 1969 F.B.I. national security wire-tapping, was constantly worried that his own telephone was tapped. Time and again he would pass me in the hall and say, 'What do your taps tell you about me today, Halde-man?'

From the first days in office the brilliant Nixon-Kissinger

team was confident they could finish, with honour, the most difficult conflict this nation has ever waged: the Vietnam War. Nixon had conceived the 'Madman Theory' as the way to do it. Henry perfected the theory and carried it to the secret series of Paris peace talks: a threat of egregious military action by an unpredictable U.S. President who hated Communism, coupled with generous offers of financial aid. Henry arrived at the peace negotiations fully expecting this plan to be successful.

But there the theory – and Nixon and Kissinger's hopes for peace in Nixon's first year – crumbled. Henry found the North Vietnamese absolutely intractable. They wouldn't even negotiate. And the reason was clear. No threat, and no offer, could obscure one great fact known to the world at large. The American people had turned against the war. The young were saying they wouldn't fight it. The response to Eugene McCarthy's Democratic primary campaign in 1968 convinced the North Vietnamese that it was only a matter of time before the U.S. would *have* to pull out, no matter what. So why negotiate?

When Henry relayed that information Nixon was as bitter and disappointed as I ever saw him. The Communists were calling his bluff. He would either have to proceed with his threat of force or take the opposite route completely, walk out of Vietnam.

I was involved in this early crisis all the way.

Because Henry viewed me as an extension of Nixon's thinking he would often drop into my office to discuss various matters and see how I as Nixon's *alter ego* would respond.

This gives me a basis for answering a question that must be in the minds of many young readers who know only that the Vietnam War was a disaster. Why didn't we just walk out of Vietnam (as many Senators, for example, advocated)?

The reason, according to Kissinger and Nixon, was far from original. Indeed, it was the very same principle which forced every other U.S. President, from Kennedy on, to stay in that war and keep fighting. The need to assure the Soviet Union that the most powerful country in the world was willing to use that power to prevent the Soviets from taking over other countries, directly or indirectly.

In January 1969, the month of Nixon's inauguration, Kissinger defined his concept:

> What is involved now is confidence in American promises. However fashionable it is to ridicule the terms 'credibility' or 'prestige', they are not empty phrases; other nations can gear their actions to ours only if they can count on our steadiness.

In a campaign speech in October 1968, Nixon had quoted an eloquent passage from Woodrow Wilson to define an even deeper personal commitment to end the war with honour – and his awareness of the challenge.

> In his first inaugural address, this is what Wilson told his countrymen: 'Men's hearts wait upon us; men's lives hang in the balance; men's hopes call upon us to say what we will do. Who shall live up to the great trust? Who dares fail to try?'

Whether the doctrine of credibility was right or wrong is for history to decide. But it was the principle which Nixon, Kissinger, and all the officials charged with the maintenance of this nation's security believed and in 1969 when we found that the North Vietnamese would not budge, Nixon was faced with a terrible decision. The North Vietnamese had called his bluff. American support for the war melted every day while the Communists waited for what they felt was our inevitable withdrawal.

Nixon knew he had to act. But the problem was tricky. If he made a warlike move to convince the North Vietnamese he was serious, the U.S. anti-war protesters would explode in riots – once again assuring the Communists that they didn't need to negotiate because Americans weren't behind the war.

He conferred with Kissinger, the Joint Chiefs of Staff, and foreign policy advisers. He decided on a move which has been bitterly – and, in my opinion, very unfairly – criticised: to *secretly* bomb the North Vietnamese supply caravans which passed through Cambodia, a neutral country.

Prince Norodom Sihanouk agreed to the bombing strategy as long as it was not publicly acknowledged because he was angry at the North Vietnamese for using his neutral country to stage their offensive against South Vietnam.

Bombing in secret would get the message to the North Vietnamese and prevent a flare-up of anti-war protests in the U.S. which would disable our peace negotiators in Paris. So the bombing began, but it wasn't a secret long. In May 1969, *New York Times* reporter William Beecher wrote a story which began: 'American B-52 bombers in recent weeks have raided several Viet Cong and North Vietnamese supply dumps and base camps in Cambodia for the first time, according to Nixon Administration sources.'

Henry Kissinger had already been angered by previous news reports that he believed hurt his negotiating posture. On April 1, for example, the *Times* had reported that the U.S. was actively considering unilateral withdrawal from Vietnam. Now Kissinger was furious. Who were the 'Nixon Administration sources,' he wanted to know. Nixon was equally angry. Both of them felt they were being sabotaged by bureaucrats in the Administration. Both of them were determined to find the source of the 'leaks' to the press. A debate still lingers as to how the wiretapping programme began.

Henry represents himself as a passive participant called into the Oval Office for a conference in late April, where he found J. Edgar Hoover with the President. Kissinger was told that a wiretapping programme was under way, and was asked by Hoover only to supply names of people he suspected of leaking.

I talked with Nixon about this after he resigned and

Nixon said he doesn't remember such a conference. Neither do I. But whether or not it took place, I do recall Henry's initial anger, which helped initiate the whole wire-tap programme. We were in Key Biscayne at the time. That morning at breakfast by the pool, Henry had been reading the morning newspapers. Suddenly he stood up, shaking. He showed me the offending story and said that the President must be informed at once.

He succeeded in stirring Nixon's wrath, too. Both men determined to find the source of that leak.

Henry telephoned J. Edgar Hoover in Washington from Key Biscayne on the May morning the *Times* story appeared.

According to Hoover's memo of the call, Henry said the story used 'secret information which was extraordinarily damaging.' Henry went on to tell Hoover that he 'wondered whether I could make a major effort to find out where that came from . . . and to put whatever resources I need to find out who did this. I told him I would take care of this right away.'

Henry was no fool, of course. He telephoned Hoover a few hours later to remind him that the investigation be handled discreetly 'so no stories will get out'. Hoover must have smiled, but said all right. And by five o'clock he was back on the telephone to Henry with the report that the *Times* reporter 'may have gotten some of his information from the Southeast Asian Desk of the Department of Defense's Public Affairs Office.' More specifically, Hoover suggested the source could be a man named Mort Halperin (a Kissinger staffer) and another man who worked in the Systems Analysis Agency. According to the F.B.I. Director, Kissinger said he had heard that Halperin had been suggested as Beecher's source but he had no proof. According to Hoover's memo, Kissinger 'hoped I would follow it up as far as we can take it and they will destroy whoever did this if we can find him, no matter where he is.'

The last line of that memo gives an accurate reflection of Henry's rage, as I remember it.

Nevertheless, Nixon was one hundred per cent behind the wiretaps. And I was, too.

And so the programme started, inspired by Henry's rage but ordered by Nixon, who soon broadened it even further to include newsmen. Eventually seventeen people were wiretapped by the F.B.I. including seven on Kissinger's N.S.C. staff and three on the White House staff (earning Henry the durable fury of one of them, speechwriter Bill Safire who, unfortunately for Henry, became a widely read *New York Times* columnist.)

My own reactions to this programme of wiretapping were exactly the same as Kissinger's and Nixon's. Kissinger said that the leaks of military secrets were undermining his efforts to make peace. Who was in a better position to know? Suppose in World War II a government civilian employee had leaked secret information about U.S. military moves in Europe which kept the Germans fighting longer? There was a real war going on in Vietnam, too. Americans were being killed. I felt that any move, such as the secret bombing of Cambodia, which from our perspective, looked like it would shorten the war, was a good move for the country. Why should the Commander-in-Chief, Kissinger, and the Joint Chiefs of Staff, be overruled by a private citizen who disagreed, and leaked secrets to the press?

I believe Americans can usefully debate whether we should or should not have simply walked out of Vietnam and let the dominoes fall where they may. But I believe there is no valid argument that government employees responsible for implementing policy can take it upon themselves at any time to reveal military secrets during the time of war. Any commander-in-chief would have a duty to do everything in his power to stop those leaks – including wiretapping.

Ironically enough, given my own involvement in the White House tapping system, I hate wiretapping because I hate prying into anyone's private life. I remember when J. Edgar Hoover called me at the White House and said he was sending over the transcripts of the Martin Luther

King tapes. The F.B.I. had bugged King's hotel room when the Kennedys were in power and caught King enjoying extramarital trysts. I don't blame the Kennedys completely for that wiretapping because I know how much Hoover was personally obsessed with King. When I received the F.B.I. Director's call, I said I didn't want to see the transcripts. The man was dead. But Hoover, no great fan of the Civil Rights movement at any time, wanted the White House to see them to show that King wasn't 'such a saint as they're trying to make him out to be today.' Presumably we would inform Civil Rights leaders that their idol had feet of clay.

Hoover sent the material over. I took one glance at the top page and pushed it back into the envelope. I found the content of that first page almost as disgusting as Hoover's attempted use of the transcripts.

So I'm not a wiretapping enthusiast. I do believe, however, in stopping leaks of security secrets, and if F.B.I. wiretapping is the only way to find them, then I believe electronic surveillance must be employed. But the F.B.I. wiretaps in 1969 turned out to be a pain in the neck for me, personally. Wiretap summaries were sent to Kissinger for a year, then Nixon directed that they be delivered to me. Almost immediately I found I was living a cloak-and-dagger existence. It was amusing, in a way, although it irritated me at the time. The F.B.I. would place the summaries in envelopes for delivery. Every now and then on my way into my office or in a hotel corridor on a trip, a man would suddenly jump out of a dark doorway, thrust an envelope in my hand, then disappear into the night.

Finding this rather ridiculous and hardly worth the effort, I directed the F.B.I. to simply send the summaries to Larry Higby, my assistant, in the regular fashion, and stop the theatrics. It was all a waste of time, anyway. I don't think we ever found anything worthwhile. Nixon and Kissinger, frustrated, kept spreading the electronic surveillance farther and farther from the original four to the final seventeen, but the taps never produced anything.

As Nixon said, gloomily, later, 'A dry hole. Just globs and globs of crap.'

There is one wiretap, however, that is important in Watergate history because Nixon personally ordered it privately – by White House aides – not through the F.B.I. The tap was on influential columnist Joseph Kraft. John Ehrlichman has gotten the blame for that wiretap by historians – but that was a Nixon project all the way. Kraft, who had been a supporter of Nixon's, had now turned against him in his columns about the war and Kissinger's peace negotiations. The F.B.I., for reasons never made clear to me, claimed that Kraft's telephone was 'untappable'. So Nixon called Ehrlichman, who eventually turned to his one gumshoe: John Caulfield.

Caulfield hired an ex-F.B.I. man named John Ragan and another man whose name has been lost to history. As I heard it later, the two of them put a ladder up against a wall of Kraft's Georgetown home and planted a bug on one of his phones. They heard nothing but the maid for weeks – and she didn't speak English. It seemed the Krafts were in Europe. Undaunted, Nixon told the F.B.I. to find out whether Kraft was 'tappable' in Paris, where he was attending the peace negotiations. Through the French authorities, a mike was installed in his hotel room.

All this for nothing. The leakers were never discovered. But unintentionally and unknowingly an important precedent for Watergate had been established: the use of private White House personnel for wiretapping.

At the same time, anti-war resentment kept rising. During an October 1969 demonstration, David Broder had written in the *Washington Star*, 'It is becoming more obvious with every passing day that the men and the movement that broke Lyndon B. Johnson's authority in 1968 are out to break Richard M. Nixon in 1969. The likelihood is great that they will succeed again . . . '

By mid-1970 the campuses were in full revolt. University research centres were being 'trashed'; at Cornell students carried rifles; elsewhere they took over offices in administration buildings, refused to move, and brought university life to a halt.

In New York a building exploded on West 11th Street as four young 'Weathermen' were busily concocting bombs. On and on the violence escalated, growing frightening in its intensity and emotion. The cry of 'Hey, hey, L.B.J., how many kids did you kill today?' had changed to a simple statement about the war: 'Hell, no, we won't go.' And through it all, Nixon, grimly, still tried to fight his war.

He had a double problem. In response to the weariness with the war, he was already withdrawing thousands of American troops. But increasingly the Communists took advantage of that withdrawal and pressed on, hoping to create a rout. They did this once again through Cambodia, their favourite route. Nixon was told the only way to stop the Communist offensive was to mount a preemptive strike in Cambodia, seize North Vietnamese supply bases, and cut off the Communist advance long enough to get us through the dangerous summer months.

Once again he conferred with all his top advisers before making what he knew would be a wrenching decision. The overwhelming advice was that the invasion (we called it an incursion) was necessary. But this time Nixon announced the military move to the public.

The result was a national uproar. On the midwest campus of Kent State, some frightened National Guardsmen fired their guns at students, killing and injuring several. Violence and hatred for the President, of an order probably never before seen in this country, exploded on campuses after this outrage. White House staffers looked stunned; heads were hanging; some said, 'Hell, it isn't worth it. Let's just bug out of the damn war.'

A huge anti-war protest bloomed in Washington. Tens of thousands of students poured into the city and camped all over town. A troubled Nixon, unable to sleep, went out for a post-midnight talk with the students.

Nixon was concerned by this hatred of him by the young. Not by the bomb-throwers, whom he called 'bums'.

They usually weren't even students, but outcasts who settled near campuses like Berkeley and inspired and led the students to their worst excesses. But he knew the great majority of young people who weren't 'bums' also hated the war.

It is also true that Nixon simply could not understand why the young people didn't see that he was really trying to end the war. Hadn't he been the first President in years to remove troops from Vietnam? And unknown to the public at the time he had made offer after offer to the North Vietnamese, only to have them turn down each offer. After all, it wasn't South Vietnamese troops invading North Vietnam, but the other way around.

And so he couldn't believe the campus revolutions were totally spontaneous. He suspected they were being aided and abetted, if not actually inspired, by Communist countries. Nixon's notion has been derided for years by the press ever since it became known as a typical example of 'Nixon paranoia'. Therefore, it was a surprise for me to read in the *New York Times*, October 9, 1977, the following:

On the first page, second lead, was this headline:

F.B.I. ASSERTS
CUBA AIDED WEATHERMEN

and the subhead:

Secret Data on War Protest Years
Cite a North Vietnam Role

It seems that the Justice Department had discovered in 1976 that, among other things:

'A group of intelligence agents in the late sixties and early seventies, assigned to the staff of the Cuban Mission to the United Nations in New York, arranged for American youths to be inculcated with revolutionary fervor.' In other words, inspired to create demonstrations. 'According to the Justice Department report, protesting students were trained in *practical weaponry* by Cuban military officers through the so-called Venceremos Brigades.'

After the Weathermen went 'underground' in 1970, they were aided by these Cuban intelligence agencies and spirited away from the F.B.I. Some were sent to Europe, given new identities, and sent back into this country by way of Czechoslovakia – all paid for by Cuban Intelligence.

North Vietnam was active, too. North Vietnamese agents advised the Students for a Democratic Society how to mount the so-called Days of Rage in Chicago in 1969. The North Vietnamese advised the S.D.S. to choose youngsters who would battle with the police. They suggested that the anti-war movement needed not just intellectual protestors but also physically rugged recruits.

And so on.

When Nixon suggested this in 1970, reporters derided him, without knowing the facts, saying that he was always obsessed with Communist infiltration. In their view, the man in whose mind the Hiss case burned as his earliest triumph reverted to the 'Communist' explanation for almost everything. But in this case, Nixon turned out to be more right than any of us knew. The anti-war sentiment was genuine, but there were professional agitators, too.

Kent State, in May 1970, marked a turning point for Nixon; a beginning of his downhill slide towards Watergate. None of us realised it then; we were all too busy trying to calm the nationwide furor over the Cambodian invasion. But then I saw that Nixon had given up on the intelligence and investigatory agencies such as the F.B.I. to help in his battle to quell the national uproar and bring the war to a satisfactory close. As far as he was concerned, the F.B.I. was a failure; it hadn't found the leakers of military secrets; it hadn't found Communist backing for the anti-war organisations which he was sure was there. In sum, it had nothing to help him. And Hoover had cut off F.B.I. liaison with the C.I.A.

Of course Nixon knew very well he couldn't count on the C.I.A. To make matters worse, he was dissatisfied with the military intelligence he was getting – not only from the C.I.A. but the many other intelligence agencies in Washington. As he told me, 'Those guys spend all their time fighting each other.' And it was true that the jealousies among various intelligence branches were always burning at a white-hot pitch (probably still are). A phenomenon in Washington rarely discussed is the active hostility among government agencies – complete with spies and 'plants' – at the expense of the country. This was exemplified vividly in the Nixon Administration when a yeoman on Kissinger's N.S.C. staff was uncovered as a spy planted there by the Joint Chiefs. Yeoman Charles Radford xeroxed top secret documents and sent them to his real chiefs at the Pentagon so they would know what Kissinger and his foreign policy experts were planning.

In the spring of 1970, a young man named Tom Huston, who had recently joined the White House staff after a tour of duty as an Army officer assigned to the Defense Intelligence Agency, outlined what he believed to be some of the problems in the whole intelligence community. Especially the complete lack of co-operation and co-ordination – and the damaging effect this was having on the need for adequate intelligence in relation to the possible foreign influence and support of the domestic agitation and violence.

He urged that something be done immediately, and recommended a conference of the chiefs of all the various intelligence agencies at which the President would bang some heads together and tell them to develop some workable plans that would produce results instead of excuses and arguments. This recommendation fell on predictably fertile soil when it reached the President. Huston was saying exactly what Nixon was thinking.

The meeting was held on June 5 with the heads of the C.I.A., F.B.I. and N.S.A. President Nixon didn't pull any punches in expressing his dissatisfaction with their work in the area of co-ordination of foreign and domestic intelligence, especially as it related to information regarding the domestic demonstrations.

He ordered them to form themselves into a task force

to develop a plan to solve the problems and produce results. And he assigned Tom Huston as the White House staffer to work with them. What resulted has become known as the 'Huston Plan' but that title tends to obscure the fact that the plans presented to the President and approved by him were produced not by Tom Huston, but by the task force composed of all the intelligence agencies and chaired by J. Edgar Hoover. All of them signed the report. Hoover signed as chairman, but indicated his disagreement with many of the recommendations in a footnote.

Little did we know when Nixon approved that plan that he was building a bomb for John Dean to detonate years later. Dean somehow acquired a copy of the report, put it in a safe, and produced it dramatically at precisely the right time to impress the prosecutors the most. Because it recommended a number of illegal activities such as mail-opening, bugging, and breaking and entering, it created a major sensation.

The Report was distorted to make it appear an effort by Nixon to take over the intelligence community for his own sinister political purposes by placing an unknown White House staffer in command of the whole intelligence apparatus. It was nothing of the kind.

Now, irony piles upon irony. The portion of the Huston Report relating to illegal activities was viewed with horror by various columnists when it was revealed. But it was not a new government policy. Indeed, until Lyndon B. Johnson stopped it in 1966, it had been official for years.

But the further irony is that we now know – but did not know then – that some of the activities by the F.B.I., C.I.A. and other intelligence agencies, had never stopped, not even in 1966. In fact, they were going on even as the President faced the intelligence chiefs in the Oval Office. But none of this was made known to the President by the intelligence chiefs and, indeed, one of them – Hoover – claimed to be indignant about the whole concept. So indignant, he complained to John Mitchell, who relayed the criticism to Nixon, and Nixon dropped the idea after five days.

The Huston plan, even though it failed, brought home to the intelligence agencies a new threat. They feared that White House 'interference' could result in disembowelment of their power. I believe that from that point on the C.I.A., for example, began monitoring the White House very, very closely through 'plants' and perhaps other intelligence agencies, too.

Were there C.I.A. 'plants' in the White House? On July 10, 1975, Chairman Carl Nedzi of the House of Representatives Intelligence Committee released an Inspector-General's Report in which the C.I.A. admitted there was a 'practice of detailing C.I.A. employees to the White House and various government agencies.' The I.G. Report revealed there were C.I.A. agents in 'intimate components of the Office of the President.'

Domestic C.I.A. plants are bad enough, but in 'intimate components of the office of the President'?

I was 'intimate', Ehrlichman was. Kissinger was. Who else was intimate in an official sense? Alex Butterfield, who sat right outside the President's office (Rose Mary Woods to this day believes he was a C.I.A. plant. As we shall see later, she may have good grounds.)

I leave the question to rest as a part of a great mystery the significance of which may one day overshadow even Watergate: the manipulation of this nation by members of an intelligence agency.

The failure to implement the Huston Plan set the stage for the drama surrounding the release of the Pentagon Papers by a Rand 'think tank' employee named Daniel Ellsberg.

Unlike Nixon's excitement about the revelation of the secret bombing in Cambodia, his immediate reaction after the release of the Pentagon Papers was muted. After all, the Papers covered events which had occurred during the Kennedy and Johnson Administrations, not his Administration, and they weren't really all that important anyway.

But Kissinger told the President he didn't understand how dangerous the release of the Pentagon Papers was.

'It shows you're a weakling, Mr President.' Henry really knew how to get to Nixon. 'The fact that some idiot can publish all of the diplomatic secrets of this country on his own is damaging to your image, as far as the Soviets are concerned, and it could destroy our ability to conduct foreign policy. If the other powers feel that we can't control internal leaks, they will never agree to secret negotiations.'

What really bothered Kissinger?

The Pentagon Papers didn't even touch on Nixon's role – or Kissinger's – in Vietnam. I think there was a personal factor in addition to his more substantive concern. Henry had a problem because Ellsberg had been one of his 'boys'. (He had lectured at Kissinger's Defense Policy Seminars at Harvard in the 1960s.)

In four and a half years in the White House I listened, often with smiles, to many Kissinger rages, but the Pentagon Papers affair so often regarded by the press as a classic example of Nixon's paranoia was Kissinger's premier performance. Unfortunately for Henry, it was recorded, and may some day be played to standing room audiences.

I was in the office when one of the angry speeches was made. As I remember, it ended with charges against Ellsberg by Kissinger that, in my opinion go beyond belief. Ellsberg, according to Henry, had weird sexual habits, used drugs, and enjoyed helicopter flights in which he would take potshots at the Vietnamese below.

Not exactly the Chamber of Commerce's Man of the Year, if those bizarre descriptions were to be taken seriously.

By the end of this meeting Nixon was as angry as his foreign affairs chief. The thought that an alleged weird-o was blatantly challenging the President infuriated him far more than it might, let's say, if Ellsberg had been one of those grey-faced civil servants who, according to Nixon, 'still believed Franklin D. Roosevelt was President'.

He launched a counterattack through the courts on both the newspapers which printed the Papers, and against Ellsberg on criminal charges.

And he wheeled his 'Big Three' into action: Haldeman, Ehrlichman, and Colson. From a Watergate standpoint it's interesting to see just how he utilised each of the talents of his top men.

For the out-in-front-smash-them-over-the-head approach, he naturally selected me. I was called into his office and ordered to confront personally every single Cabinet officer and agency head, brutally chew them out and threaten them with extinction if they didn't stop all leaks in the future.

'You're going to be my Lord High Executioner from now on,' Nixon told me. I nodded, little knowing the words would some day play on national television with me in front of a Senate Committee – and viewers visualising me with an axe and a hood, standing over cowering men with their heads on the block.

But now, I kept my own head while Nixon lost his. He was particularly incensed at Bill Rogers's State Department, which always seemed to be obstructing his and Henry's moves in the Vietnam War. Nixon said, 'God-damnit, Bob, I want every employee in the State Department who could have access to be given a lie detector test.'

There were thousands of employees in the State Department. In my mind's eye I saw lines reaching for blocks waiting to be administered lie detector tests. And newspaper reporters gleefully pouncing on this further example of Nixon's coming police state. I said, 'That's impossible, Mr President. There are too many of them. The State Department will be in an uproar, and we'll get a bad press.'

'I don't give a damn. I want it done. Those bastards over there are behind half the leaks in this Administration. I'm going to stop them once and for all.'

I said nothing more, then stepped out of the office and placed the order immediately on my mental 'no-action-ever' shelf. Nixon kept hounding me, but I stalled and stalled. Eventually he gave up, and only a few State Department officials at the top were given tests.

For a more devious approach than mine, Nixon selected John Ehrlichman. John had a subtle mind and loved intrigue. Ehrlichman told me once that the one job he wanted in the Administration was not Domestic Counsellor, but C.I.A. Director. (His fascination with the C.I.A. has continued in his post-Watergate writing career.)

By this time, Nixon had given up on the F.B.I. and C.I.A. for any real help in trying to track down and plug up the leaks from the White House and the rest of the Administration. But he was still determined something had to be done. So he told Ehrlichman, 'If we can't get anyone in this damn government to do something about the problem that may be the most serious one we have, then, by God, we'll do it ourselves. I want you to set up a little group right here in the White House. Have them get off their tails and find out what's going on and figure out how to stop it.'

This was right down John's alley. After some checking, he assigned Egil Krogh from his own shop and David Young from Kissinger's to set up the Special Investigations Unit to carry out the President's charge. (John's inclusion of a Kissinger man was a typical stroke of Machiavellian genius. He knew all too well how Henry would happily ignite a fuse, then stand off swearing he knew nothing about it, or had even been against it.)

John's two men set up shop in a little office in the basement of the E.O.B. (Executive Office Buildings), and were soon dubbed the 'Plumbers' because of their assignment to fix leaks. Not to be outmanoeuvred or left in the cold from anything as potentially juicy as this appeared to be, Chuck Colson hastily got involved, too – recommending the hiring of Howard Hunt to augment the Plumbers' staff.

As we shall see, Colson had his own assignments in the battle against Ellsberg and the Pentagon Papers. Among them, he was to try to discredit Ellsberg in the public eye, rather than letting him go down in history as a hero; to make him an example to others who might take it into their heads to follow his lead and leak more secret documents.

It is still not clear how Colson managed to sidetrack the

Plumbers into his area of the discrediting of Ellsberg. The reason for trying to get Ellsberg's psychiatrist's files is explained by the desire to find evidence to support Kissinger's vivid statement about Ellsberg's weird habits. And this information could be used at Ellsberg's trial to discredit his character.

A substantial controversy has developed as to who originated the order to break into Ellsberg's psychiatrist's office. And this is important because the Ellsberg break-in played a major role in the Watergate tragedy to come. The courts decided John Ehrlichman ordered it, but John Dean testified that Egil Krogh told him the orders for the break-in came 'directly out of the Oval Office', and Ehrlichman didn't even know about it.

5

San Clemente, November 13, 1976. I wait for the guard at the gate of Nixon's compound to admit me. The guard doesn't recognise my name. Finally he obtains permission. I assure him I know the way. The gates open, and I drive to the prefab office buildings whose construction I had once supervised.

I found Nixon in his armchair in his office. Once again he wanted to probe my memory for details of various Watergate events for use in his book. The subject today was the Plumbers, and the Ellsberg break-in.

The more Nixon spoke, the more I realised something strange. Nixon was worried that he had personally ordered the Ellsberg break-in. This came as a surprise to me because I remembered all of those Oval Office conferences in 1973 when he appeared so stunned – and even hurt – by the Ellsberg break-in. At that time, he called it absurd, bizarre.

Now he was implying his hurt action had been a pose.

Not only had he known about the 'bizarre' break-in all along but he had ordered it, himself.

He said, 'I was so damn mad at Ellsberg in those days. And Henry was jumping up and down. I've been thinking – and maybe I did order that break-in.'

I said that Dean had testified that Egil Krogh (the head of the Plumbers) had told Dean the orders for the break-in came right out of the Oval Office.

That reminder bothered Nixon. He clasped and unclasped his hands under his chin. A bee had entered the room and was executing a holding pattern over a pile of black notebooks on the floor. It buzzed off. All this time Nixon said nothing, thinking.

And I was remembering Ehrlichman, face red, saying to me during our trial, 'Nixon didn't even make a deposition at my Ellsberg trial. He let me go right down the tube and never lifted a hand.' But even in that moment of anger, Ehrlichman hadn't told me Nixon ordered the break-in. Which meant Ehrlichman was a patsy, if Nixon had really told Krogh – who worked for Ehrlichman – to do the break-in without informing Ehrlichman. And Ehrlichman took the rap.

Nixon said, 'I had Egil Krogh out here to talk about it.'

So he had been worried enough about it to ask Krogh to come all the way to San Clemente. But why was he so anxious anyway? The Ellsberg trial was over. Nixon had a pardon and was untouchable.

And then I realised the situation. If Nixon had ordered the break-in while in the Oval Office, his order was preserved on tape. And those tapes might well become public some day. Nixon was debating whether to reveal what he had really said in that office about the break-in, or wait it out. It might be years before that particular tape was finally unearthed. If there was one.

Nixon said, 'Krogh told me he didn't believe I ordered – or even knew about – the break-in.'

'So that solves it,' I said.

But it didn't. Again and again that afternoon Nixon returned to the subject. Finally, he said, 'I'm just going to have to check it out further.'

He had already talked to Krogh, so I assumed he meant he would check with other members of the Plumbers. Which seemed very odd to me. Krogh's assurance should have quieted his fears.

I went home and the next day, a Sunday, Nixon telephoned me to go over the subject *again*. I couldn't believe it. I asked him point blank why he was making an issue of it since Krogh had denied it.

'Uh . . . well . . . I'm just wondering what to say in my book.'

After I hung up the telephone I wondered whether Nixon's enduring concern was based on one fact: that he *had ordered* the Ellsberg break-in. If so, that meant he had been conning us in those Oval Office conferences when he pretended surprise and chagrin over the same break-in he had ordered.

Whether he authorised the break-in or not Nixon did take the next step which made matters infinitely more dangerous in the long run. He already had selected me for the straight-ahead approach, and Ehrlichman for the more devious route. Now he called in Chuck Colson for an even more devious attack on Ellsberg.

Colson states that the President assigned him the task with these fighting words: 'We've got a countergovernment here and we've got to fight it. I don't give a damn how it is done, do whatever has to be done to stop these leaks and prevent further unauthorised disclosures. I don't want to be told why it can't be done. This government cannot survive, it cannot function if anyone can run out and leak whatever documents he wants to . . . I want to know who is behind this and I want the most complete investigation that can be conducted. . . . I don't want excuses. I want results. I want it done; whatever the cost.'

Colson was off and running. Shortly thereafter he wrote me a memo for the attention of the President. He said that the prosecution of Ellsberg would present a great opportunity.

> He is a natural villain to the extent that he can be painted evil . . . We can discredit the peace movement and have the Democrats on a marvellous hook because thus far most of them have defended the release of the documents . . . I have not yet thought through all the subtle ways in which we can keep the Democratic Party in a constant state of civil warfare, but I am convinced that with some imaginative and creative thought it can be done.

Expanding this thesis in a telephone call to a friend, Colson said, 'We might be able to put this bastard into a hell of a position and discredit the New Left.'

Colson wasn't content with the White House amateurs like Krogh and Young. He found an ex-C.I.A. agent named Howard Hunt to assist them. He called Hunt.

> COLSON: Let me ask you, Howard, this question: Do you think with the right resources employed, that this thing could be turned into a major public case against Ellsberg and co-conspirators?
> HUNT: Yes, I do, but you've established a qualification here that I don't know whether it can be met.
> COLSON: What's that?
> HUNT: Well, with the proper resources.
> COLSON: Well, I think the resources are there.
> HUNT: Well, I would say so absolutely.
> COLSON: Then your answer would be we should go down the line and nail the guy cold?
> HUNT: Go down the line and nail the guy cold, yes.

Colson taped this call and sent a transcript to Ehrlichman along with a note: 'The more I think about Howard Hunt's background, politics, disposition, and experience, the more I think it would be worth your time to meet him.'

So Hunt came aboard and was assigned to the Plumbers. And it seemed Hunt had a friend, named Bob Bennett, who was head of a public relations agency called Robert

R. Mullen Company. Colson didn't know that Mullen was a C.I.A. cover agency, and that Bennett regularly reported to a C.I.A. case officer. From the time of the Pentagon Papers until the Watergate break-in this odd trio, Hunt, Colson and Bennett, two-thirds C.I.A. controlled, would embark on a number of strange projects which would come to be called 'other things' when Nixon worried what might be revealed by Hunt if he didn't receive his blackmail money. And to add to the mystery of the actions of this trio, one more ingredient must be mentioned. The Robert R. Mullen Company was not only a C.I.A. cover but had as its principal client, Nixon's old friend, Howard Hughes. The C.I.A. connection was totally unknown to us until years later.

During Hunt's brief career with the Plumbers, he worked with Gordon Liddy, who had been brought into the group by Bud Krogh. Supposedly they were working under the direction of Krogh and Young, who in turn were under Ehrlichman's direction. But in the Ellsberg break-in, we find them receiving orders and financial support from Colson. And, somewhere along the way, they were also getting directions from Bob Bennett, outside of the White House, on behalf of the C.I.A. and the C.I.A.'s silent partner, Howard Hughes.

Neither Nixon, Ehrlichman, nor I knew of this extracurricular affair with an outsider named Bob Bennett. We thought Bennett was being used *by* us as a source of information about O'Brien's past relationship with Hughes. We didn't know that a C.I.A. employee was, in effect, running a White House team.

The Plumbers' unit was disbanded shortly after the Ellsberg break-in in the fall of 1971. Hunt became a special projects man for Colson as a White House consultant, and at the same time went on to the payroll at the Mullen Company. Liddy went to C.R.P. as legal counsel, with the additional responsibility of campaign intelligence. But the two maintained their contact with each other – and Hunt was the man to whom Liddy turned to help him sell and later carry out his intelligence recommendations.

In effect, now that they were at C.R.P., the militant side of the Plumbers (Hunt and Liddy) was at last on its own. And it would have a big budget for the first time. (The Ellsberg break-in got by on only $10,000 that Colson squeezed out of the Milk Producers Association. The conduit for the money, I heard later, was the ubiquitous Bob Bennett.)

Bennett must have looked upon the team at C.R.P. as a plum suddenly ripened into magnificence. What could he do with them now that they would have hundreds of thousands of dollars? And Colson obviously saw their potential, too, from his own angle. Soon Hunt and Liddy were huddling in his White House office. (Colson has always denied anything 'factual' about Watergate was even discussed at the White House. Only their request to call Magruder about the campaign intelligence budget.)

And I, unaware of the crosscurrents swirling around a team with two heads, was nudging Gordon Strachan, who was 'tickling' Magruder for something which sounds very old fashioned in the ultramodern terms of both C.I.A. and Colson: political intelligence.

My request, believe it or not, was for a simple recording of our political rivals' *public* speeches to preserve for future use their attack on each other so we could check the usual inconsistencies (candidates often vary the content of a basic speech for an audience of ghetto blacks or Southern farm workers, for example). Hunt and Liddy must have laughed. Compared to their approach. I was in the political – and electronic – dark ages.

And so, these offspring of Kissinger's attempt to control the leaks he felt had sabotaged his negotiating strengths during the Vietnam peace negotiations were now full-grown as a team and ready to flex their muscles in a domestic political campaign. They did so at Watergate on Memorial Day, then went back in again on June 17, 1972. But who sent Hunt and Liddy in there and why?

Book IV

WHO ORDERED THE BREAK-IN?

1

There are two central mysteries of the Watergate tragedy: first, who ordered the break-in, and why?

Nixon had been through hell in his first four years in office. The Vietnam War had created almost unbearable pressures which caused him to order wiretaps, and activate the Plumbers in response to anti-war moves. But by June 1972, he was miraculously on top. His May 8, 1972, bombing of North Vietnam and mining of Haiphong Harbour had decisively stopped the North Vietnamese advance and caused their leaders to make their first serious move in four years towards peace. His diplomatic achievements with China and Russia had been enormously successful. His popularity was at an all-time high. And the Democratic candidates had been flattened by the McGovern steamroller, with the result that the party's weakest candidate was an odds-on favourite to win the nomination.

Nixon's own re-election was secure. Why then risk everything by sending burglars after political information in the Democratic National Committee Headquarters at a time when it wasn't needed? Especially as every professional politician in Washington (including Nixon and myself) knew that no political knowledge of any value could ever be found in party headquarters. The candidates' headquarters contained all the vital information. The Democratic National Committee, like its Republican counterpart, is little more than a ceremonial shell before the convention takes place.

The second central mystery is how this insignificant break-in somehow escalated into an unprecedented Constitutional crisis which forced Nixon out of office. Was it spontaneous? Or were unknown persons or agencies manipulating it?

When the Watergate prosecutors drew up their indictments in the cover-up case, they completely ignored the break-in itself. And to this day, there has been no charge filed against anyone for involvement in the planning or execution of the break-in other than the original group that stood trial in January of 1972.

This, despite all the talk at the time by commentators, congressmen, and senators about the necessity of pursuing the case to get the answers as to who ordered the break-in and why.

One reason no one was indicted for it later was that the D.N.C. break-in was such an obvious absurdity even the prime informers, Dean and Magruder, could not think of a motive for it that a jury could believe.

I believe that now for the first time. Americans should look closely at that break-in. When they do, they'll see that what seemed absurd contains clues to very profound mysteries.

Three theories have been advanced in an attempt to explain the Watergate break-in. The truth, as I see it, is different from any of the three. They are as follows:

1. The 'official' theory, as advanced by Dean and Magruder in testimony before Congress
2. The Democratic Party Trap Theory
3. The C.I.A. Trap Theory

Let's examine these theories in detail to see what clues they provide, and what facts I have which lead me to believe my own is the most likely.

The 'Official' Theory of the Break-in

To this day no one has explained this theory better than Dean himself on March 21, 1973, when he confronted the President in the Oval Office with the news that his Presidency was dying of a cancer. At this time, Dean was still very much a part of Nixon's team.

DEAN: First of all, on the Watergate. How did it all

start, where did it start? It started with an instruction to me from Bob Haldeman to see if we couldn't set up a perfectly legitimate campaign intelligence operation over at the Re-election Committee . . .

I was told to look around for somebody that could go over to 1701 and do this. And that's when I came up with Gordon Liddy who – they needed a lawyer. Gordon had an intelligence background from his F.B.I. service. I was aware of the fact that he had done some extremely sensitive things for the White House, and he had apparently done them well. Uh, going out into Ellsberg's doctor's office . . .

PRESIDENT: Oh, yeah.

DEAN: . . . and things like this. He'd worked with leaks. He'd, you know, track those things down. and so the report that I got from Krogh was that he was a hell of a good man and not only that, a good lawyer, uh, and could set up a proper operation . . . Liddy was told to put together his plan, you know, how he would run an intelligence operation. And . . . after he was brought over there at the Committee, Magruder called me in January and said, 'I'd like to have you come over and see Liddy's plan.'

PRESIDENT: January of '72?

DEAN: January of '72.

Dean then went on to describe Liddy's plan presented in Attorney General Mitchell's office:

DEAN: The most incredible thing I have ever laid my eyes on. All in codes, and involving black bag operations, kidnapping, providing prostitutes, uh, to weaken the opposition, bugging, uh, mugging teams. It was just an incredible thing.

'Mitchell virtually sat there puffing and laughing,' Dean said. He told Nixon that Mitchell had informed Liddy that the plan was too expensive and grandiose. Liddy came back a month later with a scaled-down plan, and this time Dean suddenly became righteously ethical:

> DEAN: I told them these are not the sort of things that are ever to be discussed in the office of the Attorney General of the United States – and I am personally incensed.
>
> Liddy sat over there and tried to come up with another plan that he could sell . . . They came up with another plan but they couldn't get it approved by anyone over there. So Liddy and Hunt apparently came to see Chuck Colson, and Colson picked up the telephone and called Magruder and said, 'You all either fish or cut bait. Uh, this is absurd to have these guys over there and not using them, and if you're not going to use them, I may use them.' Things of this nature.

Dean then went on to describe 'where the next thing comes in the chain'.

> DEAN: I think that Bob (Haldeman) was assuming that they had something that was proper over there, some intelligence-gathering operation that Liddy was operating and through Strachan who was his tickler, he started pushing them . . .
>
> PRESIDENT: Yeah.
>
> DEAN: . . . to get some information and they took that as a signal to probably go to Mitchell and say, 'they're pushing us like crazy for this from the White House.' And so Mitchell probably puffed on his pipe and said, 'Go ahead.' And never really reflected on what it was all about.

Later Dean turned to a meeting with Liddy after the break-in where he received Liddy's only published statement so far on his motive.

> DEAN: So I called Liddy on the Monday morning and

> I said, 'Gordon,' I said, 'first I want to know if anybody in the White House was involved in this.' And he said, 'No.' And they weren't. I said, 'Well, I want to know how in God's name this happened.' And he said, 'Well, I was pushed without mercy by Magruder to get in there, get more information – that the information . . . it was not satisfactory. Magruder said, 'The White House is not happy with what we're getting.'

And it's here Nixon put his finger on the central mystery:

> PRESIDENT: Why, I wonder? I'm just trying to think as to why *then*. We'd just finished the Moscow trip. I mean, we were . . .
>
> DEAN: That's right.
>
> PRESIDENT: The Democrats had just nominated McGovern. I mean, for Christ's sake, I mean, what the hell were we – I mean I can see doing it *earlier* . . . but I don't see why all the pressure would have been on *then*.

In sum, the 'official' theory is that the White House set up a campaign intelligence-organisation capability at C.R.P., that Haldeman (acting for the President) pushed them 'without mercy' for intelligence information, and Colson pressed them even further.

In their first break-in on Memorial Day they installed two 'bugs', one on Chairman Lawrence O'Brien's telephone, the other on the telephone of an executive named Spencer Oliver, Jr.

The O'Brien tap didn't work. The tap on Oliver's did but according to Magruder's testimony it resulted in nothing but romantic gossip.

While writing this book I was informed that the chatter about love issued not from Oliver, but from a secretary named Maxie (now working for President Jimmy Carter, of all people), and other secretaries. Oliver's phone was the only one with a W.A.T.S. line accessible to secretaries and Maxie later told Oliver that when he was away she and her associates would spend the time calling boy friends all over the country – and using vivid details.

Whether or not this is true, the official theory states that because no useful information was found, Mitchell was angry and ordered a second break-in to fix the bug on O'Brien's phone. And on that second attempt the burglars were caught.

This defies belief, and not just because Mitchell denies it. I believe it's probable that Mitchell, despite his denial, in some way authorised the Liddy overall budget when he met with Magruder in Florida (in fairness, it must be said that not only Mitchell denies that he did, but a third party in the room, Frederick LaRue, also denies it.)

But I will never believe that the politically astute Mitchell would specifically approve a break-in at the Democratic National Committee Headquarters. For one thing, Mitchell was usually the most cautious man in Nixon's camp. Time and again he stopped Nixon from making impulsive, angry moves. (For example, he not only relayed Hoover's complaints about the Huston Report, but added his own strong suggestion that it be killed.)

Secondly, Mitchell, as a campaign expert, would know – as we all did – that there was no useful political information to be gained from the D.N.C. Headquarters. The idea that Mitchell saw the tape transcripts, discovered to his surprise that nothing 'useful' was being received, and sent the burglars back *again*, is even more absurd. Look at the date. Mitchell, the campaign chairman, knew by June 17 that Nixon didn't need any political information, useful or otherwise, to defeat McGovern. He was about 64–36 in the pools, an unprecedented lead.

I believe Mitchell would have killed the idea of wiretapping the D.N.C. in a minute. If he was determined to wiretap for political information, he would have sent Liddy's minions into *McGovern's* headquarters. In fact the only memo of mine that I recall on the subject of the intelligence capability at C.R.P. was this suggestion, apparently not heeded: 'Transfer whatever capability you have from Muskie to McGovern,' which shows where *I* believed the 'gold' was. In that memo I was referring to such capabilities as our hard-working chauffeur in Muskie's camp and whatever system we had for recording public speeches, but the principle remains the same. If I had considered the D.N.C. a viable target, I would have targeted D.N.C., and not the candidate's headquarters. This theory is also flawed in that it provides no reason whatever for the selection of O'Brien and Oliver as the specific targets within the D.N.C.

But there's a larger reason the 'official' theory falls flat. To isolate the break-in as a simple political intelligence action is to require sweeping under the rug an absolute mountain of conflicting evidence. An examination of the Democratic Party Trap Theory will reveal one reason why.

The Democratic Party Trap Theory

Who are the four key figures in the Watergate drama who are still hiding secrets? According to Richard Nixon in a telephone conversation with me, they are James McCord, Richard Helms, Bob Bennett, and Fred Fielding, who worked for John Dean. (Interestingly, Nixon does not include Liddy.) These people, he believes (and I concur), still have undisclosed facts to tell about Watergate. But *my* list – unlike Nixon's – would also include Chuck Colson and Richard Nixon.

When last heard from, McCord was back at work as a private security consultant in Rockville, Maryland (promising future clients, no doubt, to tape doorlocks *vertically*).

Recently a man who had worked in Democratic National Committee Headquarters met McCord in Rockville, and asked why he had placed a tap on Spencer Oliver's telephone, in addition to the tap on Larry O'Brien's. The question had some basis because if it were true that the burglars were looking for political information they might better have tapped the telephone of Robert Strauss, who as finance chairman was the No. 2 man to O'Brien.

McCord said, 'We knew exactly whose phones we were going to tap when we went in there. We had made a diagram of the offices.' But he refused to give more details.

The suggestion of those who believe Watergate was a trap set by the Democrats is that one of the two taps was placed on Oliver's telephone only because it was felt nothing important would be said by a lower level employee, such as Oliver. And the second tap on the telephone of Larry O'Brien would produce nothing because, amazingly enough, *O'Brien knew that the break-in was about to take place*, and would therefore take precautions. (Indeed, O'Brien's tap didn't 'work', for some reason – and that's surprising, because McCord was one of the top wiremen in the C.I.A., and had won praise from his superiors for his electronic talents.)

I believe that in years to come historians will find themselves actually laughing at the D.N.C. Headquarters break-in when they study the facts. *Never before has a crime been so well advertised and widely known ahead of time.* The C.I.A. knew about it because Eugenio Martinez, one of their agents, was on the Watergate team and was reporting regularly to his C.I.A. case officer. That wasn't bad enough. Larry O'Brien, the actual target, was specifically told that the break-in at his D.N.C. Headquarters was going to occur.

In 1976 I tried to telephone Fred Thompson, who had been head of the minority staff of the Ervin Committee. The facts Thompson had uncovered in his investigation about the involvement of both the C.I.A. and the Democratic Party in the break-in had startled him again and again. He published the evidence in his book *At That Point in Time* and it was then I tried to reach him, because that evidence intrigues me. Thompson didn't return my call and I finally gave up. Perhaps he thought he should not be communicating with a man named Haldeman 'at that point in time', as Dean used to say. I don't know. But I'm thankful to him and his staff, anyway, for the investigative work they did because in telling my own story of Watergate, it fills in many voids which were mysteries to me.

What were the facts that support the Democratic Party Trap Theory?

It begins with a letter from Bill Haddad, a Democratic politician in New York to his friend Larry O'Brien in Washington, on March 23, 1972.

> I am hearing some very disturbing stories about G.O.P. sophisticated surveillance techniques now being used for campaign purposes . . . The information comes from a counter wiretapper who helped me once in a very difficult situation in Michigan and who had come to me highly recommended from two lawyers.
>
> Can you have someone call me so you can get the information first hand and take whatever actions you deem necessary . . .

O'Brien dispatched an aide, John Stewart, to New York to check on the information. It turned out that Haddad's source was a private investigator named Woolston-Smith, who had overheard conversations in New York's 'intelligence community' revealing that the Democratic Party Committee Headquarters at the Watergate in Washington was about to be wiretapped. He had also heard that the bugging activity was connected to the November Group, an advertising agency working for the Nixon campaign in New York.

It's interesting that McCord, who later botched (deliberately or not) the second break-in by his horizontal tape, and the first break-in by installing a tap that didn't 'work' on O'Brien's telephone, was at that time in New York checking the telephones of the November Group advertising agency. The conclusion is very tempting that he was the 'wire man,' who tipped off the break-in and if so, why?

At the meeting in New York, Haddad, who had sent

the letter alerting O'Brien, revealed to O'Brien's man Stewart that he had information of his own: namely that Miami's Cuban community would be involved. The Cubans would be told that the motive for the break-in was to find evidence that the Democratic Party was receiving money from Cuba.

This was a shocker. Six weeks before the Watergate break-in the Democrats not only knew that their Headquarters in the Watergate was going to be broken into, they also knew that Cubans from Miami would be involved, and even the motive the Cubans would be given for the operation! What was more astonishing is that Haddad said he had told his friend, Jack Anderson, the columnist, of the break-in before it happened.

Anderson's mysterious role in Watergate will be examined eventually, but now it's more significant to see what the Democrats did after being warned. According to Stewart's testimony, not much. Stewart admitted that, prior to the break-in, the Democrats had received a warning that the Nixon campaign would attempt to bug the D.N.C. Headquarters. But he said the information was 'so unsubstantiated that it certainly was not the basis for any action on our part.'

In New York the staff interviewed Woolston-Smith, the private investigator who had first alerted the Democrats. They found themselves confronted with a pudgy, dapper man with a British accent and a stubby pipe that he waved in the air to make points. Contrary to what O'Brien's aide, Stewart, had testified, Woolston-Smith said that Stewart was 'very interested' in the warning about the break-in. In fact, right up to the time of the break-in, he and Stewart frequently talked about it. In Woolston-Smith's words, Stewart's interest 'was hot right up to the end.' Not only that, but Woolston-Smith recalled that his last pre-Watergate conversation with Stewart was 'something is about to happen.'

I believe the evidence proves that Larry O'Brien and the Democrats knew the break-in was going to happen. This is staggering in its implications.

My second conclusion is tentative, but the facts seem to lean towards it. McCord, who botched up the break-in, was the man who got word to the Democrats – accidentally or not – that their headquarters was going to be wiretapped.

O'Brien had been quoted as saying he did nothing about the warning because the information wasn't specific and, besides, the D.N.C. didn't have enough money to afford sufficient security measures. But the fact is the bug on O'Brien's telephone never transmitted. The Democratic Party Trap theorists believe that the bug on O'Brien's phone was simply removed after it was installed and that's why it didn't 'work'.

And what about the strange actions of columnist Jack Anderson?

From my view, Anderson has acted strangely out of character throughout the Watergate case. He's usually been quick to point out both his successes and failures. But on Watergate, silence fell. Nothing was said about his own involvement until the Thompson Committee got on to the Haddad testimony about the break-in, and Anderson's knowledge that it was about to happen.

Even more embarrassing, it turned out that Anderson was a close friend of Frank Sturgis, one of the Watergate burglars, ever since the Bay of Pigs. Coincidentally or not, when Sturgis arrived at Washington's National Airport from Miami, Anderson just happened to be there. The columnist explained his presence at the airport by saying that he was on his way to Cleveland for a speaking engagement. The Senate staff searched for weeks and never found any evidence of that alleged speaking engagement.

Anderson admitted that after the break-in he saw Sturgis in jail. He also admitted Sturgis had introduced him to Bernard Barker, another Watergate burglar, in Miami, and had spoken of E. Howard Hunt.

But Anderson, of course, denied that Sturgis had told him anything about the break-in ahead of time. What he couldn't deny, because the investigators had it from other sources was that Bill Haddad, the New York Democratic politician, had informed him that the break-in was going to take place.

I find this incredible. Jack Anderson, of all people, in Washington, knew the Watergate break-in was going to take place. Why didn't he publish this fantastic scoop? Why did he, instead, take action to hide what he knew?

Anderson allowed the break-in to take place without publishing what he knew. If he had published his information, Watergate would never have taken place. Even more mysteriously, Anderson admitted receiving the information in a letter, but claimed he had *lost* it. Haddad, who had sent the letter, topped this by saying he had kept no copies in his files. Apparently, neither the Democrats nor Anderson wanted anyone to know exactly what was in that letter which warned about the break-in.

But if the Democratic Party was setting a trap, why didn't they spring it? Why didn't they post guards nearby who would capture the burglars red-handed?

The answer is: they might have posted guards – but in a more sophisticated manner that would not reveal to the Republicans that the Democrats had been forewarned. I'm referring to a policeman named Carl Shoffler.

On May 20, 1973, the Watergate staff interviewed Edmund Chung, an acquaintance of Shoffler's. Chung told the staff that he had dinner with Shoffler earlier that year at which he 'got the impression that Shoffler had advance knowledge of the break-in . . . ' Shoffler had said that if Chung checked police records, *he would wonder why Shoffler was on duty the night of June 16–17.*

That last statement was another bombshell because the investigators did check the police record and found something very odd. Shoffler was the plainclothesman who had answered the call from Watergate about the break-in – in a car that just happened to be the nearest one to the crime. What made it more mysterious was that Shoffler *wasn't supposed to be on duty at that time.* He had concluded his regular eight-hour tour at 10 p.m. But for some unknown reason he asked for a *second* tour of duty. Two eight-hour stretches back to back. Why?

When the call came in about the Watergate burglary, it was Shoffler who grabbed the phone in the car and volunteered his unit's assistance.

Shoffler denied Chung's story, but the fact remains that the police record reveals he was not supposed to be on duty that night; he had finished his tour for the evening. It's extremely intriguing, to say the least, that he volunteered for a second tour and just happened to be the man nearest to the crime.

And so, the proponents of the Democratic Party Trap Theory say, it's certain that the Democrats knew the Watergate break-in was going to take place and that they even alerted Jack Anderson who could exploit it *after* it happened. And they also believe it's probable that plainclothesman Carl Shoffler was deliberately stationed in the area that night by the Democrats to capture the burglars red-handed.

What's wrong with the thesis? Not much.

I've no doubt the Democratic Party, once getting wind of a stupid scheme like the break-in, would let it happen in hopes the resulting publicity would damage the Republicans – and might even have hired a plainclothesman to be *sure* it was exposed.

But the theory doesn't explain the other side of the mystery – the *motive* for breaking into the D.N.C. Headquarters.

The theory I describe next, the C.I.A. Trap Theory, has answers to both questions, motive plus a possible deliberate trap.

The C.I.A. Trap Theory

On June 23, 1972, at the White House meeting I've already mentioned, I had requested that the C.I.A. attempt to stop the F.B.I. investigation of the Mexican bank through which C.R.P. cheques had been laundered.

In the summer of 1973 I watched C.I.A. Director Helms and Deputy Director Walters testify in outraged tones to the Ervin Committee that the C.I.A. had been duped at that meeting into assisting the White House cover-up.

The impression the two C.I.A. officials gave was that the C.I.A. was pressured into co-operating with us, even though they righteously insisted over and over again that the C.I.A. had nothing to do with Watergate.

Today this is still the understanding of the vast majority of Americans about the C.I.A.'s role in Watergate.

Even when Helms admitted to the Committee that one of the Watergate burglars, Eugenio Martinez, was still on the C.I.A. payroll when the break-in occurred, no one drew the obvious conclusion. C.I.A. operatives regularly report to case officers. Martinez had been working with the Hunt-Liddy team for months. He almost certainly was reporting to his C.I.A. case officer all along – and that means the C.I.A. had advance knowledge of the break-in.

Interestingly, the C.I.A. never allowed the Ervin Committee investigators to see the reports of Martinez's case officer at the time. And when they asked to interview the case officer they were told he was on safari in Africa, almost the only place in the world you can't be reached by telephone or radio. That 'safari' never ended during the entire run of the investigation.

But even Republican Senators on the Committee were tricked by what seemed to be the legitimate outrage of the C.I.A. officials who testified in public. Unfortunately for those officials, two ex-C.I.A. agents shortly thereafter published 'inside' reports on the C.I.A. involvement which told quite another story.

On September 14, 1973, Miles Copeland, a former C.I.A. agent, hinted in the *National Review* that James McCord might have received a 'non-order to sabotage the Watergate burglars' operation.' In other words, that C.I.A. chiefs told McCord to abort the burglary, without a specific order in writing.

Still, this was general speculation. But then another ex-C.I.A. agent added more specifics. In November 1973, Andrew St George said in *Harper's* magazine that he had visited C.I.A. headquarters and discussed the break-in with his former associates. What he discovered was that

Martinez had indeed reported to the C.I.A. hierarchy on the planning of the Watergate break-in. Even more interesting, St George was told that C.I.A. Director Helms, himself, had been informed of the break-in before it happened.

This prompted Senator Howard Baker to send a letter to William Colby, the new C.I.A. Director. (Helms had asked for a diplomatic post about as far from Washington as you could get without going on safari – an ambassador to Iran.) The letter to C.I.A. asked if any individual had ever informed the Agency about the break-in.

A month later, the C.I.A. responded with a surprise. Bob Bennett, President of the Robert R. Mullen Company, had communicated to an employee of the C.I.A. (namely, his case officer) information which had come to his attention concerning the Watergate five. This was the first revelation that E. Howard Hunt's employer at the Mullen Company, Bob Bennett, was a C.I.A. 'asset'.

According to the Senate minority staff, this was the first item of what turned out to be a mountain of incredible C.I.A. entanglement with the Watergate matter.

The Senate minority staff investigation began in full force in January 1974, uncovering one fact after another which left the investigators astonished. These revelations eventually led Fred Thompson to state that in his mind, 'the question was becoming one of whether the C.I.A. had been a *participant* or a benign *observer* of the break-in or, in view of the bungling of the burglary and the mysterious circumstances surrounding it, whether C.I.A. operatives had perhaps *sabotaged* the break-in to weaken the White House and strengthen the Agency in its struggle for survival.'

And soon the Committee had a strange – and not too welcome – partner, Chuck Colson. Colson was involved because of a strange twist of fate. The first C.I.A. memo uncovered by the Senate staff stated that Bob Bennett of the Mullen Company was going to direct reporters, including Bob Woodward of the *Post*, towards Colson as the

Watergate villain and away from the C.I.A.. Bennett was also feeding Woodward other information for which the reporter was 'suitably grateful'.

2

Who Is Deep Throat?

The memo of Bob Bennett's C.I.A. case officer points almost overwhelmingly to Bennett as Deep Throat, the phantom source for Woodward and Bernstein. In that C.I.A. memo it states that Bennett is feeding information to Woodward for which the reporter is 'suitably grateful'.

'Suitably grateful' of course, implies that Woodward is protecting the C.I.A. in exchange for the information. And, in fact, an examination of Woodward and Bernstein's book, *All the President's Men*, shows a remarkable coincidence. The C.I.A. is barely mentioned, even though Woodward admits his first interest in the case came when he heard McCord, at the precinct station, say he had been employed by the C.I.A.

Strange.

Nevertheless Woodward has denied that Bennett is Deep Throat. I agree with him. I have my own candidate, based on my knowledge of what was going on at the time Deep Throat was feeding Woodward his stories.

Nixon has this same knowledge, too, and from time to time he swings away from Bennett and points to my candidate.

His name is Fred Fielding. He was John Dean's staff assistant; a shy, slightly prissy fellow.

Why do I think Fielding is Deep Throat?

1. I begin by accepting Woodward's own description of Deep Throat as a 'source in the Executive Branch who had access to information at C.R.P. as well as the White House.' That, if true, eliminates Bennett, who was not in the Executive Branch. Woodward later said in the book

that Deep Throat also had special access to the Justice Department and the F.B.I. Only Dean, or his associate, had access from the White House to C.R.P., the F.B.I. and the Justice Department during Watergate.

2. The second fact that makes me suspect Fielding is that Dean told us he personally had kept Fielding 'out of things' during Watergate. If that's true, you had a man with access to a lot of information from different sources but kept away from other vital information. And that accounts for a mystifying aspect of Deep Throat's behaviour that has gained little or no notice. Not what he told Woodward that was accurate – but what he told Woodward that was *wrong* and almost every White House staffer *knew* was wrong. This could only happen if Deep Throat had access to much information, but was deliberately kept 'out of things', as Dean had said. Fielding would then let his imagination fill in the gaps.

There are dozens of examples. I'll cite just a few. Deep Throat tells Woodward in one of his first meetings:

> Much of the intelligence-gathering was on their own campaign contributors, and some to check on the Democratic contributors – to check people out and sort of semi-blackmail them if something was found . . . a very heavy-handed operation.

'Heavy-handed', and complete baloney, as it was later discovered.

Following up that false information, Deep Throat plunges on with this beauty:

> Mitchell conducted his own – he called it an investigation – for about ten days after June 17. And he was going crazy. He found all sorts of new things which astounded even him. At some point Howard Hunt, of all the ironies, was assigned to help Mitchell get some information. Like lightning, he was pulled off and fired . . .

Mitchell never spent one moment 'investigating' Watergate, let alone ten days. Ehrlichman and Dean did that. And the idea that Hunt would have been assigned to Mitchell to investigate his own break-in is rather comical, to say the least. Hunt stayed out of sight from Day One.

And so on.

Their most famous error – naming me as one of five controllers of the Watergate fund – caused Woodward some agony. Especially as Deep Throat had 'confirmed' the errant story before the *Post* published it.

But, as I've said, Deep Throat *did* furnish Woodward with legitimate information. So, grasping this puzzle in two hands, I believe Fred Fielding is the likeliest candidate in the White House to 'know and not to know' – and therefore his name henceforth should be 'Double Throat'.

3

Chuck Colson – referred to in the C.I.A. memo as the man they would blame – had sources in the government everywhere and he used them, constantly surprising the Ervin Committee staff investigating the C.I.A. connection with knowledge that even they didn't have. For example, Colson told Fred Thompson that the C.I.A. was financing a Hughes project, the Glomar Challenger, a fact Thompson found incredible until he read it in a newspaper a year later.

One a.m., California, the summer of 1973. I was sound asleep. The telephone rang. I reached for it in a half daze, but snapped awake quickly when informed that the President was on the telephone from the White House. I glanced at my watch. With the three-hour time difference, it was four in the morning in Washington. What was keeping Nixon up all night?

Nixon's voice was hushed, almost supernatural. I had an eerie sensation of mystery as the President of the United States said in a whisper, 'Bob, I want you to answer these questions – and I also want you to telephone Ehrlichman and call be back with his answers. This is very, very urgent.'

And these were the questions that a haunted President, sitting up at four in the morning, unable to sleep, asked me that night.

> 'Do you know anything about the Bennett P.R. firm, the Mullen Company?'
>
> 'Did you ever employ them at the White House? Were they ever retained by us for any purpose?'
>
> 'Did you know they were a C.I.A. front?'
>
> 'Did you know that Helms [the C.I.A. Director] *ordered* Bennett to hire Howard Hunt?'
>
> 'Did you know that Hunt was on the payroll at the Bennett firm *at the same time* that he was on the White House payroll?'

I told Nixon that I only knew about Bob Bennett and the C.I.A. connection because Fred Thompson had interviewed me before I left Washington. He told me Senator Baker, the minority chairman of the Ervin Committee, was convinced that there was a C.I.A. connection to Watergate. For example, that Martinez was more active in the C.I.A. than they had been told. And Martinez was in constant contact with his case worker regarding Hunt before the first break-in. 'The premise is that all this was reported to C.I.A. headquarters.' I said that Thompson had lots of other facts, many hard – but others circumstantial, because the C.I.A. had destroyed the evidence. But 'Baker's investigators have uncovered so much evidence about the C.I.A. they're afraid it will come out later and make them appear to be dummies if they didn't investigate it at the time.'

In 1974 Chuck Colson came to my house to see me on the same subject. We sat in my living room as Colson told me he was absolutely convinced that the C.I.A. ran the whole Watergate operation from the beginning. He told me we had to act quickly to expose them. Ehrlichman and I should join him in digging out the truth before our trial. If the C.I.A. initiated the break-in, the court would realise we were the victims rather than the villains of Watergate. 'We need to hire private investigators,' Colson said. 'Do it right.' Colson said he knew two investigators who were the best in the business, but the problem was they were expensive. 'Can we get somebody to put up the money to hire these guys? For example, Ehrlichman's contacts in Texas? It would probably take $15,000 to $20,000.

We never could raise the money, so private investigators were never hired. I doubt that two private detectives would have had much success. However, I discovered – as did the Senate Committee staff – that Colson hardly needed assistance from anyone. He applied the same energy he had once utilised for his White House projects to his search for facts on the C.I.A. involvement in Watergate, and he almost outdid the entire Senate Staff.

He had an eager extremely helpful associate, a President who once had whispered his suspicions to me across the continent at four in the morning: Richard Nixon.

I believe Nixon opened up all the related White House C.I.A. files to Colson. As Colson's investigation broadened, he kept me informed of many facets of the C.I.A. connection that he turned up.

By the time Colson wrote his book, *Born Again*, he had apparently decided to turn the other cheek, as the Bible suggests, and ignored almost completely all the facts he had discovered about the C.I.A. involvement.

Before examining Colson's information, let's study the C.I.A. Trap Theory. Proponents of this theory believe the C.I.A. feared Nixon because of his known distaste for the agency and his effort to bring them in line via the Huston plan.

Utilising Bob Bennett of the Mullen Company, the theory says, the C.I.A. controlled the Hunt-Liddy team in all of its ventures from Ellsberg to Watergate. In the words of the official Senate Watergate report: 'Bennett's accessibility to the C.I.A. has raised questions concerning possible Agency involvement in . . . Bennett's activities in regard to Hunt/Liddy . . . ' To wit:

> Bennett suggested and co-ordinated the DeMotte interview regarding Chappaquiddick. [DeMotte was a man whom Hunt went to Rhode Island to interview. He supposedly knew the truth about Chappaquiddick, as well as stories of Kennedy's sexual escapades. It turned out he knew nothing.]
>
> Bennett co-ordinated the release of Dita Beard's statement [about the I.T.T. case]; suggested that [Las Vegas newspaper editor] Hank Greenspun's safe contained information of interest to both Hughes and C.R.P. [Greenspun's safe was supposed to contain the private papers of Robert Maheu, Hughes's top employee in Las Vegas, who was fired and then began a bitter court war with Hughes];
>
> . . . asked for and received from Hunt a price estimate for bugging Clifford Irving [Author of a forged autobiography of Hughes];
>
> . . . set up dummy committees with Liddy as a conduit for Hughes's campaign contributions to Nixon;
>
> . . . served as the point of contact between Hunt and Liddy during the two weeks following the Watergate break-in.
>
> Furthermore, Robert Oliver, who worked for Bennett, was the father of R. Spencer Oliver, Jr, whose telephone was tapped at the Democratic National Committee Headquarters.

The official report revealed other strange facts:

1. The original Watergate team was composed not of five men, but six. Who was the sixth man? Tom Gregory. Apparently he became nervous for some reason about the proposed burglary. And this is what is so interesting. This original member of the Watergate burglary team went to Bob Bennett to ask permission to quit. He did not

go to Gordon Liddy who was supposed to be the man in charge of the team.

2. A few days after the break-in, a C.I.A. employee named Wayne Pennington went to McCord's house and burned all documents connecting McCord to the C.I.A. It must have been some mountain of paper; the smoke from the fire was so voluminous it blackened the walls in the house – and the C.I.A. ended up paying for the damage.

3. After the break-in, Hunt flew to California to hide out with a C.I.A. agent.

4. The C.I.A. had a taping system on its offices and telephones just as the White house did. On January 15, 1973, Senator Mansfield sent a letter to the C.I.A. ordering all evidentiary matter to be retained and protected. Defying Mansfield's letter, the C.I.A., in an unprecedented action, *destroyed all of its tapes* the very next week. Question: What were they hiding?

5. The C.I.A. provided Hunt with disguises and equipment for various White House missions. C.I.A. officials admitted this but testified they had broken off relations with Hunt just before the Ellsberg break-in. The Senate investigation proved that they continued to work with Hunt right up to the Watergate break-in.

This was a provocative investigation indeed; so disturbing to the C.I.A. that eventually the Agency brought down an iron curtain on further co-operation. And, in character, they somehow managed to persuade influential newsmen to lambaste Senator Howard Baker, the spearhead of the Senate Investigation, for using the C.I.A. investigation to 'draw attention away from Nixon.' It was a ploy that anti-Nixon columnists eagerly fell for, perhaps to their regret.

But nothing could stop Colson. His research on Howard Hunt was particularly interesting because if the C.I.A. connection to Watergate was a reality, then it followed that Hunt was 'planted' at the White House by the C.I.A. What made Colson angrier was that he was the 'patsy' who was conned into hiring Hunt. Who was the man who suggested Hunt as a White House employee? Bob Bennett.

Colson reported that, 'Early in 1971, Hunt and Bennett began visiting me from time to time to offer their services on a volunteer basis to help the White House in outside efforts or in political matters.' By offering 'volunteer' help they gradually eased themselves into his confidence, Colson said.

But Colson had dug up more interesting facts about Hunt. For example, C.I.A. Director Helms had testified to Congress that he hardly knew Hunt. But, according to Colson, Helms not only knew him, he had loaned Hunt $20,000 when he was having financial difficulty because of heavy medical expenses incurred by his daughter.

There was mysterious business in Hunt's very first assignment – to find out the truth about Chappaquiddick. It began when Hunt told Colson that Bob Bennett knew someone in Rhode Island who could offer inside knowledge of Senator Ted Kennedy and Chappaquiddick. Hunt volunteered to go to Rhode Island and interview the person, Clifton DeMotte.

Colson later found out, however, that DeMotte knew absolutely nothing about Chappaquiddick or any other area of Ted Kennedy's private life and there was no reason ever to believe that he did know anything. So why the charade?'

Simple. It turned out that DeMotte was a *former employee of Bob Bennett's*, and Colson believed the project was framed by Bennett only to drag the White House into a compromising position with the C.I.A. by asking for C.I.A. assistance on a private political mission.

In fact, all the time Hunt was on the White House payroll, Colson said, *Hunt's secretary was on the C.I.A. payroll!* Her code name in C.I.A. files, according to Colson, was 'Menopause Mary'. Question: Was Hunt, supposedly a retired C.I.A. agent, actually an *active* agent while in the White House?

And when Colson looked through Hunt's files after Watergate he saw that on the very day Hunt had been hired at the White House, July 1, 1971, there was a telephone slip asking Hunt to return a call to Mr Osborn of the C.I.A. Osborn was the C.I.A.'s Director of Security. 'Hunt told me he had been out of touch with the C.I.A. for years. But this note showed that he was in contact with the C.I.A. from the very first day,' Colson said.

Finally, Colson discovered that four months before he hired Hunt to work for the White House, Hunt had already contacted one of the Cubans, Bernard Barker, in Miami. To Colson, it seemed suspiciously like a 'get ready for action' call – even before the White House hired Hunt.

The full story of the C.I.A. connection to the break-in is so labyrinthine that it would take a book of its own to fully explore the intriguing leads.

The C.I.A. Trap Theory suggests the intelligence community instigated the break-in in order to embarrass the President they feared.

Did the C.I.A. fear Nixon? Here's a little noticed portion of the statement made by James McCord.

> (McCord Memorandum submitted May 7, 1973 to the Senate Watergate Investigating Committee and Federal Prosecutors):
>
> Further, based on an earlier discussion with Robert Mardian in May 1972, it appeared to me that the White House had for some time been trying to get political control over the C.I.A. assessments and estimates, in order to make them conform to 'White House policy.' One of the things this meant to me was that this could mean that C.I.A. estimates and assessments could then be forced to accord with D.O.D. (Department of Defense) estimates of future U.S. weapons and hardware needs. This could be done by either shifting an intelligence function to D.O.D. from C.I.A., or by gaining complete political control over it at C.I.A.
>
> Among other things, this also smacked of the situation which Hitler's intelligence chiefs found themselves in, in the 1930s and 1940s, when they were put in the position of having to tell him what they thought he wanted to hear about foreign military capabilities

and intentions, instead of what they really believed, which ultimately was one of the things which led to Nazi Germany's downfall.

When linked with what I saw happening to the F.B.I. under Pat Gray – political control by the White House – it appeared then that the two Government agencies which should be able to prepare their reports, and to conduct their business with complete integrity and honesty in the national interest, were no longer going to be able to do so. That the nation was in serious trouble has since been confirmed by what happened in the case of Gray's leadership of the F.B.I.

What he wrote, in arcane bureaucratic language, is that the C.I.A. feared Nixon would preempt the C.I.A. as it had the F.B.I.

What's my opinion about the 'mountain of evidence' connecting the C.I.A. to the break-in?

It's very persuasive. But perhaps because I don't have a conspiratorial nature, I just can't imagine the C.I.A. *initiating* the break-in. I feel certain they monitored it with 'plants' to keep it under control. I also think the overwhelming weight of the evidence points to a deliberate sabotage of the break-in. But McCord, perhaps the most ardent ex-C.I.A. agent who has ever surfaced, may have sabotaged it on his own (for the reasons stated in his Ervin Committee testimony).

What evidence is there that both break-ins were sabotaged? In the first break-in on Memorial Day McCord placed two taps, then checked them with a portable receiver. He told his associates they both worked. Yet strangely, O'Brien's tap never did function.

When O'Brien's telephone was swept later by F.B.I. agents the tiny mike – nothing more than 'a little toy' as one Democrat on hand said – was operating, but it didn't even have the range to reach *across the street* where the receivers were installed. Shouldn't McCord – an expert wireman – have known this?

McCord's actions on the second break-in are even more

suspect. Virgilio Gonzales and Frank Sturgis had taped the doors during the Memorial Day break-in. For some reason, McCord volunteered to do it this time. He did it in spades. Reportedly, he went to the eighth floor by elevator, then taped every door on every floor leading from the stairwell to the corridors so that they could be opened from either side. Incredibly, he installed the tapes horizontally, so that large swatches were exposed on either side. By the time he finished, the doors on eight floors gleamed with new tape for a guard to discover. A guard, Frank Wills, naturally found the tape on the first door he saw on the garage level. He believed it was put there by a building engineer, and merely removed it.

Meanwhile the Watergate burglars waited across the street for the last late-working D.N.C. employee to leave. He did so at about the same time Wills was removing the tape. The D.N.C. employee turned out the lights in the D.N.C. and left. Across the street in a room in the Holiday Inn, McCord saw the D.N.C. was at last dark and silent. He and the other burglars converged in the basement level – and here is where McCord's actions become even more suspicious. For some reason, he claims he checked the garage door *and the tape was still there*. But the guard, a disinterested witness, states he removed it, and Hunt agrees, adding that the tape was not only removed, but caused them to rethink the whole plan – which they did. (What happened next is interesting quite apart from McCord: Martinez testified that the burglars went back to the Holiday Inn room across the street to decide what to do. Hunt and Liddy went into another room *and called someone*. After the telephone call to the unknown person [not Magruder, so who could it be?] Hunt emerged to say the operation would go on.)

Incredibly the door was once again taped horizontally! The guard inevitably saw that the tape he had just removed had miraculously reappeared – and alerted the police.

Meanwhile other evidence of sabotage occurred in the D.N.C. Headquarters. McCord had supplied a walkie-talkie. But when the lookout across the street, Alfred Baldwin, saw people searching the building, he warned Hunt, and Hunt shouted through the walkie-talkie to the burglars. For some reason, the walkie-talkie which they carried for just such an alert had been silenced and the burglars didn't get the message.

This series of clear, unmistakable errors appears to be deliberate sabotage and if so the C.I.A., or a C.I.A. agent acting alone, may have interfered in an historic way which was eventually to bring down the government.

Nevertheless, the chain of events leading from the discovery of the break-in to the fall of the Nixon Administration was probably as much of a surprise to the C.I.A. as it was to the rest of the country. Their activities were aimed at crippling the President, not removing him.

Why would the C.I.A. sabotage the Watergate operation? As McCord's testimony shows, ever since the Huston report, C.I.A. was very concerned about the White House 'gaining complete political control over . . . C.I.A.' We've seen how every one of the Hunt-Liddy projects up to and including Watergate mysteriously failed. The C.I.A. might have thought that this President, with his mind set on White House control of intelligence, and willingness to employ private intelligence teams in the White House, represented such a great danger to them that one of his secret operations must be exposed. C.I.A. would have known the resulting publicity from the exposure of Watergate would seriously hamper the President in the future in any further intelligence grab.

Furthermore, Larry O'Brien was of particular interest to C.I.A. in another way. He had worked for Hughes, who was C.I.A.'s secret partner in the Glomar Challenger and many other projects (Hughes corporation's earnings from C.I.A. were in the tens of millions). C.I.A. certainly wouldn't have liked a private White House team finding out everything that O'Brien knew about Hughes's C.I.A. connection.

In a twist of fate, this O'Brien-Hughes connection interested Nixon, too – from a different direction. Which leads me to my own theory of the break-in which is different from any of the others. It's based on my experience in the White House – and a strange conversation with a frightened White House aide. To understand the background we must go back to the spring of 1972.

4

The Haldeman Theory

'I've got it,' Chuck Colson said. He stood by my desk, grinning.

'Got what?'

'The proof we need that Dita Beard's I.T.T. memo was a forgery.'

International Telephone and Telegraph is a huge multinational corporation whose problems, as far as I was concerned, had brought us nothing but grief. In 1969, the Justice Department had filed antitrust suits seeking to divest the corporation of three recent acquisitions: Canteen Corporation, which manufactured food-service machines; Grinnell Corporation, whose main product was automatic sprinkler systems; and the Hartford Fire Insurance Company, one of America's largest property and liability insurance companies.

I.T.T. fought that antitrust suit bitterly with the President of the United States in its corner. What infuriated Nixon was not that Justice Department brought this suit, but that after it lost the case, it decided to appeal, in direct contradiction of Nixon's policy against such harassment of industries.

Who was the man telling the President of the United States what he could or could not do? as Nixon complained to me. A medium-level Justice Department employee named Richard McLaren. Who won? McLaren, of course.

(Past and future Presidents will not be surprised.)

But Nixon, as the English might say, 'gave it a go'. His anger mounting, in April 1971 he called in Ehrlichman and George Shultz, Director of the Office of Management and Budget.

NIXON: They're *not* going to file [an appeal].

EHRLICHMAN: Well, I thought that was your position.

NIXON: Oh, hell.

EHRLICHMAN: I've been trying to give . . . them a sign on this and, uh, they've been horsing us pretty steadily.

NIXON: I don't know whether I.T.T. is bad, good, or indifferent. But there are not going to be any more antitrust actions as long as I am in this chair . . . Goddamnit, we're going to stop it.

Nixon followed up with a call to Richard Kleindienst, the Deputy Attorney General, who was supervising the I.T.T. suits because John Mitchell's former law firm had once represented one of I.T.T.'s subsidiaries.

NIXON: I want something clearly understood, and, if it is not understood, McLaren's ass is to be out within one hour. The I.T.T. thing – stay the hell out of it. Is that clear? That's an order.

KLEINDIENST (no quick study): Well, you mean the order is . . .

NIXON: The order is to leave the Goddamn thing alone. Now, I've said this, Dick, a number of times, and you fellows apparently don't get the message over there. I do not want McLaren to run around prosecuting people, raising hell about conglomerates, stirring things up at this point. Now you keep him the hell out of that. Is that clear?

KLEINDIENST: Well, Mr President . . .

NIXON: Or either he resigns. I'd rather have him out anyway. I don't like the son-of-a-bitch . . .

Why was Nixon so angry? Because he had a special deal with I.T.T.? If so, I never heard an inkling of it in the Oval Office. I believe what caused his anger was that by 1971 Nixon had realised he was virtually powerless to deal with the bureaucracy in every department of the government. It was no contest. Nixon could rave and rant. Civil servants, almost all liberal Democrats, would thumb their noses at him. Washington insiders all acknowledge that the man who is still King in Washington has been dead for 32 years. Franklin D. Roosevelt's legacy lives on.

Republican Cabinet officers, installed at the head of departments, soon find that they rule nothing. The real decisions are made below by people who cannot be fired under Civil Service rules and who will be there long after the Republican Cabinet officers depart. As far as civil servants are concerned, every Republican administration is a transient phenomenon of no lasting importance.

We found this out at another agency, the I.R.S. I was involved in some of these efforts – and what a waste of time. Example: an important Republican backer of Nixon would find himself being audited. The explosion would send shock waves to the White House. Why him? Why not the notorious Mr John Doe, a Democrat, who we had been told was cheating on his taxes?

The measure of Nixon's powerlessness is simply stated in this fact: After repeated efforts to have the I.R.S. look into the tax returns of Mr Doe, the alleged 'cheater', we would get nowhere. And it boiled down to a humorous circumstance. Imagine first the well-known concept of the all-powerful President. Then listen to John Caulfield, John Dean's gumshoe. Caulfield's suggestion on how the President could get action at the I.R.S.: 'Why don't I write them an anonymous letter?'

And thus the descent: from the President's alleged power to an 'anonymous' letter by John Caulfield.

Now Nixon came up against hard rock again on the I.T.T. case. Mitchell got the word from McLaren. He went to see the President and said, 'if you stop the appeal, it will be "political dynamite". You will have people quit, you will have a Senate investigation . . . ' What he didn't have to add is that Nixon would also inspire a thousand leaks of documents and evidence, the bureaucrat's great tool of self-defence.

After all the Presidential storming, McLaren worked out a deal that he defended as completely fair: I.T.T. would retain the Hartford Fire Insurance Company, but would have to divest itself not only of Grinnell and Canteen, but two other large subsidiaries, Avis Auto-Rental, and Levitt builders.

Unfortunately for all, another factor clouded the picture and I was neck-deep in that, so if blame is to be affixed, I'm certainly one of the people responsible.

In 1970, Nixon told me he wanted the 1972 Republican convention in San Diego. 'I can stay in San Clemente and fly over to the convention by helicopter when I'm needed.' He also saw the political benefits. California was a critical state with the biggest bloc of electoral votes in the country. And in 1968 Nixon had barely squeaked through. 'I think we can help hold California if we give them the convention,' Nixon said.

One day I received a call from a fellow Californian, Cap Weinberger, the Deputy Director of the Office of Management and Budget. 'Bob, an old friend of yours is in town.' The friend was Ed Reinecke, California's Lieutenant-Governor. I went over to Cap's office to say hello to Ed. As we were leaving, I needled him. 'You California people are backward. No one's doing anything to get the Republican convention – and the President wants to hold it there.'

Reinecke said he'd 'get going on it right away'.

Some time after he returned to California we received word that San Diego was interested in becoming the host city for the convention. But they were having problems raising commitments for the necessary funds to underwrite their bid.

Various corporations were approached, including I.T.T., which owned the plush Harbor Island Hotel. I.T.T. made a proposition. If the President would make his convention headquarters in the Harbor Island Hotel, I.T.T. would put up $400,000 of the two million needed.

Many commentators have concentrated on that $400,000; few have mentioned how comically it dwindled. Somehow the offer went down to only $100,000 guaranteed. And even there, I.T.T. was cautious. The money would go not to the Republicans but to the San Diego County Tourist and Convention Bureau.

In effect, the Republican Party wouldn't receive a dime. All I.T.T. was doing, and in a dwindling fashion, was helping to make it possible for San Diego to obtain the convention and to create business for its own hotel.

Richard Nixon is guilty of many mistakes in Watergate but, from my own knowledge, the I.T.T. affair was a cheap shot. Because what happened was an I.T.T. public relations employee named Dita Beard wrote a memo, which stated in public relations braggadocio that the I.T.T. pledge to the San Diego Tourist Bureau was tied to the antitrust situation. 'I am convinced,' she wrote, 'that our noble commitment has gone a long way towards our negotiations on the mergers eventually coming up as Hal [Geneen] wants them. Certainly the President has told Mitchell to see things are worked out fairly.'

What we now know is that Mitchell had told the President that McLaren would make his own deal in his own way and Nixon had to stay out of it.

Nevertheless, Jack Anderson got the Dita Beard memo and played it for keeps. An antitrust case had been fixed, and the fix was a payoff for I.T.T.'s pledge of up to $400,000.

Chuck Colson was in my office within minutes telling me the President had said that he, Colson, should handle this crisis. And the headaches began for me.

Colson's aim was to prove the Dita Beard memo was a fraud. And the first step was to get her to deny she wrote it. To do this he let out all the stops. Soon his man, Howard Hunt, was at the C.I.A. rounding up wigs and voice changers to fly to Dita Beard's bedside in Denver. (She had been taken ill when the uproar struck. No one knows to this day whether she was actually sick or not, but I got the feeling in Washington she really was ill. She had every right to a stomachache. Her future in corporate public relations must have looked rather dim at that point.)

A strange and basically stupid sequence then unfolded. Hunt in a red wig calling on Dita Beard and running out into the hall to call Colson every two minutes. Hunt wanted her to fly back East, tell reporters that she hadn't written the memo, then collapse. Whether she was to collapse in front of the microphones, or while riding in a cab, was not made explicit.

Meanwhile, Colson was charging into my office everyday on his way to and from the President's office. Not only would he obtain Beard's denial, he was going to ask the F.B.I. lab to test the Beard memo and prove it was a forgery.

I was cynical about Colson's campaign, but Nixon was enthused. Colson was his new man in a crisis. He was going to nail that I.T.T. story as a fraud. Nixon was finally getting action.

Colson got his denial – but no collapse – from Dita Beard and the release of her denial was co-ordinated by his new friend, Bob Bennett of the Robert Mullen Company. It was greeted with general derision. No problem, Colson assured me. When the F.B.I.'s respected lab said the memo was a forgery, all would believe. But the F.B.I. stalled. And stalled. Colson was impatient. He charged out to hire a private company to test the memo and prove it was a forgery.

Bob Bennett suggested Intertel, the famous private security company whose main client – as Bennett's – was Howard Hughes. Intertel dutifully ruled that it couldn't be proven that Dita Beard typed her memo. But the F.B.I. lowered the boom on Colson by an ambiguous report which seemed to suggest that Dita Beard *did* write the memo.

Colson had turned the White House into a turmoil during the weeks of charging around trying to discredit Dita

Beard's memo. Now he was clearly defeated and, worse, he looked bad in the eyes of Nixon. Colson was furious.

The man who did capitalise on the I.T.T. scandal was the one you would expect – Larry O'Brien, the Democratic National Chairman. He made more points on the I.T.T. scandal than any other Republican venture, including Watergate. Colson was angry at O'Brien, but this was nothing new. Their enmity went back a long way – to the time when Colson worked for Republican Leverett Saltonstall and O'Brien for the Kennedy's in Massachusetts politics.

The disappointment of his defeat at the hands of O'Brien almost drove Colson crazy. I know because of a strange scene enacted in my office.

By the spring of 1972 Colson had angered nearly everyone inside the White House – and out. Mitchell and Ehrlichman were only two of his legion of powerful enemies – and their anger at Colson had always landed on my shoulders. I was the one who had to carry their complaints to Colson.

Dealing with Colson was no fun for White House staffers at any level. If he was superior in rank, he would bully them. If he was inferior, he would smile – and remind them he had 'the ear of the President'. Which he did. Never more so than in the I.T.T. case.

In the I.T.T. case I think it was Mitchell who complained about Colson charging around and upsetting the F.B.I. in his zeal to prove Dita Beard's memo was a forgery. He wanted me to call Colson on the carpet. What made it worse was that Nixon was flogging from the other end. Assured by Colson that his 'evidence' would be 'on his desk tomorrow' Nixon was enthused. When evidence didn't come in – as usual – I decided I had to have a showdown with Colson, once and for all.

I called him into my office and proceeded to 'chew him out' in real anger. Colson's heavy eyeglasses were slightly askew. He sat there, listening sullenly, as I told him the White House staff was an organisation, and we couldn't have a loose cannon careening around the deck, smashing into everyone else's area.

'But the President . . . ' Colson interrupted.

'I don't give a damn whether the President told you or not. Check with Ehrlichman, if you're going to do something that's in his bailiwick. Check with Mitchell, check with me, check with *somebody*! You're not going to keep charging off on your own, or I'm walking into the President's office, and you'll be out of here.'

Then I saw something beyond belief. Tears glistened in Colson's eyes. To my astonishment, he was sobbing.

My riot acts had been read to tender young secretaries as well as to august Cabinet officers. No one had ever collapsed the way the iron-man bully did. He found a handkerchief as I told him that what I said stood, and don't forget it.

But Colson never stopped. And every time he went into Nixon's office, his battery was recharged. And on I.T.T. – and Larry O'Brien – Nixon was firing Colson up to his limit.

During that spring, Larry O'Brien became a symbol of hate (political, not personal), for both Colson and his boss, Nixon, who had to hear the tales of defeat in Colson's efforts to fight off what Nixon considered an unfair rap on I.T.T. O'Brien kept riding the issue hard, as he should have as Democratic Chairman. Nixon decided, as always, to counterattack. What was bothering Nixon was the fact that he thought O'Brien was getting away with something. There just had to be hanky-panky involved in O'Brien's fantastically large ($180,000-a-year) Howard Hughes retainer for a part-time job.

Which leads me on to my own theory of who initiated the Watergate break-in.

Richard Nixon, himself, caused those burglars to break into O'Brien's office.

5

The fact that it was Larry O'Brien, of all people, who was leading the Democratic charge on I.T.T. embittered Nixon. O'Brien touched a raw nerve: Nixon's dealings with Howard Hughes, which had cost him two elections.

In the case of O'Brien, Nixon was acting very much like Captain Queeg in his search for the strawberries. He *knew* the strawberries had been stolen, but he just couldn't get anyone to take the event seriously.

And here was Larry O'Brien, a secret Hughes lobbyist – and no one cared enough to dig out the *proof* about O'Brien's connection with Hughes.

And yet, as Nixon had often said to me, how the press took after him on any possible connection to Howard Hughes! He strongly felt that the build-up to the $205,000 loan to his brother was a typical 'cheapshot' by the press. Now he felt he had a scandal of his own to reveal which could turn the tables on the Democrats. He called me into his cabin in Air Force One and laid out the programme. 'We're going to nail O'Brien on this, one way or the other.'

For assistance, I turned to Dean who turned to Caulfield who turned to jelly when he found 'skeletons in the Hughes closet' (ironically both Republican and Democrats) – and quietly let the issue die. But the subject was never dropped. In 1972, as the election approached, Nixon became more heated on the subject. 'O'Brien's not going to get away with it, Bob. We're going to get proof of his relationship with Hughes – and just what he's doing for the money.'

This was at the summit of Colson's influence with Nixon. Colson was in and out of the office time and again in the I.T.T. battle and other projects. Hunt was being employed on many of these ventures. I believe it is almost certain that Nixon asked Colson to help him 'nail' O'Brien. Colson naturally turned to Hunt. And Hunt tried to do it by tapping O'Brien's telephone at Watergate.

This isn't mere conjecture on my part. It's backed up by Nixon's own words, as revealed over and over again in the tapes. Nixon *knew* what had happened. He had told Colson to get the proof. Colson would have gotten the word to Hunt, and Hunt would have told Liddy to make his number one priority target Larry O'Brien. For good measure they placed a bug on Spencer Oliver, Jr, whost father worked for a company whose main client was Howard Hughes. In effect, those two telephones were the 'Hughes' telephones in the D.N.C. Headquarters. (In addition to the wiretaps, Frank Sturgis, one of the Watergate burglars, later said in a magazine article that the burglars were ordered to look in the files for 'anything about Hughes'.)

Time and again after the burglary Nixon would make such statements as, 'Colson must have done it.' Or a variation, 'There's no way he wasn't involved.' This was his prime and practically sole point of concern about Watergate until March of 1973.

On March 21, 1973, in his first long round-up with John Dean of the facts in the case, Nixon twice revealed to Dean his own feelings about the actual origin of the Watergate break-in. But Dean was so intent on his quest for immunity he brushed Nixon aside.

NIXON: The absurdity of the whole damned thing. Bugging and so forth. Well, let me say that, uh, Colson *et al* . . . were doing their best to get information . . . but they all knew very well they were supposed to comply with the law.

DEAN: U . . . uh

NIXON: You think . . . you feel that really the . . . triggerman was Colson on this, then? [Probing, fearful of the positive answer he expected to get.]

DEAN: Well, no. He was . . . just in the chain. He . . . helped push the thing.

NIXON: Called him up and said, 'We've got [unintelligible]' I don't know what the Christ he would be doing. Oh, I'll bet you I know why. That was at the time of I.T.T. He was trying to get something going there because I.T.T. – they were . . . giving us hell.

Later, Nixon returns to the subject of Colson.

NIXON (to Dean): I'm rather surprised at what you have told me today. From what you said I gathered . . . your analysis does not for sure . . . indicate that Chuck knew that it was a bugging operation for certain. [Great feeling of relief, but still not too sure.]

DEAN: That's correct.

NIXON: On the other hand, the other side of that, is that Hunt had conversations with Chuck . . . *Chuck might have gone around and talked to Hunt and said, 'Well, I was talking to the President and the President feels we ought to get information about this or that or the other thing.'* [The real reason for the fear.]

Dean tried to turn Nixon's attention away, but Nixon was obsessed with Colson.

NIXON: *I have talked to Chuck . . . and I am sure that Chuck may have even . . . talked to Hunt along those lines.*

The next day, March 22, I was recapitulating for Nixon what we had learned from Dean, and other sources. I said that Dean had told me there was no White House involvement in Watergate.

NIXON: Even Colson?
HALDEMAN: He's satisfied with that.

But Nixon was far from satisfied. 'I recall myself, Bob, the I.T.T. thing. I can . . . remember how he was. Hell, he'd go on for an hour about what he was trying to do . . .'

I'm sure that the same kind of instructions given me to nail O'Brien were given also to Colson – and Nixon's own words in out later conversations show that he knows it, too.

It's an interesting fact that no one who attended the Liddy-Mitchell meetings in January in which Liddy presented his original plan mentioned a D.N.C. break-in or wiretap. The original plans, apparently, were aimed towards the Democratic convention wherein the prostitutes and kidnappings would flourish, as well as electronic bugging of candidates' suites.

If so, the suggestion to bug O'Brien in Washington came as a later revision. And we know that Liddy and Hunt were both in Colson's White House office when the telephone call was made from Colson to Magruder, urging Jeb to get the programme started.

The Colson call came after the first two meetings in Mitchell's office, when Dean thought the entire plan had been killed. Magruder's testimony on the call is interesting because it points to Colson's real interest in the D.N.C: O'Brien.

QUESTION: After the February 4 meeting in Mr Mitchell's office, when the plan was still not approved, did there come a time when anyone else at the White House urged you to get the Liddy plan approved?

MAGRUDER: Yes. Mr Charles Colson called me one evening and asked me 'would we get off the stick . . . that we needed information on Mr O'Brien.'

And McCord's recollection is even more to the point. McCord said that in meetings with Hunt and Liddy he got the impression that Hunt had knowledge from Colson about the forthcoming break-in that even Liddy didn't have.

> QUESTION: What did he say . . . to indicate to you that he had any independent knowledge other than what Mr Liddy might have told him?
>
> MCCORD: . . . I mentioned to this committee the name of another individual . . . that Mr Hunt referred to in conversations in which they were talking about the Watergate operation . . .
>
> QUESTION: I think you should refer to the name.
>
> MCCORD: He referred to the name of Mr Colson . . . in the meetings with me and Mr Liddy in Hunt's offices . . . specifically, when Mr Hunt had a typed operational plan for the entry of the Democratic National Committee headquarters . . . at one point he held this plan in his hands and . . . he interjected the name of Mr Colson into the conversation at that point with words to the effect, 'I will see Colson.' And he held the paper in his hand in this sense.

An interesting irony is that Bob Bennett – accused by Colson and rightly so, of steering reporters away from C.I.A. towards himself as the villain – in fact really believed that Colson *was* the man behind the break-in. And who was closer than Bennett to the Hunt-Liddy team, which he had controlled (or 'advised', take your pick) over the last year? Yet we see these words in Bennett's first report to his C.I.A. case officer after the break-in: 'Colson most likely suggested the break-in to Hunt on an "I don't want to know, just get me the information" basis.'

The Haldeman Theory of the break-in is as follows: I believe Nixon told Colson to get the goods on O'Brien's connection with Hughes at a time when both of them were infuriated with O'Brien's success in using the I.T.T. case against them.

I believe Colson then passed the word to Hunt who conferred with Liddy who decided the taps on O'Brien and Oliver, the other 'Hughes' phone, would be their starting point.

I believe the Democratic high command knew the break-in was going to take place, and let it happen. They may even have planted the plainclothesman who arrested the burglars.

I believe that the C.I.A. monitored the Watergate burglars throughout. And that the overwhelming evidence leads to the conclusion that the break-in was deliberately sabotaged. (In this regard, it's interesting to point out that every one of the Hunt-Liddy projects somehow failed, from the interrogation of DeMotte, who was supposed to know all about Ted Kennedy's secret love life and didn't, to Dita Beard, to Ellsberg, to Watergate.)

None failed so comically as Hunt's interview with Lieutenant Colonel Lucien Conein, a C.I.A. official in South Vietnam at the time of President Ngo Dinh Diem's assassination.

Nixon had run into a stonewall at C.I.A. while trying to track down all the facts about the Bay of Pigs. Now, through Colson and Hunt, he went after another alleged weak spot in Kennedy's record: the assassination of Diem in 1963.

Hunt later testified that he and Colson were attempting to show that 'a U.S. Catholic administration had in fact conspired in the assassination of a Catholic Chief-of-State of another country'. Colson felt this would damage Senator Ted Kennedy with Catholic voters if he ran in 1972.

Hunt soon discovered that Kennedy had known of and approved the coup against Diem. But had he gone further, and approved the assassination of the South Vietnamese leader?

Hunt went to work. First he interviewed General Paul D. Harkins, the Commander of U.S. forces in Vietnam in 1963. Apparently, Harkins didn't give him what he wanted because Hunt then contacted another source, the flamboyant Conein, the C.I.A. operative in Vietnam who had maintained liaison with the rebels at the time.

Conein was reportedly a legend in Vietnam. He was certainly not the 'quiet American'. Once, angry that a tyre had blown on his jeep, he leaped out into the road, drew his pistol and shot out the other three tyres in a rage. Before his days in Vietnam Conein had been in the French Foreign Legion. When Hunt contacted Conein, Ehrlichman came to me, ecstatic. 'We're getting the whole story of the Diem assassination.'

'How come?'

'Hunt's going to get the real facts from Conein.'

'How?'

'I don't know but Hunt says he has a plan.'

I found out later the amusing details. Hunt arranged with the Secret Service to have Ehrlichman's office 'wired'. Then, according to the story I heard, he poured Conein many drinks of good cheer. According to Hunt, Conein then told him the whole story of the Kennedy role in the Diem affair. But when Hunt called in the Secret Service later to obtain the tape, he was dismayed to see the technician probe beneath a seat cushion.

'What are you doing?' Hunt asked.

'I hid the tape recorder under the cushion,' the technician replied.

Hunt groaned. That was the cushion on which Conein had sat. He groaned louder when the technician extracted the remains of a shattered recorder from under the seat – not one word was on the tape.

But Nixon was convinced that Kennedy had ordered the Diem assassination. At a September 16 press conference Nixon said, 'I would remind all concerned that the way we got into Vietnam was through overthrowing Diem, and the complicity in the murder of Diem.'

Hunt was allowed to see all the cable traffic between the U.S. Embassy in Saigon and the State Department between April and November 1963 when the coup occurred. What

Hunt immediately noticed was that among the 240 cables, 'the closer one approached the assassination period, the more frequently were cables missing from chronological sequence.'

According to Hunt, he reported to Colson that none of the cables still existent definitely established Kennedy's complicity. 'You would have to take a sequence of three or four cables . . . and speculate on what was contained in the cables missing from the sequence.'

Colson suggested that maybe Hunt could 'improve' the existing cables. Hunt went to work with a razor blade and a Xerox machine and made a tidy collage of two cables, and at last had his incriminating cable. 'At highest level meeting today, decision reluctantly made that neither you nor Harkins should intervene on behalf of Diem or Nhu in event they seek asylum.'

Colson then took the bogus cable to Bill Lambert of *Life* magazine for a 'major' *Life* expose. However there was one problem. The two conspirators couldn't allow *Life* to photograph the fake cable because a close examination would show it was a forgery. Even more unfortunately, *Life* specialised in *photographs.* No picture, no expose. And another Colson idea went down the drain – to resurface in a gurgle when the 'other things' became news.

C.I.A.'s role in all the Hunt failures, including Conein, is intriguing, to say the least. But I believe the *initiative* for the Watergate break-in came from Nixon through Colson. Nixon lit the match, handed it to Colson, who in turn touched off the fuse.

And the final clue to their role, insofar as I am concerned, is a strange conversation I had with Ken Clawson, Colson's ex-aide.

It was a few weeks after I had resigned. I was still in Washington. I received a call from Clawson: something was bothering him, he said. He had to see me.

Larry Higby had been talking with Clawson when he suddenly blurted out that there was something about Colson and Nixon that no one knew but him. He had to talk to somebody who would advise him what to do. Higby suggested he speak to me. Thirty minutes later Clawson and Higby entered my Georgetown home. Clawson sat down on the edge of a couch and nervously said, 'I've got to tell somebody, Bob.'

'What?'

There was a pause. Then Clawson said, 'Chuck Colson is blackmailing Nixon. He's got Nixon on the floor.'

'What do you mean?'

'Nixon didn't know that Colson was taping all of his telephone calls with Nixon before and after Watergate happened. He's got on tape just what Nixon said all through the whole Watergate mess.'

Incredible. Was Nixon being blackmailed? Memories flooded back. Not only of Nixon's many remarks about his concern for Colson's Watergate involvement, but of the fact, generally unknown, that one of Nixon's first orders during the reorganisation period after the election was that 'Colson's got to go'. It surprised me at the time, because Chuck had been a key figure in the development of the highly successful 'New American Majority' strategy for the election, and Nixon was fully committed in his own mind to pursuing that strategy in his second term. I had figured that I would have to contend with the Colson problem for four more years as a result.

When I expressed my surprise and started to outline the reasons I thought Chuck should stay, Nixon said, 'I've already decided this. I don't want to keep anyone on the staff here who may be hit with some of the Watergate fallout in the future. I just don't know what might come up – and it's much better for Chuck to leave now, when all the changes are being made, and appear to be doing it on his own initiative, than for him to be forced to leave under a cloud at some future time.'

Nixon argued that it was for the best interest of the man – and obviously also for the Administration. And he wanted it handled in such a way as to be the least harmful and most helpful to Colson.

Colson strongly resisted the decision that I had to relay to him. He pushed the President hard to be allowed to

1. Haldeman and Nixon review speech draft aboard the campaign plane, Tricia, in October 1968.

2. Nixon visiting Eisenhower at Walter Reed Hospital just before his death.

3. Nixon and his staff on visit to Charles de Gaulle in 1969.

4. Record-breaking stacks of telegrams of support received after Nixon's 'Silent Majority' speech.

5. At San Clemente Nixon and Haldeman welcome Kissinger upon his return from secret mission to China.

6. Ambassador Kenneth Rush being informed that he will not become Secretary of State. Photo taken at Aspen Cottage at Camp David during reorganization of staff after the 1972 Nixon victory.

7. Richard Helms being informed of his removal as CIA Director and appointment as Ambassador to Iran.

8. President Nixon and the three key advisers of his Administration.

Aboard Air Force One, Kissinger's delight at being named *Time*'s 'Man of the Year', with Nixon.

10. John and Jean Ehrlichman and Jo and Bob Haldeman pose for an Easter photograph beneath the Aspen Cottage balcony on which Nixon decided to fire them a week later.

11. Returning home after his resignation, Haldeman and his wife accidentally meet a most gracious Hubert Humphrey.

12. Two veteran advance men compare notes in front of the D.C. Court House: Republican Haldeman, who is on trial, and Democrat Dick Tuck, who is covering the trial for *Rolling Stone*.

13. The Haldeman family poses at Susan's graduation from UCLA Law School in June 1977. Left to right, Peter, Susan, Hank. Jo, Bob, Ann.

stay on. Nixon was generous in his sweetners to soften Colson's reluctance to leave. Colson was given strong assurances of a long and close relationship with the White House from the outside – as a sort of senior 'Kitchen Cabinet' member – working especially in the area of the New American Majority. As a further sweetener, the President offered him his choice of an overseas trip on 'special assignment'. Chuck chose Moscow for his farewell tour.

Not only that but I also understood that Chuck would be opening his new law practice with a very healthy $100,000 annual retainer from the Teamster's Union, which he had been instrumental in bringing into the Nixon fold in 1972.

I don't know if Colson was ever, or is now, blackmailing Nixon. But I noticed something very strange about the Nixon-Frost television interviews. In all those hours discussing Watergate, Colson's name was mysteriously absent.

Times passes. Colson is now completely absorbed in his Prison Christian Fellowship Programme. Needless to state he's a changed man. I believe the shock of what happened to him at Watergate precipitated his very real conversion from a political bully-boy to a religious evangelist.

But in a perverse way it's sad that the old Colson is gone. There may never be his like again. I see him now in my mind's eye as he appeared at the Doral Hotel swimming pool in Miami in August 1972. The Republican convention was under way. The young White House staffers were correctly togged out for the pool area in conservative bathing trunks, bright white sneakers, crisp white towels. Enter Chuck Colson at four in the afternoon in black street shoes, black socks, old trunks, and a pipe jutting out of his mouth. He'd sit on the edge of a chair, chewing the pipe stem as he tore savagely through a newspaper while the White House staffers watched their all-American image go up in a cloud of Colson smoke.

Book V

THE HIDDEN STORY OF WATERGATE

1

After the break-in, the second great mystery of Watergate began to unfold. How did this small crime escalate into a constitutional crisis and force the resignation of the President?

I believe the solution begins with a White House effort the effect of which on Watergate has never been mentioned: the reorganisation of the government.

By 1972, the Federal bureaucracy had long since mushroomed out of control (in which condition it still remains). President Jimmy Carter made the fact of this rampant bureaucracy one of his winning arguments for election, pledging he would reorganise the government for efficiency.

We tried. In fact, we came closer to succeeding than any administration ever had. And we did it in a ruthless fashion, angering not only Democrats but many of our own people who had served us loyally and honourably. But ruthlessness was the only attitude that would work, and because of it in January 1973 we were well on the way to the point where the Administration could, for the first time in decades, be controlled by a President. And that caused pure fright in Washington – because this President was Richard M. Nixon.

November 5, 1972. The Roosevelt Room of the White House. The senior White House staff was assembled, basking in the glory of Nixon's landslide re-election the night before. Many of them had hangovers. Eyelids drooping, they looked on sleepily as Nixon entered to make his ritual speech of thanks for their efforts.

Instead, they were shocked awake as Nixon, instead of lauding them, stated quietly that they were all required to resign. He then left the room and turned the floor over to me. I stood up, and in chilling tones that actor Robert Vaughn might envy told the numbstruck staff members that each and every one of them must have his resignation on my desk by nightfall. Period.

Then the same scene was replayed with the Cabinet in the Cabinet room.

At least that's the way it seemed to most of those present, judging from their later accounts. Actually it really wasn't quite that brutal in concept, although it may have appeared that way because of my undoubtedly brusque approach.

Nixon was determined to make major and sweeping changes in both structure and staffing, but he had every intention of using the talents of most of those who had served in the first term and wanted to stay on for the second.

Nixon was not only demanding the resignation of Cabinet members, presumably to place stronger men in their place (four of them, in fact, would be re-appointed), he was about to initiate a dramatic, even revolutionary, new structure of government. In this structure there would be four 'super-Cabinet' officers with offices in the White House supervising activities of their own departments as well as those of associated independent agencies in four functional areas.

Economic Affairs
Human Resources
Natural Resources
Community Development

In addition, four traditional cabinet posts would be retained: State, Defense, Justice, and Treasury.

In effect, this would accomplish two goals: streamline all of the dozens of helter-skelter and redundant independent agencies into four departments that were manageable; concentrate them so that all departments of the executive branch of government would be controlled by the White House.

In the middle of his first term Nixon had introduced a

reorganisation bill to accomplish that revolution. It was hastily rejected by a nervous Congress. Talk of power accruing to 'a small handful of White House aides' filled Congressional halls with fear; even more so when Nixon angrily said that he would accomplish the reorganisation by executive order and to hell with Congress – if he won the election.

He won. And he did.

Reorganisation is the secret story of Watergate. That reorganisation in the winter of 1972 – very little known to the American public – eventually spurred into action against Nixon the great power blocs in Washington. All of them saw danger as the hated Nixon moved more and more to control the Executive Branch from the White House, as he was constitutionally mandated to do.

What they feared was real. Nixon genuinely meant to take the reins of government in hand, and if members of the Congress had been privy to a Presidential conversation on September 15, 1972, they would have been even more fearful.

This conversation was Dean's first extended meeting with the President. The transcript of the tape released by the White House deals only with Watergate, but the second portion of the tape, which wasn't released by Nixon, is more important to the real understanding of the Watergate story. It contributes clues to the mystery of how Watergate expanded into a national crisis.

At that time, Ehrlichman and Roy Ash, Director of the Office of Management and Budget, were beginning to shape up the reorganisation plan we would put into effect if Nixon won. Nixon's conversation moved from Watergate to his frustration with the I.R.S. Specifically, he inveighed against the entrenched servants in the I.R.S. who thwarted his every move.

Dean said, 'The problem is this. There are so damn many Democrats down there . . . the Commissioner and Secretary can't figure out how they can get down in there to get files. I don't know. That's what I haven't ever been told the answer to. And we've been round and round on this for at least the two years I've been over here.'

He was referring to the fact, as I have said, that when Republicans screamed about tax audits and pointed fingers at 'deserving' Democrats, Dean couldn't get any action at all against those Democrats. On the other hand, it seemed almost certain that as soon as a notable person in any field, from Billy Graham to John Wayne, announced his backing of Nixon, a tax audit notice would arrive in the next week's mail, courtesy of a loyal Democrat civil servant in the I.R.S.

Even so, I sounded a cautionary note when Nixon and Dean started expounding on what they could do about getting the tax files of certain Democrats. Nixon said, 'There are ways to do it. Goddamnit, sneak in in the middle of the night . . . ' (A perfect example of classic Nixonian rhetorical overkill.) I said, 'We sure shouldn't take the risk of getting us blown out of the water before the election.' (A perfect example of classic Haldeman effort to defuse another potential bomb.)

Nevertheless the subject of the I.R.S., as always, brought Nixon to a boiling point. Now he referred to Secretary of the Treasury, George Shultz: 'He's got to know that the resignations of everybody . . . The point is, I want there to be no holdovers left. The whole Goddamn bunch is to go out. And if he doesn't do it, he's out as Secretary of Treasury. And that's the way it's going to be played. Now, that's the point. See.

'Now they always get around this by saying the White House can't appoint. Well, Goddamnit, the Secretary can appoint those jobs. We're not going to have a Secretary of the Treasury who doesn't do what we say. Absolutely, every Goddamn one, and if George doesn't want them out, that's too damn bad.'

I said that the excuse of waiting to appoint a new I.R.S. commissioner was that we didn't have a man who could fill the position: 'That doesn't make any difference either now. We can leave it empty.' Dean was looking at me, a half-smile on his face. He was enjoying his first taste of proximity to the President, especially as he had caught Nixon in a black mood. I smiled, too. 'Actually we can leave the whole Goddamn government empty and it wouldn't hurt the world one bit.'

Dean took me seriously and said with a straight face, 'That's an exciting concept.'

I laughed and said, 'It sure is.' But I was serious when I said about the reorganisation, 'It'll be so positive that this country will say, 'My God, finally somebody is cleaning house.' Clean enough so they can't zero in on any one of them and say, "You've been political." '

Nixon said, 'The point is, I have an uneasy feeling there's no real plan developed yet. I talked to Ehrlichman about it, but he's so busy with other things. The whole plan has got to be a concerted plan to find out not only who the President appoints, but who every Goddamn Cabinet officer appoints, and every damned agency head appoints up and down the line.'

I told Nixon that we had the plan underway. The plan Ehrlichman and Ash were working on not only streamlined the executive branch at the top, but struck, for the first time, at the lower levels where the government is really run. Nixon expounded on the problem. 'Mitchell was captured by the bureaucracy (at Justice). Mitchell was told, quote, get over there and help me break some of these guys. They're not worth a damn because I've known them for years. Rogers (at State) was totally captured by the American bureaucracy. Mel Laird (at Defense) he didn't change anybody. You know what I mean?'

I said, 'He put some of his people in,' but Nixon shrugged that off, 'Yeah. On the top level. But the people who ran the Pentagon before are still running the Goddamn Pentagon.' And he went on, 'H.E.W., the whole damn bunch. And you see this is the problem. The difficulty is you've got to do it fast because . . . after the first year it's too late. You've got to do it right after the election. You've got one week, and that's the time to get all those resignations in and say, "Look, you're out, you're out, you're finished, you're done, done, finished." Knock them the hell out of there.'

Dean said that 'one of the problems when we came in was that no one knew all of the key sensitive spots in each agency and department. You know, a key administrative appointment can influence the whole operation . . . '

I told him that Bryce Harlow had made a study and had come up with a concept of placing loyal men in these key spots: general counsel, public relations, personnel, legislative liaison, and administrative executive officer. Nixon said, 'That's exactly what we have to do. I know that Malek is busy over at the committee. The point is, we've got to get the names ready now.'

I told Nixon that Fred Malek, White House Personnel Chief, was already doing that, getting the names of people in key spots. He was reviewing them with each member of the staff 'who had had any relations with these departments and can say whether they're strong or weak.'

Nixon leaned back. 'Let's remember the V.A., any Goddamn thing. Clean those bastards out . . .

'Now on that, take that Park Service, they've been screwing us for four years. Rogers Morton won't get rid of that son-of-a-bitch. But he's got to go.'

Nixon's personal obsessions aside, it was apparent that the sprawling Federal bureaucracy had to be streamlined and brought under control.

I told Nixon to be prepared if he did decide to go through with the reorganisation. 'You'll see a rash of stories this fall about the ruthless White House staff, referring to these dirty bastards who are undercutting the whole U.S. Government. But if you're prepared to ride through a few weeks of those, you'll end up with one hell of a government. And the American people would shout right on.'

Nixon agreed. 'I'll suggest that we're going to have a house cleaning. It's time for a new team. Period. I'm going to say we didn't do it when we came in before, but now we have a mandate. And one of the mandates is to do the cleaning up that we didn't do in '68.'

I said, 'And we can be nice about it. It's no reflection on anybody. It's just that the time has come for new leadership.'

And so, on September 15, 1972, less than seven weeks before he was re-elected, Nixon pondered the re-organisation that was to take place. Earlier in the conversation, in the segment of tape released to the press, Nixon complained: 'we've had the power but we've never used it before.' He was referring to his blocked efforts at the I.R.S. and the Justice Department. Now he was ready to go.

It's interesting in the light of future events, that just before the meeting closed, John Dean said, 'I think, just watching a case like this thing I've been on (Watergate), you learn an awful lot about people when you see the crunch come down.'

2

Almost immediately after Nixon's re-election, five men travelled by helicopter to Camp David: Richard Nixon, Ehrlichman, Haldeman, and two aides, Todd Hullen and Larry Higby. For the next two months we would reside at Camp David, trying to take the Executive Branch of the government apart and put it back together in a model that would work. Nixon divided his time between this effort and the final actions and negotiations that would bring the Vietnam War to an end.

It happened that I was also deeply involved in this final Vietnam effort, not because of any foreign affairs expertise (which of course I did not have), but because Henry Kissinger adopted a shrewd procedure in his Paris negotiations of telephoning me from Europe to report on the negotiations and discuss any new proposal to be made to the North Vietnamese. I would then take my notes into

Nixon and obtain the President's thoughts and recommendations, then return to my office and telephone Henry in Paris. By that simple move, Henry could truthfully say to the Vietnamese that the proposal he was offering was his own, and he had not yet talked to the President about it – a negotiating position which gave him needed flexibility.

But from a Watergate standpoint, the Camp David sojourn turned out to be damaging. Those two months were the period Dean would be confronted with renewed money demands by the Watergate burglars, and other problems connected with their upcoming trial. Because Ehrlichman and I were feverishly working at Camp David on the reorganisation, Dean had to strive almost alone.

Was the reorganisation really 'feverish'? Yes, because a government is not simply boxes on a chart. It is the people who fill the boxes. Each one of them had to be found, considered, checked out, and interviewed. Nixon kept whipping us to do it *now* ('after Christmas will be too late'); we worked night and day.

My assistant Larry Higby's recollections give that period almost a Keystone Cops flavour. It was as hectic as Higby recalls, but there was, in addition, much tedious and agonising appraisal of individual candidates, particularly for the big jobs. But I enjoy Higby's account:

> It was a terribly tense time. Haldeman was constantly with the President. I mean for hours. And then he'd get back to his own office and be called right back to the President's office. It was just a yo-yo thing, you know. I was stacking up the calls and doing stuff that was way over my head. I mean, I handled the firing of Dole (Republican National Chairman) through Bryce Harlow, which I had absolutely no business being in. But there was nobody else to take care of it. And so it was a madhouse up there. Bob was just bang, bang, bang, all day.
>
> Constant turmoil, politicians calling to recommend people, other politicians calling to bitch if their candidates weren't acceptable for one reason or another.

> So there was a real frenetic atmosphere, and for some reason it was almost depressing. It started out as a very exciting kind of thing because we were gonna rip the place apart and put it back together again. But Bob had so much pressure on him, that it got to be very depressing, and you almost didn't want to go on with it. It turned from a real upper into a downer. I'm telling you the phone got to be so you just didn't want to talk . . . never wanted to hear a phone ring again.

Higby was amused because near the end, when we thought we had chosen the best men for the right jobs regardless of the traditional ethnic and regional considerations, Nixon was suddenly nervous. He called me in and said, 'Well, hell, we don't have one Catholic.'

(Incidentally, there *was* one limitation hammered over our heads by Nixon: 'No Goddamn *Harvard* men, you understand! Under no condition!' And, of course, the first two men Malek recommended to the grumbling Nixon were from Harvard because, as Fred said, they were the best men for the job.)

At any rate, we had one major post left, Secretary of Transportation. This wouldn't be as important a job as it had been in the past, because the Secretary would now be reporting not to the President but to a super-Cabinet officer. Still, it was a chance to appoint a Catholic and make a bow to ethnic standards. I called Higby (and he takes up the story):

> Poor Fred Malek. He was head of personnel on the White House staff, and he was the one we always went to with problems. He was swamped. Now I called him about the Catholic problem, and he said he'd get on it. An hour or so later the phone rang, and it was Malek, enthused. 'I've got your man,' he told me. 'His name is Claude Brineger, he's president of Union Oil of California, and listen to this: he's not only Catholic, but he's young and from the West

Coast.' [Two great points as far as Nixon would be concerned.] 'On top of that, they say he's a great manager and would be perfect for the job.'

So I trotted the paperwork over to the President, but when he looked at it he was concerned. 'Are you sure he's Catholic? His name doesn't sound Catholic to me.' So I got back to Malek. I said, 'The President doesn't believe that Brineger is a Catholic name.'

Malek not only confirmed it but added another political plus. Brineger was Irish, and that was even better because we didn't have an Irish name on board.

So Claude Brineger was appointed Secretary of Transportation because he was an Irish Catholic, and two weeks after he was in office, he informed us he was a German Presbyterian.

What I didn't find amusing were some of the classic feuds which came to a climax at Camp David in that period. The mightiest was the long-running show: Kissinger v. Rogers.

In a way, of course, the very existence of Kissinger testified to the possible benefit of a reorganisation plan which would place the key officials in the White House. Nixon had brought this concept into play on foreign policy from the beginning of his first term, and it had worked. He was able to achieve control of foreign policy, work hand-in-hand with the man who would carry his policy out. The result had been one success after another.

But it had also created problems, and from the beginning I was in the centre. Both Rogers and Kissinger would bring their complaints to me. Rogers, a very nice, considerate man, could still explode, with some reason, when he learned that secret negotiations were going on without his knowing it. 'How can I testify on the Hill, or communicate with the Soviets, if I don't know everything that's going on?' he would say.

Henry, on his part, viewed the entire State Department monolith as a conspiracy of thousands of men and women 'out to get me. They're jealous, Bob. They keep stabbing me in the back. I can't operate with them nitpicking me to death.' And so forth. State Department officials were, in fact, jealous of Henry's position next to the President, and because they were excluded from many secrets, some did try to discredit Henry whenever they could.

In November 1972, we moved to resolve this long standing feud by replacing Rogers as Secretary of State with a man who could work better with Henry.

Despite the popular press belief, Henry Kissinger did not *want* or expect to be Secretary of State in 1972. Reporters have generally assumed that position was Henry's goal from the moment he came to the White House. And sinister motives, from jealousy to anti-Semitism have been ascribed to Nixon for not awarding Henry the office that was his due.

This is not true. From my many conversations with Henry in those days, I know that he realised that the true foreign affairs power position was his National Security Council post at the White House. The Secretary of State was a figurehead. Worse, it was an administrative job: the bureaucratic chief of thousands of employees. Henry preferred his special role in the White House, which not only gave him the greatest range for his unique talents, but won him the Nobel prize, world respect, and beautiful women.

But there was a burr under his saddle: Bill Rogers, who kept insisting on his 'rights' as Secretary of State. What Henry wanted was a Secretary of State with whom he could work, one who wouldn't challenge and postmortem his every move.

Nixon wrestled with the problem for months. Bill Rogers was his oldest friend in government. Nixon didn't want to hurt Rogers, but he knew Henry was right in this instance. Henry, after all, was representing the President's various positions in foreign affairs, and when Rogers challenged these positions on behalf of the State Department, he was actually resisting the President.

Nixon spoke to me about the conflict one day, and I said, 'Go with Henry. The situation's getting worse every day. I can't keep them off each other's backs.'

I had often had to play mediator between Rogers and Kissinger, calling Rogers to explain the reason why Henry had acted without informing him first – or placating Henry after Rogers had complained to the President about some Kissinger move. John Mitchell also acted as mediator from time-to-time. It was full-time work.

So Nixon called in Henry and we talked it out. It was decided Bill Rogers would be asked to resign at the end of Nixon's first term. Henry agreed strongly with Nixon's choice of a successor, a man he liked and could work with, the Ambassador to Germany, Kenneth Rush. But Henry had spoken to me in a corridor of the White House: 'I won't believe it until I see it, Haldeman. That Rogers will never quit. He'll be with me until I die.'

I told him 'no.' It was set. I would make certain of it.

November 1972. A cold sunny day at Camp David. I was in the lounge at Laurel Lodge trying frantically to get caught up on the backlog of telephone calls that kept piling up while I was in and out of meetings with the President and one Cabinet officer after another as we put the reorganisation into effect.

The steward came in with a cup of coffee and said, 'Secretary Rogers is just arriving from the helipad, Mr Haldeman.'

This was going to be a tough one. We had already established the operating pattern for these sessions. The Cabinet offiçer or agency head arrived at Camp David, and was brought directly to a private meeting with either Ehrlichman or me. Our task was to give the full explanation of the overall reorganisation – and then to drop the bomb on the man we were talking to. In a few cases it was good news, but for most of them the changes were something less than totally welcome since they generally meant a reduction in apparent position.

Rogers would be particularly rough because in his case the decision was that he would have to go. I was not at all sure what his reaction would be. I suspected that he had decided to leave anyway, but that he would adamantly resist being forced out. In any event, I had the enviable task of telling Richard Nixon's closest personal friend in the government that Richard Nixon had decided it was now time for him to leave. I had always liked Bill, so that made it especially hard, even though I was on Kissinger's side in this decision.

I approached my unpleasant assignment frontally – never one for the more delicate arts of diplomacy – and told Bill as soon as we had sat down in the little office off of the lounge what the decision was.

Bill was always straight with me too – and he was today. He didn't show much surprise, but he sure didn't smile either. In rather cold tones, he told me, 'I was rather expecting this decision, and I have given it a great deal of thought. I feel very strongly that it is not in either my interest or the President's for me to resign at this time.'

Here it comes, I thought. Now I'm going to get the long agonised reasoning why he should stay on. I'm in for a tough battle, since the President is determined he must go, and it's my responsibility to convince him of that before he sees the President.

But there was no long agonised reasoning. Rogers was not about to debate the subject with me. He simply told me his view that while he was ready to leave soon, he should not do so now, at the time all the others were leaving. He wanted to stay on for six months or so, and then leave at his own initiative. And if there was going to be any discussion of that view, it was going to be with President Nixon, not with Bob Haldeman.

I realised there was no point in my trying to go any further. So I asked the aide to tell the President we were ready to see him – and Bill and I walked from Laurel over to Aspen, the President's cabin.

The scene with the President was equally straightforward. But Rogers added one important point. He would not leave now because it would look like a victory for Kissinger, and that would be bad for all concerned. As I rather expected, the President was not up to fighting it out with his old friend, and he agreed to Rogers's concept of a commitment to leave by mid-June.

I didn't blame Nixon. But I wasn't happy either because I dreaded the words Nixon would say next: '*You* tell Henry.'

Telling Henry was like placing a flaring match inside a high-octane gasoline tank. The explosion was predictable, but nonetheless searing. 'You promised me, Haldeman. You gave me your *word*! And now he's hanging on just like I said he would. Piece by piece. Bit by bit. He stays on and on and on.' Henry turned away. He lowered his voice. 'There is a price you must pay, I suppose. Mine is Rogers. He will be with me forever – because he has this President wrapped around his little finger . . . '

I told him Bill Rogers would leave in June for certain. How ironic is history on all levels. I ended up in Camp David five months later with Bill Rogers and Richard Nixon talking resignation, all right. Only this time it was Rogers telling Nixon that *I* must resign instead of the other way around.

And, to further compound the irony, this time the President asked Rogers to tell me of the decision that I must resign – just as once he had me tell Rogers of the decision about him. But, unlike me. Rogers refused, and told the President that was a job he would have to handle for himself. I wish I had done that once in a while.

Ironically, it was because Rogers did *not* resign as we wanted him to in November that Henry ended up Secretary of State himself. If Kenneth Rush had come in as Secretary of State in November, he no doubt would have stayed in office throughout Watergate. But Nixon, as Watergate flowered, knew Henry was his most precious asset with the press, the Congress and the public – and when Rogers did finally resign, Nixon gave Henry both jobs, Secretary of State and National Security Adviser in the White House.

And Kenneth Rush became the Secretary of State-who-never-was.

3

The State Department problem temporarily solved, we persevered, and in January 1973, the *U.S. News and World Report* told the world what had been going on at Camp David.

BEHIND NIXON'S REORGANISATION

> They're calling it a 'managerial revolution' – the way the President is shuffling jobs and duties. His goal: Get Government operating the way he wants it.
>
> Behind the continuing shake-up in top administration jobs is this –
>
> Richard Nixon, in his second term as President, is determined to assert more effective control and policy direction over the massive Federal bureaucracy.
>
> The President is doing this, in part, by placing trusted White House Lieutenants – trained for four years in the Nixon way of doing things – in key positions in the operating departments.

That article appeared on January 1, 1973. A few weeks later, after months of *Post* and *Times* news stories about Watergate, the Gallup Poll reported that Nixon's popularity (or approval rating) reached an all-time high.

The Watergate break-in, and the associated revelations of Woodward and Bernstein, had failed to ignite the public. And now Nixon, a President more feared by Democrats and the bureaucracy than any President in this century, was at the peak of his power with control of the government tightly in his hands.

What would happen if Nixon's reorganisation went through, and Nixon remained in office? Washington insiders shuddered. Not only would he tightly control all reins of the government through eight top officers in the White House; he would plant his own 'agents' in key positions in every agency of the government.

It was too much for those who feared Nixon. Then suddenly, like a ripe plum dropping from a tree, Watergate split wide open in late January 1973.

A reprieve. Nixon could be deflected, perhaps even crippled. At the worst he could be thrown on the defensive, unable to pursue his plan to grip the government in a way that had never been done before.

4

There are four major power blocs in Washington: they are, beginning with the most important:

1. The Press
2. The Bureaucracy
3. The Congress
4. The Intelligence Community

Each of them was under threat by the President in January 1973, who was at the height of his popularity with the American people. Each of them reacted with special ferocity because that President was Richard Nixon. And in the months of January, February, and March of 1973, they would mount a war on the White House.

I'm not suggesting there was a conspiracy. The reaction might better be described as organic: an awakening at various times among various people that Nixon was vulnerable because of Watergate.

In some areas, such as the intelligence community, the awakening came early. In others, such as the press – with a few exceptions such as the *Washington Post* and the *New York Times* – it came late.

But when the press did move massively into Watergate, all other power blocs were seen as frail in comparison. And in the end, it was the press, more than the three other power blocs combined, that did the most to bring Nixon down.

He had been their adversary for decades.

It began in 1952 when he was nominated for Vice-President by the Republican Party and emerged from an obscure California legislator to become a nationwide political force.

Decades ago, in the days of F.D.R. and Truman, the ownership of the press was conservative. But in the intervening years, the dominant thrust of the media had become liberal. The nation's two most influential newspapers, and all three television networks, were owned and run by liberals (still are). Add to that the fact that the newsmen who actually write and report the stories have always been self-styled 'working stiffs' with every antipathy towards most Republicans and especially Richard Nixon.

When Nixon was nominated in 1952, the liberal press cringed. Nixon was the man who had put Alger Hiss into jail. Something about that case always bothered them. Ask any twenty newsmen, and half of them will admit they believed Hiss was guilty. Nevertheless, and strangely, they despised the man who proved it.

In 1952 they started looking into the young hopeful of the Republicans, and discovered he had done some rough, if not unethical, campaigning against Jerry Voorhees and Helen Gahagan Douglas. At the time they were finding this out, the *New York Post* broke the story that Nixon had a fund which was donated by California fat cats.

They nearly rid themselves of Nixon right then and there. But Nixon bounced back with the Checkers speech and, insult to injury, served the full eight years under Eisenhower.

Eisenhower soon started using Nixon's talent's for tough campaigning. Nixon became the Agnew of the fifties, on the road constantly, blasting the Democrats from stem-to-stern, and by 1960 the anti-Nixon image was set. Tricky

Dick, the hatchet man. Would you buy a used car from this man? Mort Sahl said: 'Politics aside, is Richard Nixon worth $100,000 a year?'

The war between Nixon and the press reached some sort of a climax in 1962 when Nixon blurted out his anger at the press after losing the California governor's race.

But there, the press made an error. A.B.C. placed Alger Hiss on the air to celebrate Nixon's downfall, and the American people thought that was going too far. Instead of burying Nixon, A.B.C. launched his comeback.

By 1967, after Goldwater's defeat, Nixon was thinking of running again. But the press would view him differently, at least to an extent, and for a while there was, as they said, a 'new Nixon'. He had gained a great deal of inner self-confidence and outer self-assurance, and that was reflected in his dealings with the press. They responded with much kinder treatment than in the old days. But this never fooled Nixon. He knew they were still the enemy and they could not be trusted. This was only a temporary aberration. Things would revert to normal before long. And, of course, the prediction was 'father' to the result.

Throughout the campaign, and in the early months in office, the press was generally quite fair to Nixon.

But the Vietnam War – and Nixon's hawkish moves to end that conflict – brought the press again into solid ranks against him. Nixon, in character, fought back, this time using his own Vice-President, Spiro Agnew.

The concept of Agnew's inflammatory speeches against the Eastern 'elite' centred in New York and Washington, which controlled communications in this country, came right from the Oval Office. The speeches were written mostly by Patrick Buchanan, Nixon's most hard-line speech writer (Bill Safire wrote some, too).

The first speech Agnew was to make attacking the press caused even *my* short hair to stand on end when I saw an advance copy, and I'm not easily shocked. I took the script right into Nixon's office and said, 'We can't go with this. It goes too damn far.'

Nixon said he hadn't read the speech yet. The two of us

went over it, deleting some of the more vivid phrases. To those who heard or read Agnew's now-famous first speech attacking the press and thought it was too strong, all I can say is: you should have seen the first draft. (A year later in a speech in another context, Agnew was to call New York Republican Senator Charles Goodell 'the Christine Jorgensen of the Republican Party'. We took the phrase out, but it was used later anyway.)

Agnew, of course, was right when he said that a small elite controlled U.S. communications. This is a fact, unalterable by Agnew prose, *pro* or *con*. (I said much the same thing in a speech at U.C.L.A. – and was amazed at the furious reaction to my intentionally joking reference to a small secret group that met weekly to decide the 'line' for the coming week.) Their power was – and is – awesome. An important Presidential speech on policy would be televised – one reflecting days and sometimes weeks of discussion among top government officials – and be jeered at as soon as it ended by television news commentators who had consulted no one. Instant Analysis, they called it. The 'analysis' seemed never to be favourable.

Similarly, the regular television news shows presented commentators who would 'analyse' the President's statements at a press conference, as well as the papers he would release on various topics. The celebrated incident with Daniel Schorr, a C.B.S. newscaster began this way. Nixon had announced his policy in regard to parochial schools, and Schorr went on the air to say that he didn't believe there was such policy.

The President was furious. And, to his own detriment, he lapsed into old-time vindictiveness. 'I want an F.B.I. check on that bastard. And no stalling this time.'

I called Higby who said, no problem. Schorr had a White House pass which meant he had been 'cleared' for security by the F.B.I., so there must be a file. He called the F.B.I. and asked for Schorr's file.

Now began a strange development which some of the more conspiratorial-minded of my colleagues feel was a deliberate attempt by the F.B.I. to injure Nixon. Instead of transmitting the routine background file, the F.B.I. began a full field-check on Schorr, interviewing neighbours and employers. Within minutes Schorr found out about it, and the White House was again in the limelight, this time accused of using the F.B.I. to harass a newsman. We cancelled the investigation instantly when we learned about it. But it was too late.

We had to concoct a cover story one shade away from absurdity: the White House was considering Schorr for a Federal job. Not one of our grander moments. But by then I was used to the trauma inspired by the hatred between Nixon and the press.

I can't remember all of the reporters and newspeople he asked me to 'go after' in one way or the other. Mike Wallace said something about the White House Princess: Tricia? 'Call him up and tell him to apologise'. John Osborne, or Hugh Sidey, or you-name-it wrote something Nixon didn't like? 'Bar him from the press pool. Bar him from Air Force One.'

I ignored most of these petty, vindictive orders, but there were some I couldn't ignore – and one was particularly embarrassing to me.

At one of Joe Alsop's Sunday dinners I was seated next to Kay Graham, owner of the *Washington Post*, our prime tormentor. I talked to her at length, trying to show that we were reasonable men at the White House, and therefore her treatment of us at the *Post* should be reasonable. I think I made some headway; at least it was a start. Mrs Graham told me to be sure to call her directly anytime I felt the *Post* was not being fair in its treatment of us.

Bang! Some weeks later Nixon called me into his office. Tricia's upcoming wedding ceremony would be the social event of the year, but now Nixon was boiling. 'That damn *Post* is going to be barred from Tricia's wedding.'

It seemed that in a family conference regarding the wedding plans the night before, the unpleasant subject of press coverage had come up, and somebody raised the horrible spectre that the *Post* would probably assign its most vitriolic anti-Nixon society reporter to cover the affair. This would be a disaster. This same reporter had violated the ground rules at Julie Nixon's wedding in New York, and then had written an article that rankled.

Presidents seem to share one understandable quirk – protective instincts towards their children. Harry Truman, of course, sent a letter to Paul Hume, music critic of the *Post*, announcing his plans for Mr Hume if he wrote one more unflattering review of daughter Margaret's voice.

I guess father had reassured the family that he would take care of the *Post* problem. And that meant buzzing Bob Haldeman first thing in the morning.

I objected that banning the *Post* would create all kinds of repercussions and blow up into a public relations mess that would spoil the wedding. It would ruin the great public image that the wedding would inspire. Nixon said, 'I don't care. I will not have those people ruining the highlight of my daughter's life. The *Post* is barred.'

I went back to my office and tried to figure out how to handle this one. I remembered my earlier conversation with Kay Graham and her offer of consultation anytime there was a problem. Although this was not exactly what she had in mind, I decided it was the best hope for a solution. So I violated my decision not to take advantage of her offer, and placed the call.

'Kay, you suggested I call you if we had any problems with the *Post*, and although I would not normally do that, I have a unique personal problem that I hope you can help me with.' I then explained the Nixon family concern with what might happen if a certain reporter were assigned to the wedding, and asked if anything could be done to avert it. I tried to appeal to her personal side, citing the family's natural desire that the wedding be a happy occasion. I didn't mention my orders from the President that the *Post* was to be banned altogether because I hoped we could work out something that would solve the problem.

Mrs Graham rather coolly replied, 'I'll see what I can do, but as a publisher, I can't interfere with the decision of who covers a story – and we can't allow the White House to dictate our press coverage. But I understand the problem.'

I don't know what she did, but the problem of the reporter was solved. I didn't ban the *Post* from the wedding as Nixon had wanted me to.

Predictably, the press had been the first to respond (in public) to the threat of Nixon's second term. Woodward and Bernstein of the *Post* hammered the Watergate story for months, joined by the *New York Times*, *Time* and *Newsweek* magazines and, occasionally, the television networks.

In private the intelligence agencies had been on the case from the beginning with both 'plants' and outside agents, such as Bennett.

Congress and the bureaucracy, the other power blocs, were slower to move into action. Because of its make-up, Congress can't react quickly to anything. And the bureaucracy is so secure in its jobs that the people don't respond swiftly to a threat either. They know the threat will pass long before they do.

But in January, with information seeping through the arteries of government that 'something was going on at the White House' – the reorganisation – members of these last two power blocs – Congress and the Bureaucracy – reacted to save their lives. And they had a common cause. It's little known that the greatest power centres in Washington are the liaisons between Congressional Committee Staffs and the Federal bureaucratic departments they deal with.

These staffs work together for years, understand each other, operate in unison for common goals not necessarily those of the elected administration The staff of the House Armed Services Committee, for example, maintains liaison with Pentagon officers and civilians on a day-to-day basis. Together they shape bills, budgets, weapons proposals into meaningful legislative action. They are power centres within the larger power blocs.

And now Nixon was going to plant his own White House people right inside all government departments and agencies, who could shatter these long-standing alliances.

Congress, which had stalled on previous motions for Watergate investigating committees, now appointed Senator Sam Ervin to head a projected Committee to investigate campaign abuses. The hearings would be on television, bringing to play another power bloc, the press. Bureaucrats, the third power block, started leaking from every direction, ranging from F.B.I. documents to Nixon's tax returns. By March 21, 1973 the White House was under siege by the press, the intelligence community, the Congress, and the bureaucracy – all scenting blood.

Nixon dug in. He still had the protection of the most powerful office in Washington: the Presidency. He could fight back with executive privilege and use his massive command of public attention to go over the heads of the power blocs to the people. I believe that even under a full-scale attack by the power blocs, Nixon would have survived the onslaught. But we made every mistake possible, some before Watergate even happened.

Yet, even with the mistakes, it took a series of almost incredible 'breaks', happening at precisely the right times, to escalate a war with the power blocs into a Presidential catastrophe even his enemies could not envision.

Book VI

THE REAL STORY OF THE TAPES

1

The story of Nixon's own Watergate mistakes begins, of course, with the tapes. That story has been fudged by Nixon in a variety of ways, climaxing with the assertion on television in 1977 that he had ordered me to destroy all of the tapes except the 'national security' matter.

The White House. July 1973, shortly before I was to testify before the Ervin Committee. Fred Buzhardt, one of the President's legal counsels, smiled as he handed me a letter. 'I think you'll find this interesting.'

It was from a former vice-president of R.C.A., and went something like this:

> I was very interested to read in the news about the Nixon taping system because it reminded me of an unusual experience I had many years ago as a senior R.C.A. engineer. I was called to the White House by President Roosevelt to install a recording facility in the Oval Office, which I believe to have been the original system installed there.
>
> Of course at that time it was wire recorders we used. I installed the wire recorders in the basement, and had to drill a hole through the incredibly thick cement floor of the Oval Office to run the wire up to the desk. The microphone was located in the lamp on the President's desk, and there was a switch on the lamp by which the President could turn the recording system on and off.
>
> You can verify this story, I am sure, by examining the cement floor of the Oval Office. The hole should still be there, under the rug. There was some machin-

> ery also located in the drawer of the desk. I was never called upon to remove this system, so I always wondered how long it stayed there. The only clue I had was that I was always amused to see in pictures of President Truman that the same lamp was on the desk.

I never learned whether anyone rolled back the rug to check the R.C.A. engineer's story, but my own belief is that the telltale hole drilled in the Oval Office cement floor is still there, four decades later, mute evidence of the urge of more than one President to protect himself from the convenient lapses of memory of his associates.

For that was the most important reason the Nixon taping system was installed, before Watergate partisan arguments from both sides blurred the truth. It was not to provide tapes for historians to peruse, but for the President's use alone – for reference when visitors ranging from foreign statesmen to his own Cabinet officers and advisers made statements that conflicted with their private talks with the President. And that was Richard Nixon's primary intent when he installed the tapes in 1971, with a secondary benefit of providing him with valuable reference material for his own use – but never for the use of historians.

Of course, his predecessor, Lyndon B. Johnson, didn't install taping facilities solely for historical purposes either. Among the White House assets we inherited from Johnson's administration were many secretaries, some of whom had transcribed L.B.J.'s tapes. One of them told this fascinating incident which demonstrates one of the real reasons Presidents install tapes.

L.B.J. was, as usual, furious at Bobby Kennedy. Apparently Bobby had said something to reporters quite at variance with what he had told the President in private. L.B.J. decided to trap Bobby, using his Oval Office taping system.

He called Bobby into the office, pressed the switch under his desk that activated the tape machine and proceeded to record the conversation. To his delight the trap worked better than he expected. Bobby made one self-incriminating statement after another.

The President was enthused. At last he had Bobby where he wanted him. The door of the Oval Office had hardly closed when L.B.J. ordered the tape transcribed. But when the transcriber donned her headset she heard nothing but static. The news of the malfunctioning equipment made L.B.J. so angry, according to my witness, that he slammed his fist on the desk. It was only later that L.B.J. discovered that Bobby Kennedy had entered the meeting with a *scrambler* in his pocket. He carried a tiny radio transmitter that completely jammed the microphones while he smiled his famous smile and made his 'incriminating' statements to the eager L.B.J.

I like that story because I had a certain respect for Bobby. Although we had been on opposite sides of several political campaigns, as an advance man and as a campaign manager, I admired his intelligence and his rare ability to react quickly to problems. And this example of his outwitting the heavyhanded L.B.J. makes me smile. But I'm not surprised, either, that Bobby won this electronic shoot-out. After all, he'd had three more years of practice around the White House and the Justice Department.

Of course both John F. Kennedy and L.B.J. taped White House conversations. In Kennedy's case it was not known even by his closest advisers. Ted Sorenson and McGeorge Bundy. Kennedy, like Nixon, would no doubt have claimed that the taping was done for purely historical reasons, L.B.J.'s trustees seem to use the same rationale to explain the 'selected' tapes now in L.B.J.'s library. But real history? I'm afraid Presidential scholars will have slim pickings or – in the words of General Haig once employed in discussing Watergate evidence, 'thin gruel'. Undoubtedly the tapes the scholars will be allowed to analyse, from both Kennedy's and Johnson's administrations, will contain exclusively statesmanlike utterances made in conferences and telephone calls. No messy Watergate-type political discussions, no expletives, deleted or undeleted, and certainly no mention of wiretapping or other skulduggery!

But in 1968 Nixon was shocked to hear about L.B.J.'s taping equipment. And one of his first decisions was to order all of L.B.J.'s electronic harware in closets and offices ripped out.

I passed his instructions to my assistant, Larry Higby, and the Secret Service removed all of Johnson's taping equipment. And so the Nixon Oval Office conversations were to remain unrecorded until February 1971. And if they had continued unrecorded until November 1976, it's generally conceded that Richard Nixon would have served out his term until the end; come Dean, mean or clean. So why did he decide to go back to L.B.J.'s practice of taping his conversations?

As in some other actions relating to the Watergate crisis, there are two versions of the facts, Nixon's and mine. Let's examine Nixon's version first. Don Kendall, Chairman of the Board of Pepsico, and personal friend of Nixon's, was a trustee of the Nixon Foundation, and served on a committee to set up the Nixon Library for the post-Presidency period. In the process of that committee's work, they had spoken to ex-President Johnson, who told them that Nixon had been foolish to remove the taping capability that had been in the White House. The tapes would be invaluable as an aid to Nixon in writing his memoirs. Kendall then came to me, so Nixon's story goes, and told me what Johnson had said. I passed on Johnson's recommendation, and we installed the system.

Now Nixon has gone over this with me several times, and the story certainly sounds perfectly plausible. The only problem with it is that it isn't true and I have told Nixon that repeatedly to his great discomfort. I remember all too well whose actions resulted in the reinstallation of an Oval Office taping system and it wasn't Don Kendall.

Don Kendall did not report L.B.J.'s views on the tapes to me, and I did not relay that report to Nixon. Perhaps someone else did – and perhaps that *was* a factor in the decision to install a taping system. There was definitely a desire on Nixon's part to have the tapes for his own use in whatever historical work he might do after leaving office, and for reference while he was in office.

But the main driving force that led Nixon to approve the use of a taping system was his desire for an accurate record of everything that was said in meetings with foreign guests, government officials and his own staff. He recognised the problem of either intentional or unintentional distortion or misunderstanding and became more and more concerned about the absence of such a record.

It was a final attempt by a frustrated Nixon to pin down the opinion of Henry Kissinger and other advisers who often seemed to come up with their own versions of both their own and the President's position on controversial military and foreign policy decisions.

Potential distortions of fact about the Oval Office conferences caused Nixon to start worrying about the need for an accurate record of everything said in important meetings. But without taping facilities, how was it to be done?

This was a problem I had recognised back in the transition period. And I sought advice then on how to deal with it, beginning with General Andrew Goodpaster, President Eisenhower's former staff aide who was then N.A.T.O. commander.

He told me President Eisenhower had utilised people like himself and the President's son, John, to sit in the meetings and take notes. But Nixon rejected that idea. He thought that a note-taker would inhibit his visitors. And I agreed that it makes people nervous when they keep looking over at someone scribbling down everything they say. I'm often pictured as 'the man with the yellow pad', busily recording everything said. In fact I did make notes in my own meetings with the President, but usually not in meetings with other advisers or Cabinet members. And, more important, in a Watergate context, is the fact that in either case I only took 'action notes' on Presidential orders I would execute. I didn't record wide-ranging discussions or comments on topics. As we have seen, this misconception about my 'comprehensive' note-taking is one key to the confusion about the missing 18½ minutes in the June 20, 1972, tape.

One of the prime focal points of Nixon's concern was the unpredictable Henry Kissinger. Nixon realised rather early in their relationship that he badly needed a complete account of all that they discussed in their many long and wide-ranging sessions. He knew that Henry was keeping a log of these talks, a luxury in which the President didn't have time to indulge. And he knew that Henry's view on a particular subject was sometimes subject to change without notice. He was frequently given to second thoughts on vital matters that the President assumed had been settled.

But, unless expressly asked, I never took notes in meetings with Kissinger or anyone else and, of course, in many of those meetings I was not present, so how was a record to be maintained? L.B.J.'s taping system began to look better and better. It not only kept a complete and accurate record, but was invisible so that visitors or advisers wouldn't be inhibited in their conversations with the President. Consequently, in a meeting between Nixon and me, he decided to install a taping system.

It was done in utmost secrecy. Among the President's top advisers, only I knew of its existence. And I soon learned why he insisted on such absolute secrecy. Nixon never intended anyone to hear the tapes except himself. They were never even to be transcribed.

I remember the day clearly when his attitude towards the tapes was made evident to me. Early in 1972, before Watergate, Alex Butterfield, the White House assistant who maintained custody of the tapes, entered my office. 'We're piling up a horrendous amount of tape,' he said. 'Obviously, nobody is going to sit and listen to all of it. It would take years. So I assume you're going to want it typed up.'

He asked me if he should get a crew started transcribing the tapes. 'Otherwise, it's going to just build up to an insurmountable task.' I raised the question with the President that day. 'Do you want to start making transcripts of the tapes?'

He startled me by saying vehemently, 'Absolutely not.' He didn't want transcripts made at any time. Nobody was going to listen to those tapes, *ever*, except himself. Then he added, 'I'll never even have Rose Woods listen to them. Rose doesn't know I'm making the tapes. I say things in this office that I don't want even Rose to hear.'

At that point Nixon looked up at me sharply as if becoming aware of what he was saying. 'Uh . . . possibly *you* can hear them, too, but no one else.'

Thus the tapes were kept secret even from Rose Mary Woods, until Watergate. And then Rose and I were the first persons to whom Nixon turned regarding the tapes. He asked me to listen and take notes on the March 21, 1973 'troublesome' conference with John Dean – and I ended up with a perjury charge. Rose did little better – ridiculed in the press as she desperately reached for a foot pedal while stretching back for a telephone to demonstrate how 18½ minutes of the June 20 tape had been 'accidentally' erased.

Rose would never have had to go through that ordeal if the tapes had not survived as evidence. In the whole story of the White House recording system the one question asked over and over again by both friends and foes of Nixon is 'Why didn't he destroy the tapes?'

In a telephone call long after I left the White House, and during the period when Nixon was going through the agony of listening to many of the White House tapes prior to releasing the transcripts or turning the tapes over to the prosecutors, Nixon laughed wistfully and said, 'You know, it's funny, I was just listening to one of the early April tapes of a meeting between you and me. I had completely forgotten this, but in that meeting I said to you, "Bob, maybe we should get rid of all those tapes and just save the national security stuff." And you said no, you thought we should keep them. Oh, well.'

As far as I know, that April conversation was the closest he ever came to any idea of destroying the tapes. I think the subject was never raised again. It certainly was not an order in any sense, and based on Nixon's report of the conversation to me, there is no way he could possibly consider that he had ever given such an order. In any event, very soon after that conversation about destroying the tapes time ran out swiftly on Nixon. On April 15, only a few days later, Henry Petersen, the assistant Attorney General in charge of the Criminal Division at the Justice Department, came into the Oval Office in tennis shoes and jeans (he'd been working on his boat) to inform the President that John Dean was co-operating fully with the prosecutors. Already Dean had made the charges against Ehrlichman, Mitchell and me in his escalating efforts to gain immunity and the President knew full well who would be next.

Nixon quickly realised that the still secret tapes, which he had been about to destroy in early April, could be the weapon he needed against Dean on the Watergate charges. The only occasions in which Dean could say he spoke to the President about Watergate were Oval or E.O.B. Office conferences – and those conversations were on tape. While Dean would have to rely on his own memory the President might be able to use the tapes to trip him up.

A telephone call from Nixon to me on June 4, 1973, shows Nixon's strategy at work. This was before the tapes were revealed. Both Dean and I had yet to testify before the Ervin Committee.

TELEPHONE OPERATOR: Yes, please.

PRESIDENT: Mr Haldeman, please.

OPERATOR: Thank you. Mr Haldeman?

PRESIDENT: Hello. Have you got a minute?

HALDEMAN: Sure.

PRESIDENT: I thought you should know that starting at, uh, 9.30 this morning, I have been working until just now. I listened to every tape.

HALDEMAN: Good Lord!

PRESIDENT: You know, the thing that you did [I had

listened to the March 21 tape for the President and made notes] and, boy, I know the agony you went through. I put the earphones on, you see.

HALDEMAN: Did you? That's the way to do it.

PRESIDENT: And I listened to every damn thing, and Bob, this son of a bitch [Dean] is bluffing.

HALDEMAN: Well, sure.

PRESIDENT: Also, we sent Buzhardt over – and this is just for your private information –

HALDEMAN: Yeah.

PRESIDENT: He went through the files and not a Goddamn memo in the files! [The President was excited because Dean had made no written memos on the Oval Office meetings, which meant Dean had no documentary evidence of any kind to back up his story.]

HALDEMAN: Really?

PRESIDENT: None. Period. He didn't make any.

(Later)

PRESIDENT: But I thought you'd be interested, pleased to know that I, I went through this agony for eight hours, nine hours today. I did nothing else. Just damn near broke me down. But, you know how tough it is to listen to that stuff.

The President was especially worried about two telephone calls he had made to John Dean from the Key Biscayne after his March 21 conversation with Dean. His telephone call to me continued:

PRESIDENT: And the telephone calls from Key Biscayne [to Dean] I don't have because they don't have those recorded. I called him twice from Key Biscayne and, uh . . .

HALDEMAN: Yeah, but that . . .

PRESIDENT: But I think it was about McCord, but I don't know . . . It could have been about Bittman [William Bittman was Howard Hunt's lawyer who had been relaying demands for money and clemency.] You know, I could have mentioned that to him.

HALDEMAN: That's possible, yeah.

PRESIDENT: And, uh, but suppose I did. You know, suppose I said, "Well, listen, I understand Bittman's taken care of" or something. That's a question of evidence, right?

HALDEMAN: Yeah, but that isn't likely . . .

PRESIDENT: I might have, no, no, I might have mentioned that because I was concerned about it, you know. About whether, uh, Bittman had, uh . . .

HALDEMAN: Yeah.

PRESIDENT: . . . was gonna blow – not because of Watergate, because he was going to blow on, uh . . .

HALDEMAN: . . . on the other project.

PRESIDENT: Yes, that's right.

Now four years later, I find this concern of the President's about Bittman interesting. In the telephone call I interrupted the President to say 'on the other project' – referring to the Ellsberg break-in. But even then I realised the President was most likely thinking plural of those other projects that had worried him in April when he first thought of destroying the tapes. For Hunt could have told his lawyer much.

Obviously still nervous about his remark that Bittman was 'taken care of' Nixon returned to the subject later in the conversation. He asked me, when I had listened to the March 21 tape, 'did Dean mention all this Bittman stuff.'

HALDEMAN: No. Not at all.

PRESIDENT: Shows ya, maybe . . . the Bittman thing is something that concerns us more than him.

(But now the President returned to his main theme):

PRESIDENT: But the point is that this whole jazz to the effect that – from January throughout thirty-five meetings and telephone calls in which we discussed the cover-up, Bob – [Dean's charges are] totally false . . . And I wasn't sure, you know, until I heard it.

HALDEMAN: All right, what're you gonna do with that now, other than know it.

PRESIDENT: I can't do a thing except . . . reassure our own people, and to know that, uh, we know what the hell the facts are.

HALDEMAN: Yeah.

PRESIDENT: And we're going to let him go out on his string a little further now. You know what I mean.

'At that point in time', June 4, 1973, Dean had been talking to the prosecutors for seven weeks; now after listening to the tapes the President believed his decision to save them had been the right decision. The tapes of the Oval Office meetings Dean had attended would prove the President was clear. Or would they? That March 21st conversation in which Nixon had been so strident in pursuing clemency and cash for the Watergate defendants still bothered him. Couldn't Haldeman get him over that hurdle in some way? One minute after he hung up, the President was on the telephone to me again in that regard.

PRESIDENT: Bob?

OPERATOR: Just a moment. Here you are.

PRESIDENT: Sorry to bother you again . . .

HALDEMAN: Okay.

PRESIDENT: . . . but the one thing which, of course, is a sticky point, is with regard to the 21st and if you'd give some thought with regard to how you could pre-empt that sometime, uh, I think it would be very good.

HALDEMAN: Um hmm.

PRESIDENT: I don't know how the hell you can, but, uh . . .

HALDEMAN: I think we can somehow, and I think . . .

PRESIDENT: Somehow just put it out, you know?

May 4, 1977. The ex-President, perspiring, as David

Frost presses him to say one word. The word Frost wanted was 'guilty'. Instead he received an emotional Nixon performance whose impact on the American public was that Nixon's only real guilt in Watergate was his failure to fire those two arch villains, Haldeman and Ehrlichman, who ran the cover-up, earlier than he did. He just couldn't be a butcher, Nixon said.

In the light of Nixon's statements on the Frost TV interview, let's examine the transcript of the telephone call above. He is telling me to 'pre-empt' the March 21 conversation. 'Somehow just put it out, you know?'

In other words 'put out' a version of the troublesome conversation that would make the President look innocent.

The President well knew I was going to testify before the Ervin Committee soon. Out of my testimony concerning the March 21 tape to which I had listened arose a perjury charge. I testified that the President said we could raise the money for the defendants but it would be wrong (which I firmly believed he *had* said). My associate and friend, Larry Higby, considers this testimony one of my gravest errors. He recalls that when he finally read the statement of that conversation he called me and said, 'Bob, I've stuck with you through thick and thin, but this was an outright lie.'

What brought on this 'outright lie'? My notes made when I heard the tape had been impounded, and I was not allowed to listen to the tape again to refresh my memory before testifying. While it's true that I purposely construed that conversation in an attempt to 'pre-empt' Dean's version, which I knew was distorted, I believed I was truthfully reporting what had been said. My recollection was faulty and the court later decided my response to Nixon's prodding me to 'pre-empt' Dean was perjury, despite my great concern to avoid this possibility.

Like members of Napoleon or Kerensky's government, or any of the hundreds that have fallen in history through their own mistakes, the key members of the old Nixon Administration spent as much time looking for the 'fatal flaw' as the Impeachment Committee did in search of 'the smoking pistol'. Through an interesting chain of logic, Nixon credits me with setting in motion the events that led to the discovery of the taping system.

Nixon claims I said to him before his meeting with John Dean on April 16, 1973, began: 'Make sure the tape machine is working.'

Did I make that remark? It very well could be. The day before, April 15, I learned that Petersen had called for my resignation. Dean was the man whose 'co-operation' inspired that suggestion by Petersen; I certainly wouldn't have minded any use of the tape machine to sabotage Dean in any way.

It's hard for me to believe I could have made such a remark because I knew full well that the system was automatic – and there was absolutely nothing that either the President or I could have done to make it work or stop it.

But still, I wonder. What I really believe is that the President made one of his greatest mistakes during the meeting with Dean on April 15 and hates to admit he did it all by himself. According to Dean, it was in that conversation that Nixon walked behind his chair and lowered his voice in such a suspicious way while talking about clemency that it made Dean think the conversation was being taped. Then, on April 16, Dean says Nixon asked him a series of 'leading questions which made me think this conversation was being taped.' And that suspicion led to the key question by a Senate investigator to Alex Butterfield: 'Do you know of any basis for the implication in Dean's testimony that conversations in the Oval Office are recorded?'

No doubt the President would like to think that if I hadn't reminded him of the tape machine, he wouldn't have lowered his voice, Dean wouldn't have become suspicious – and the question about the tapes might never have been asked. It's a fascinating 'if' I admit – an 'if' on which the entire unlocking of the tapes hinged. But, true or false, it illustrates Nixon's extreme sensitivity to those tapes. They destroyed him in office, and they plague him today. For I know that even today he returns in his thoughts to the strange circumstances surrounding the manner in which their existence was revealed.

I agree that nothing could be stranger than the background and subsequent actions of the man who exposed the tapes to the Ervin Committee: Alex Butterfield.

I am told that Rose Mary Woods believes Butterfield was a 'plant'. And I have to agree she may have a point. I hired him and I know why I hired him. I've been puzzled for years over his version of the circumstances.

> It was about in the middle of my last assignment, that of the senior U.S. military officer in Australia, that I received a telephone call from Bob Haldeman who had been a friend of U.C.L.A. back in 1946 and 1947. I had had no contact with Mr Haldeman whatever, although I believe that our wives had corresponded at least occasionally during Christmas time. Our wives had been very close friends at U.C.L.A.
>
> And so, on January 12, 1969, I heard from Mr Haldeman who was calling from the Pierre Hotel in New York. I knew from the Australian papers that he was, in effect, the head recruiter for the President elect, and destined to be the Chief-of-Staff once the President elect came to office. I was surprised to receive the phone call. We chatted for a moment. I told him that he would certainly have a wonderful tour in Washington, that I had just lived there, and it was certainly the hub of activity. And he said, well, that is why I am calling; how would you like to be a part of all of this; and proceeded to tell me a proposition which was to the effect that I would serve with him in a sort of personal assistant to the President capacity with the title of Deputy Assistant to the President. That if I wanted to accept I would have to leave the military altogether, retire, which I was eligible to do at that time, and come on to the staff as a civilian.

Was the White House filled with plants from other

agencies, most particularly the C.I.A.? The overwhelming evidence is that it was. But was Butterfield one of them? It's hard for me to believe it – but the 'facts' in the story he constantly gives the press disconcert me. Although I still consider him a personal friend.

In the first place I definitely didn't telephone him after receiving his file; I had virtually forgotten his existence. Then a letter from Australia arrived at our New York headquarters where we were working on staffing the new administration. It was from an old college acquaintance, Alex Butterfield. I had not seen nor heard of him in twenty years.

Alex was writing to tell me of his great interest in the possibility of serving the new administration in some meaningful way; and he outlined his extensive experience during the years since college. Remembering him as a nice guy, and impressed with his record, I ran some additional checks and found he was highly recommended. In his letter, he had urged that I let him fly to New York to meet with me personally. I called him in Australia (we now had the use of the White House telephone system) and told him to come on. At that stage I was still impressed with the thought of someone hopping on an aeroplane and flying himself around the world for a job interview.

We had a good talk, and I felt he would be an excellent choice for the job of my deputy. I suggested that to him. He was interested. But, oddly, he insisted that he would have to resign from the Air Force to take the job. I assured him this was not the case, and urged that he stay in the service and just let us have him assigned to the White House – a procedure with more than ample precedent. I didn't want to see him cast aside a military career he had built up over the years, and I had learned from the Pentagon that he had a great future. But he insisted, so I agreed.

It didn't make sense to me then. I told him so. And it still doesn't. Why did he do it? Why does he distort the facts now, unless he has something to hide?

Whatever Butterfield's motivations, his answer to a Senate staffer's questions about a taping system triggered

Nixon's downfall. And that collapse was to be presided over in a more straightforward fashion by General Alexander M. Haig, Jr. Haig made his presence felt forcefully right from the beginning in the indisputably greatest riddle of them all – a Nixon decision which has puzzled and fascinated everyone from John Connally in 1973 to Special Prosecutor Leon Jaworski in 1977. While the tapes were secret, they might have been saved, but why didn't Nixon, who had so much to fear, destroy the tapes after their existence had been made public?

One reason is that, by a stroke of bad fortune, Nixon was ill in the hospital with pneumonia when the news of Butterfield's revelation arrived at the White House. Some reporters have suggested that Haig took surprisingly drastic and precipitous action which prevented Nixon from destroying the tapes in secret. It is true that Haig immediately ordered the taping halted and the tapes sealed under Secret Service guard. But from my many conversations with Nixon, including the one in April when he toyed with the idea of destroying some of them and then rejected it, his real reason for not destroying the tapes at that time was that he just never dreamed it was possible that the tapes would ever be heard by anyone other than himself. And, meanwhile, he could use them in his Watergate battle.

I remember John Connally, temporarily out of favour at the White House (sabotaged by Haig and associates, he claimed), telephoning me in California during those critical days. 'Please, Bob, use your influence to convince the President to burn the tapes. Tell him to do it right. Have Ziegler assemble the White House press corps in the Rose Garden, pile up all the tapes, set a match to them, and let them film the bonfire. Say they must be destroyed now that their existence has been made public.'

I heard later that Connally got his message through to Nixon without my help, but to no avail. And then after the tapes were subpoenaed by the Special Prosecutor, Archibald Cox, the new legal team in the White House convinced Nixon that their destruction would be a clear obstruction of justice which would lead to his impeachment.

Nixon's lawyers should have known better. I'm surprised they didn't because now, in an absolute classic irony of history, Leon Jaworski, who replaced Cox as Special Prosecutor, states:

> When Butterfield revealed the tapes' existence, why did not Nixon immediately destroy them? If he had done so, saying conversations dealt with national security and matters highly embarrassing to members of his Cabinet, to individuals in Congress and others, a majority of Americans would have accepted his word. Despite all the criticism such a desperate act would create, I believe he would have survived and remained in office.

If Jaworski is right, and I feel now that he is, Nixon made a mistake – based on surprisingly wrong advice – beside which all other errors pale.

Nixon fought an epic battle to prevent disclosure of the tapes. And when finally he was forced to turn over some of them, there was further embarrassment. Unexplained gaps and erasures, including the famous 18½-minute conversation of June 20th.

The courts struggled to discover who erased that tape, hauling Rose Mary Woods, who had transcribed it, to the witness stand twice (the second time accompanied by a lawyer).

On November 5, 1972, Rose had been asked whether there was a possibility that she had accidentally erased any portion of the tapes while transcribing them. She was indignant. 'I have a head, don't I? I know what an erase button is.'

Later, of course, she was far more humble, but complicated everything by saying she had only erased about five minutes of the gap. This left 13½ minutes to be accounted for, even if she was right. And it gave General Haig the opportunity to express one of the great quotes of Watergate: he told the court he believed the tape had been erased by 'some sinister force'.

Who was that sinister force?

My own perception had always been that Nixon simply began to erase all of the Watergate material from the tapes when he started to worry that they may be exposed.

But Nixon was the least dextrous man I have ever known: clumsy would be too elegant a word to describe his mechanical aptitude. Reportedly, Pat Nixon once said that when they were courting, 'Dick almost killed himself trying to learn to roller skate.'

I knew from personal experience that Nixon was especially inept at operating tape recorders. In the latter part of the first term, the President decided he should make a practice of dictating his thoughts and reactions as often as he could during the evenings and on weekends. So he instructed me to obtain several tape recorders of the cassette type to be placed at convenient locations for him to use at Camp David, San Clemente and Key Biscayne.

This turned into a major project because Nixon just couldn't get the buttons straight. Both the Signal Corps and I tried to find the simplest operating tape recorder, and even then we had to specially mark the various buttons so that Nixon could handle the simple recording process without mixing things up.

So I believed that Nixon had started *trying* to erase the tapes himself, but realised – at the rate he was going – it would take him ten years. (The investigators counted five different starts in the 18½ minutes alone.)

But now I'm confused, because of the way Nixon referred to that 18½-minute gap (in a telephone call after I resigned): 'Rose's eighteen minutes.'

It could be he's shifting the blame for a Watergate mistake again, this time to Rose, but that's how he characterised the gap. After all, he could have said, 'A sinister force's eighteen minutes.'

So the tapes survived, and now the Supreme Court has ruled that they will eventually be released. Nixon, of course, is desperate to prevent their exposure; he's fought legal battles against their release all the way.

Incidentally, I think all the hue and cry of indignation over the fact that Nixon installed such a taping system is absurd. The question is not really whether he had tapes made, but what he planned to do with them. If the purpose had been to use them *publicly* at some future date, then he was certainly abusing his relationship with – and the confidence of – all of us who were recorded on them. But this was not his purpose. As long as only he used the tapes in private, it's hard to make any rational case against their being recorded. Obviously he had already heard everything that was on them. He wasn't gaining any new information by listening to them; he was just being reminded of what he had already said and heard.

The only thing really wrong with the tapes was the possibility of losing control of them. If any outside individual or institution were to gain possession of them (as the courts ultimately did, of some, and may yet of the rest) then their existence would create enormous problems for everyone whose voice was recorded – practical, moral, legal, and personal. Much that was expressed in the Oval Office, and recorded by the tapes, was said in supreme confidence between the two parties. And as long as Nixon controlled the tapes, it remained so.

To those who found reading the tape transcripts a shocking and disturbing experience, I urge consideration of a basic point.

Those transcripts are the first thing you have ever read that was not originally prepared for the purpose of your reading it. Everything else you have read: books, newspapers, letters, notes, even scripts of plays was written with the idea that it would be read.

But those transcripts were produced by court order from tape recordings of live conversations that were not conducted with the intent – or knowledge – that they would ever be written up and read by anyone.

Imagine your own feeling if you were to open your Monday morning paper and find that someone had taped all the conversations in your home over the weekend – then selected the very worst segments and printed them in the paper. That's just about what happened to us.

Just as you would have changed your weekend conversation had you known it was going to appear in the Monday paper for all your neighbours to read, so we would have changed our very frank, uninhibited, often highly embarrassing, and unadmirable, conversations with the President.

We were floundering in the midst of a bewildering crisis. We obviously didn't know what to make of it or how to handle it. And our efforts, as recorded, were frequently far less than admirable. But we were exploring and discussing alternatives. We were talking in the way that close associates do – a sort of shorthand that left out things we knew needn't be said. We were freely expressing our feelings of confusion, dismay and sometimes despair. *Not* for history, nor for the public record, but to try to figure things out, and sometimes just to let off steam.

And remember that, by court order, you have been allowed to see only a tiny portion of the total quantity of Nixon tapes. Only the small fraction that dealt directly with possible criminal actions was allowed to be released – a highly distorted sampling of Presidential conversations.

I apparently have had the wrong judgement on every facet of the tapes episode from start to finish. Therefore, I express my current view.

I strongly feel that Nixon should not destroy the tapes now, even if he some day gets custody of them, and has the opportunity to do so. I told him this in a telephone call after the custody deal had been made with President Ford, and before Congress reneged on it.

My reasoning is that the world has now heard a great deal of material from the Nixon tapes, and from that, has formed a strong impression of Nixon, his associates, and their way of working together. But what is not realised, is that the sampling process has been grossly distorted. By law, and order of the Supreme Court, the only tapes that have been made available are those that bear directly on possible criminal matters. That has produced about sixty hours of tapes. There are thousands of hours unheard.

While undoubtedly there is some very undesirable material in those remaining thousands of hours, I know that there is also some very great material. And I feel sure the 'good' heavily outweighs the 'bad'. Thus Nixon has everything to gain and little more to lose from release of additional tapes – even on a random basis. He's already paid the price, he might as well get the benefits.

This time my view is apparently not shared by the man who was one reason for the original decision to start the taping process. Henry Kissinger is determined to stop the tapes from reaching the public.

Nixon told me the story in San Clemente on November 13, 1976. He was sitting beneath a Vietnamese plaque on the same brown velvet easy-chair that used to be in the Lincoln Sitting Room, books and papers all around, a yellow pad on his lap. I had been there from 2.30 to 5.30, with no interruption except when I asked for a cup of coffee late in the session. The President went out to the little pantry adjoining his office and poured each of us a cup himself. Manolo, his valet, must have been off that day. (Manolo is well-known – and damned – by all listeners to the tapes as the creator of the thunderous, ear-splitting crashes which usually occurred as the sound was turned up in order to hear a low pitched voice. The thunder was caused by Manolo delicately placing a cup of coffee on Nixon's desk in which the microphones were installed.)

Nixon made the point that Kissinger was really the one who had the most to lose from the tapes becoming public. Henry apparently felt that the tapes would expose a lot of things he had said that would be very disadvantageous to him publicly.

Nixon said that in making the deal for custody of his Presidential papers, which was originally announced after his pardon but then shot down by Congress, that it was Henry who called him and insisted on Nixon's right to destroy the tapes. That was, of course, the thing that destroyed the deal. Apparently, when the agreement was being put together Henry was adamant that this had to be done.

Oddly, if Nixon had not demanded the right to destroy the tapes when negotiating for their return, he might well have obtained possession of them as part of the body of Presidential papers ordinarily returned to a President leaving office. But Henry called Nixon from Washington to insist that Nixon's right to destroy the tapes be part of the agreement. Nixon went along with Kissinger's demand – and this proposed 'right to destroy' the tapes was what frightened Congress into hastily enacting legislation denying Nixon possession of *any* of his papers or tapes.

Years later, the enduring drama of the tapes is still building. And now the two greatest figures in the Nixon Administration are the ones who must sit. And wait. And wonder.

Book VII

THE MYSTERIES OF THE COVER-UP

1

A cold but clear winter night in Connecticut. I was visiting Larry Higby and his family while on a trip to the East in 1976, nearly three years after I had left the White House. Larry, his wife Dolores, and I had driven to Westport to go to a movie. We were late, the line was long, and the night was cold, so we gave up and started to go back to the house and have some hot chocolate. But I had been spotted.

Someone in the long line outside the theatre had recognised me as we stood there trying to decide whether to brave the cold. Unfortunately, he turned out not to be a fan. As we started to walk away I heard someone shouting something I didn't catch, but that didn't sound overly friendly. I ignored it, and suggested we just walk back to the car. But my 'admirer' wasn't going to give up that easily. As the three of us started through the alley back to the parking lot, I realised we were being followed. And our pursuer was regaling me with a flood of highly uncomplimentary and generally unprintable comments.

Nothing came of it, but it showed the Higbys rather dramatically that the hatreds and misunderstandings of Watergate were still alive.

A few months later. At Pauley Pavilion, the U.C.L.A. basketball arena, I was enjoying one of the real pleasures that resulted from my departure from Washington – the chance to resume my longtime status as a devoted U.C.L.A. basketball fan. I had been going to all the games for years before we started winning national championships.

I had been a little concerned about what the reaction on campus might be to the return of a now-notorious alumnus, especially among the students. But there had been no real problems. Only one character who passed me in the aisle said 'How dare you show your face here!'

I was apprehensive during half-time when a student came charging down the steps to my seat on the opposite side of the 13,000 seat arena from the student rooting section. But he was very pleasant, and just wanted me to autograph his programme.

When he was half-way up the steps, after I had signed his book, he turned and shouted across the arena, 'I got it!' and held his signed programme over his head. A small group of students in one part of the rooting section responded with cheers and waves.

Then I waved across to them, and they, with some of their neighbours, set up another cheer and more waves. I was happy to see that they weren't all 'haters'. I decided to impress my wife, who had been talking to a friend and was unaware of this episode.

I leaned over to her and said, 'See that group of students straight across in the rooting section, about half-way up? Watch what happens.' I lifted my hand. To her amazement, they all waved at me cheering. Jo couldn't believe it, so she tried it and it worked for her, too.

My post-Watergate days have had their lows – symbolised by that cold Connecticut night, and too many moments like the U.C.L.A. experience. The press has created the image of me as a monster, and I've had to live with it. And all of it began in the days in which actions were taken that we called containment – and the press called cover-up – and the courts called conspiracy to obstruct justice.

Richard Nixon's one-word description of his role in Watergate has a simple majesty: innocence. And his rationale for that innocence has a majestic simplicity: ignorance.

In his story, a break-in was attempted by over-zealous campaign workers.

Then unknown to Nixon between June 17, 1972, and March 21, 1973, Haldeman and Ehrlichman directed Dean and others in a variety of cover-up activities. When Nixon was informed of the cover-up he should have immediately fired the culprits. Instead, out of loyalty to his subordinates, he allowed himself to become enmeshed in the cover-up.

In short, Nixon's only guilt in Watergate was – citing the words of a former British Prime Minister, Gladstone – he wasn't a good butcher.

But this is not exactly the way it happened. Watergate cannot be contained in this neat little package.

The President was involved in the cover-up from Day One, although neither he nor we considered it a cover-up at that time.

By June 20, 1972, he knew about Hunt and Liddy – but never ordered me or anyone to inform the F.B.I. On the night of June 20, he telephoned me to suggest raising money for the defendants and using a Cuban cover for the money. In that conversation he also indirectly suggested possible pressure on the C.I.A. by telling me to remind 'Ehrlichman the Cubans are all from the Bay of Pigs.' And on June 23, he imposed a 'national security' cover on the suggestion to use the C.I.A. to limit the F.B.I. investigation.

And more. On July 30, 1972 (this was unknown to me until four years later, when Nixon told me), Ehrlichman told Nixon of Magruder's guilt in these words: 'Magruder is in this up to his neck,' and 'Magruder should take a slide.'

What were Nixon's personal motives for a cover-up at the outset? In my opinion:

First, to prevent any possible connection of himself to the break-in through Colson.

Second, to forestall disclosure of whatever John Mitchell's responsibility might have been, if any. Mitchell was Nixon's closest political associate in government.

In a priceless note of telephone conversation with Nixon in the summer of 1973, after I had resigned, Nixon who was staying at Camp David with his family, apparently had been brooding about Watergate until his son-in-law, David Eisenhower, reminded him of a fact which cheered him up. My note from Nixon reads: 'David says if I had exposed Mitchell, I might have lost the election.'

Which, as the lawyers say, goes to motive.

Third – and perhaps most important – to avoid exposure of the 'other things' (as he always called them), the actions ranging from the Ellsberg break-in to Chuck Colson's projects which had brought such a gleam to his eye when they were happening. In other words, to 'contain' the investigation to Watergate.

It was this motive of 'containment' that led me into the actions I took, which are now regarded as the 'cover-up'. I thought our objective was to prevent the Watergate investigation from spilling over into other areas. Not to obstruct the process of justice in pursuing Watergate itself.

As I saw it, we had no intent to impede the Watergate investigation itself – only to avoid the very real possibility that it would lead the investigators, and later the Congressional inquiry, into these 'other things', which were not a part of the Watergate crime, and thus not a legitimate part of the investigation of that crime.

In retrospect, I must admit that there were certainly many indications along the way that, had I heeded them, would have at the very least caused me to wonder exactly what was really going on. But at the time, I didn't want to know, and I made no effort to find out. I did not consider that I had any responsibility to aid in the criminal investigation. My responsibility was the operation of the office of the President – and the continuance of this particular President in that office.

How often Nixon would agonise: 'What will Hunt say? What does Hunt know?' Nixon knew the chain clearly. Nixon tells Colson, Colson orders Hunt, Hunt executes.

These acts ranging from Hunt's bizarre action in the I.T.T. case (disguising himself in a wig to interview Dita Beard) to forgery of C.I.A. cables linking John Kennedy to the assassination of South Vietnam's President Ngo Dinh Diem were bad enough. But what else did Hunt do? (I was shocked when they opened Hunt's safe and found a gun. For what?)

Colson and Hunt had apparently launched many ventures, some of which, to this day, if reported accurately, defy belief (Colson suggesting to Hunt that they break into Arthur Bremer's house after the Wallace assassination attempt to look for evidence linking the Democrats to the shooting. And firebombing the Brookings Institution).

It so happened that I was involved indirectly in the Brookings Institution situation.

In January 1969, I had one of my first prolonged conversations with the President after he assumed office. He spoke first about distribution of office space in the White House to various officials, and warned me that his wife would be in charge of the Oval Office. By that he meant Pat would decorate the office for him. (Eventually she did it in bright blue and yellow because she wanted it to be 'cheerful.')

Nixon is cheerful himself, today. He leans back in his chair, hoists his feet on to his desk, and gestures expansively as he speaks. He has a long-term project for me. L.B.J's. bombing pause in late 1968, part of a last minute 'peace effort' by L.B.J. which had almost sunk Nixon. Nixon's lead against Senator Hubert Humphrey had dwindled to tiny percentage points in the last weeks of the campaign.

Nixon still bears the scars. 'There was a lot of phony stuff going on by L.B.J., Bob. I want you to make a full report with all the documents showing just what he did. He let politics enter into a war decision, and I want the whole story on it.'

'But that's all behind us,' I say.

I make a pitch for my own hoped-for project; to get the real facts from the files on the Kennedy assassination for history's sake. The idea bores Nixon. History, to him, is what has happened to Nixon – and what *might* happen later.

He sits up, fiddles with his penholder, then clasps his hands on the desk. 'I'd start at the Pentagon,' he says. 'They'll have the military moves L.B.J. made.'

I launched some staff people on the project and soon felt the first shiver of a future governmental war. I was told a man named Leslie Gelb had left his post at the Pentagon and transferred many pertinent files to a private organisation, the Brookings Institution, known in the White House as a Democratic Party 'think tank'.

That sounded odd. Government documents had been transferred to a private institution. Among them was a critical document on the bombing halt.

I asked to see a copy of it.

Well, no, the only copy was at Brookings.

I thought of Ehrlichman's similar trauma with the C.I.A. The key document was, somehow, unavailable. But this was the Pentagon, an open institution, not the C.I.A.

Then I realised that the Pentagon generals, with a new Commander-in-Chief installed in the White House, had reputations to protect. Obviously they had placed the evidence we needed out of reach by transferring it to a private institution.

I reported this to Nixon who was irritated. He slammed a pencil on his desk, and said, 'I want that Goddamn Gelb material and I don't care how you get it.'

Good luck, I thought, as I left the office. And goodbye to Nixon's long-term project. I knew of no way I could get my hands on the document we needed. Over the months ahead I would explore with Alexander Haig, who had helped to compile other material, various James Bond-type techniques to retrieve the document. The only really likely idea was to have a Pentagon military security inspector tour Brookings on a routine check for security infractions, and simply 'lift' the document when inspecting the safe.

But nothing was done about it and as far as I was concerned, the whole search for Gelb's document ended.

But not for Nixon. 1971 saw the rise of Colson as Nixon's 'can do' man. Colson answered Nixon's request for the Gelb report with his famous rallying cry: 'No problem!'

Where I had talked gingerly of a security inspector, Colson had a better idea: bombs. Jack Caulfield said to

Dean that he had been told by Colson to plant firebombs in the Brookings Institution. In the smoke and confusion, some White House assistants disguised as firemen would remove the document. The fact that the entire Brookings Institution might burn to the ground was beside the point.

Colson later said his suggestion was only a joke. He must have appeared at least rather serious because when Dean heard it he flew to San Clemente to alert John Ehrlichman of Colson's latest far-out venture. Ehrlichman killed the project – and if he hadn't the Watergate tragedy might have had a different, fiery, beginning.

2

The summer and fall of 1972 were occupied with the final plans for the Republican convention – and the convention itself – after careful observation and analysis of the Democrats' takeover by George McGovern. Then came the campaign, which involved a lot of White House time and thought despite the fact that the President did not spend many days out of Washington actually campaigning.

The Vietnam peace efforts appeared to be rapidly coming to a successful conclusion, and this was Nixon's primary interest throughout this period. He had no doubt about the outcome of – nor any other concern with – the GOP convention. I was at Camp David with Nixon during the weeks preceding our convention. The President was working on his acceptance speech and Vietnam. I was monitoring the pre-convention activities of the rest of our troops, in Miami.

Ehrlichman called one morning in great distress. 'Your Vice-President has now come up with the all-time classic,' John blurted out. (He had no great love for Spiro Agnew.) 'He's decided to have his nomination seconded by none other than Dr Joyce Brothers [the famous TV psychologist]. That hardly seems to be the gentle touch after the Eagleton flap.' I agreed and took on the delicate task of turning off one more potential blunder.

Just to make sure there was no idle time, we were also deeply involved in the preliminary planning for the inception of the second term – there was no doubt in our minds about the outcome of the election. The whole concept and structure of the reorganisation that was to take place had to be ready right after the election – as I tried to assure Nixon it would be in the September 15 meeting that has been thoroughly covered by release of the tape.

During these summer and fall months Dean was deeply occupied in the cover-up in various ways, coaching Magruder into perjury, supervising Herb Kalmbach, who was raising money for the defendants, and staying on top of all facets of the investigation and the civil suit. Elsewhere I've pointed out occasions when Dean said he checked with me but didn't: Kalmbach is an instance when he did. The request, shortly after the burglars had gone to jail that Kalmbach be asked to raise funds for their legal fees and family support seemed reasonable enough. They were our people, working for the Committee for the Re-election of the President.

And even more important, Nixon had told me on June 20 that we were going to raise money for the defendants.

My implication in the money-raising occurs twice. Once, in the early days when I – and Ehrlichman – approved the choice of Kalmbach to solicit funds for the defendants. The second occasion, interestingly, occurred *after* the election, when obviously we had no fear of losing the race. At that time I directed the transfer from the White House to C.R.P. of $350,000 cash we had salted away from 1968 surplus campaign funds. (On this I agree with all Nixon's critics: we had too much *cash* floating around for our own good. Here was an example of hundreds of thousands of dollars in a safe-deposit box – most of it never used.) Chuck Colson had withdrawn twenty-two thousand for his 'Tell it to Hanoi' advertisement, supporting our stand in the bombing of North Vietnam, May 8, 1972. He only spent about $7,000 and the $15,000 balance found its way to John Dean for safekeeping. John Dean nipped a few thousand of this, on the sly, for his honeymoon. And may have nipped even more than has ever been revealed. Try as we might, neither that accounting genius, Maurice Stans, nor I can figure out what became of another $22,000 that went to Dean, supposedly to replace the original $22,000 that had been withdrawn by Colson. It has never been accounted for.

In November, Gordon Strachan, who was leaving the White House to become General Counsel at U.S.I.A. reminded me of the $350,000 we had put away for polling and had never utilised. I told him to transfer it back to C.R.P. and get a receipt. But C.R.P. – with reporters on its back – didn't want any more cash from anybody. They had enough trouble accounting for what they had. And, meanwhile Dean heard about this gold mine, and asked me if he could use some of it for the Watergate defendants.

I told him to transfer it to C.R.P. and after that it wasn't my concern. Later I heard that instead of transferring it as directed, he sent over $40,000 for the defendants. Larry Higby recalls my exploding over the telephone at Dean when I heard he had done this.

Then the rest of the money went to C.R.P. in a bizarre way: a man wearing gloves furtively receiving the briefcase full of cash and handing over no receipt. Why did grown people act that way? Even Strachan, the deliverer of the money, was startled to find a man outfitted in gloves to receive the booty.

Perhaps Fred LaRue, the man in the gloves, wasn't so dumb. Because in the end all that money was inevitably branded just as my wife predicted: 'Bob, people will always believe that was "hush money".'

As far as I know, Nixon knew nothing of any of these fund-raising, payment, or money-transfer activities at the time. Although he did know there were plans for some sort of Cuban Defense Fund as far back as June 20, 1972.

I'll only pause to bring out one more fact about the $350,000, this one for the 'Watergate buffs'. From letters

I receive I am aware there is a cult of people in this country who collect every scrap of information about Watergate because of its many fascinating mysteries.

Study this fact about the $350,000. In mid-March 1973, according to John Dean, he was approached by Paul O'Brien (a C.R.P. counsel, later revealed to be an ex-C.I.A. employee) and told that Howard Hunt must have $122,000 or he would 'blow' what he knew about the 'seamy things he had done for Ehrlichman'. This drove Dean into deciding he must tell Nixon everything, and we thereupon had the March 21 'Cancer on the Presidency' meeting.

But two things are odd. One is known, the other not.

First, for the public item. Howard Hunt, supposedly so desperate for $122,000 he would threaten the White House with blackmail, should have been floating in money. He not only had received thousands of dollars from Kalmbach and LaRue, but his wife had been tragically killed in an aeroplane crash, and the insurance Hunt collected was substantial.

Mrs Hunt was carrying thousands of dollars in cash when her plane crashed en route to Chicago. She was the paymaster for the burglars. But the burglars were in Washington and Miami. Why was she taking the money to Chicago?

Hunt reportedly said he intended to invest the cash in a real estate venture in Illinois. If he had enough money for real estate speculation, why was he so desperate for funds as we were led to believe?

The unknown fact about the Hunt blackmail request for money is that there was no need to *raise* any more money to meet Hunt's demand because C.R.P. had all that unaccounted-for cash on hand – and more. Only a small part of the $350,000 had been used. Indeed even *after* all the payments were made, there would be some $50,000 left, which was still on hand when the Watergate conspiracy trial began. So why the panic? Why the urgency that drove Nixon to jump out of his shell and cause all kinds of problems for himself by saying he could raise the money for Hunt?

In Hollywood's vaunted motion picture, *All the President's Men*, Deep Throat whispers huskily: 'Follow the money.'

He was referring to the original funding for Liddy. But I would say to those who want to understand every last secret of Watergate, follow that $350,000, only part of which was used for the defendants. (Note: Hunt denied he made a blackmail threat. If he didn't, and an ex-C.I.A. associate, Paul O'Brien, *invented* a blackmail threat from Hunt, you would be heading for intriguing paydirt.)

3

The Colson Tapes

President Nixon enters the cover-up in a new manner in January and February of 1973. In a series of meetings with Chuck Colson in those months he discussed *clemency*, as well as other matters of interest in Watergate.

Portions of these conversations were released during the Frost interviews. Here are additional segments of interest:

PRESIDENT: Well, first of all, they've got to make a production in Liddy's case. But none of them are going to testify. Isn't that correct?

You know, Chuck, it's something they all undertook knowing the risks. Right? What do you think?

COLSON: I don't think there's any doubt about it.

PRESIDENT: Did you think they'd get caught?

This is an interesting question by the President. It appears evident to me he's assuming that Colson *had foreknowledge* of the break-in by asking it.

COLSON: No . . . I think they figured that these are guys who were with, uh, C.I.A.

Then Nixon makes his comments on clemency – and it's obvious he's brought up the subject with Colson before.

PRESIDENT: . . . basically I question clemency. Hunt's is a simple case. I mean, after all, the man's wife is dead, was killed; he's got one child that has . . .
COLSON: Brain damage from an automobile accident.
PRESIDENT: We'll build that son-of-a-bitch up like nobody's business. We'll have Buckley write a column and say that he should have clemency, if you've given 18 years of service. We'll talk about it after. That's it. It's on the merits. I would have him talk to some of the others.
COLSON: . . . Well, the others aren't going to get the same terms.
PRESIDENT: Why?
COLSON: Well because Hunt and Liddy did the work. The others didn't know much. They can't hurt us . . . none of those discussions are very incriminating to us. Awkward, but . . . Liddy . . .
PRESIDENT: Liddy is pretty tough.
COLSON: He is apparently one of those guys who's a masochist. He enjoys punishing himself. So that's O.K. As long as he remains stable . . . He's tough.
PRESIDENT: Yeah. He's an ideologue. Hunt's an ideologue.

(A note about the transcripts you are reading, and all the other transcripts you may see or have seen of the White House tapes. I have listened to most of these tapes, and followed the 'official' transcripts as I did so. I can assure you that there is often no way of being exactly sure of what was said – or even who said it in many cases. The effort to produce accurate transcripts has involved many tedious hours of work by supposed experts, but the fact remains that the tapes are just not clear enough to make it possible to assure complete accuracy.

A striking example – only one of hundreds – is where Chuck Colson once said, 'They're both healthy Right-Wing Conservatives.' The 'official' special prosecutors' transcript changed this simple sentence to 'Rosie's red healthy red neck zoo'. It's amusing to think how Watergate historians would interpret that mistranscribed statement when first confronted with it. Let's see, Hunt and Liddy were the 'red neck zoo', and Rose Mary Woods ('Rosie') – unknown to everyone – must have been running them.

The transcription errors became an issue when David Frost quoted the words 'hush money' from this transcript. President: 'Goddamn hush money, uh, how are we going to [unintelligible] how do we get this stuff?' The words 'hush money' were so blurred that the special prosecutors didn't use them in the trial. Colson angrily denied that the words 'hush money' were used, and I agree with him.)

On February 13, Nixon speculated with Colson about the guilt of Mitchell and Magruder.

NIXON: Magruder's perjured himself, hasn't he?
COLSON: Probably.
NIXON: Mitchell seems to have stonewalled it up to this point.
COLSON: Well he's – ya know, John has got one of those marvellous, ah, memories.

And now, after all the talk, after all the brave discussion of other people stepping forward to proclaim their guilt, Nixon and Colson gingerly approached a fact about Watergate: who initiated the break-in?

COLSON: That's another problem. You, y-y-you you can't control who says, 'Well . . .'
PRESIDENT: 'Colson wants this done.'

COLSON: 'Colson wants this done.' And, uh, either that, or I just [hastily corrects the incriminating 'I'] – *somebody* just . . .

PRESIDENT: Well, they even say, 'The *President* wants this or that done.'

COLSON: Yeah. *I* never did that deliberately. But . . . a lot of people did do that, of course.

On January 26 in the middle of those Colson conversations came the news from Paris. Peace in Vietnam after 13 years of war. The troops would be coming home. The P.O.W.s would be released. America was at peace.

It was a day of jubilation for Nixon, by all odds the happiest I had ever seen him. And he had a right to be. Soon the P.O.W.s were arriving at airports in the U.S. and thanking Nixon fervently for what he had done. Nixon-haters cringed at every one of those scenes, but even they couldn't attack young American soldiers who had spent years in enemy prisons.

Not long after I left the White House, and was still living in Georgetown during Grand Jury and Senate investigations and conferences, an official White House car pulled up to my door one morning. Not to pick me up, as in the old days, but to deliver a letter.

I saw immediately that it was the familiar pale green envelope used only by the President himself for his personal mail. It was hand addressed in writing that could only be one man's.

It said – in Nixon's scrawled penmanship:

Dear Bob

As I sit here preparing remarks for the P.O.W.s I realise this day would never have come without your steadfast support and also John's.

The nation, the P.O.W.s and I shall always be in your debt.

RN

He was referring to the integral part I had played, at his

right hand, through many of the critical decisions in the war. The November 3, 1969, speech in which he turned public opinion 180 degrees with his plea to the Silent American Majority to stand behind him in his efforts to end the war on a sound basis. The Cambodia incursion and the resulting domestic upheaval climaxed by Kent State. The Laotian operation a year later. The secret planning and execution of Kissinger's meetings with the North Vietnamese in Paris over months and months. The heart-rending meetings with the P.O.W. families, and their strong support.

I especially remember May 8, 1972, as one of the greatest crises in the war, which ended in one of Nixon's most successful decisions.

The North Vietnamese had unleashed a full-scale offensive. Kissinger and the Joint Chiefs of Staff had advised drastic action by the President, including the mining of the harbour of the North Vietnamese city, Haiphong, to prevent all shipping, as well as heavy bombing of North Vietnam. But there was a problem. A summit conference with the Russians was scheduled for the third week in May, barely two weeks away.

Kissinger soon had 'second thoughts'. Not that he wanted to cancel the mining of Haiphong and the bombing. He was all for that – but the timing worried him. The Soviets would cancel their summit conference, using the American actions as the excuse, and we would look bad in the eyes of the world. So he strongly recommended that we announce a postponement of the conference at the same time we announced the Vietnam action. He felt this would save us from inevitable embarrassment of a Soviet cancellation while preserving the summit for later in the year.

I was in Nixon's office when Kissinger presented this argument. To Henry's surprise, and mine, when Henry concluded Nixon said to me, 'What do you think, Bob?'

I argued with Henry to this effect: he was *assuming* the Soviets would cancel the conference. He didn't *know* they would. It was worth a gamble on our part. *Maybe* we could still have the summit conference despite the bombing. We had little to lose by trying except for some potential embarrassment – and we had much to gain.

I suppose Henry might have been angry at my intrusion into affairs in which I was far from an expert, but Nixon's next words tipped him off. He said, 'Well, there seems to be a disagreement. Why don't you both go to John Connally and see what his view is.'

Henry and I immediately walked out of the E.O.B. office to the Treasury Building. Henry described the problem and his recommendation to Connally. I started to outline my argument against announcing a delay of the summit. But Connally interrupted to present almost the same argument I had just used in the President's office.

Henry knew when he was licked: the decision was to announce the Vietnam action, and *hope* the Soviets would go along without cancelling the summit. It was a gamble. My argument for it was based solely on logic, not any presumed expertise in foreign policy or military strategy. My role was important not because my view prevailed, but because I had presented an option that had not been considered, and should have been.

The May 8 action stopped the North Vietnamese cold and brought them to the negotiating table seriously for the first time in four years, enabling Kissinger to announce shortly before the election, 'Peace is at hand.' (It took one more Nixon act, the Christmas bombing, to finally end that incredible war.)

And the Soviets did not cancel the summit conference, which proved a great success.

January should have been a month of exultation; and February, when the P.O.W.s started returning, a month of gratitude by the nation.

But in those same two months, four events began taking shape that would have a bearing on Watergate. Each of them would explode with a twist-ending at precisely the right time to do Nixon the most damage. As their impact built step-by-step, they would in a matter of weeks shatter the most powerful man on earth and turn him into a haggard defensive politician afraid for his survival.

For a while Nixon did survive. If he, through Colson, did initiate the Watergate break-in, Colson at least got away and that worry was off Nixon's mind. But the 'other things' were catching up to him, ranging from the Ellsberg break-in to all the other bizarre ventures of Colson and Hunt, *et al.*

4

All during the time Nixon was being toasted at the peak of his triumph as President, we were concerned by the initiation of trials and hearings that we felt boded trouble (we never guessed how *much* trouble).

The four events (which were to explode in surprise endings) began in January and February and were, in chronological order:

1. The original Watergate trial (which started January 8).
2. The Ervin Committee hearings. (On January 11, Senator Sam Ervin agreed to head a Senate investigation of Watergate.)
3. The Ellsberg trial. (It opened in Los Angeles, January 18.)
4. The Senate confirmation hearings on Patrick Gray as F.B.I. Director. (They started February 28.)

The two trials and two hearings began quietly. We looked at them with anxious eyes, but gradually we relaxed. Each of them seemed harmless.

The Watergate trial involved only seven men. As far as we knew, Liddy was a strange man who wouldn't talk. Period. And as to Hunt, on January 11, he testified that he had no knowledge of any higher-ups involved. The

Cubans didn't know anything except what Hunt had told them. McCord was a low-level security man.

As for the Senate hearings, there were all kinds of protections available to Nixon: primarily executive privilege, which had been used in the past to limit or prevent testimony of White House personnel.

The Ellsberg trial was no problem at all. In fact, we viewed the Ellsberg trial as a plus. We were finally thrusting the hero of the Left on the defensive.

The Gray hearings foretold no ill for us, as far as we could see. Although no one was happy with Gray's appointment, he was, in Nixon's words, 'one hundred per cent loyal.'

Buoyed by these false estimates of the charge to come, we weathered the storms of press criticism, hoping that they would eventually die, and constantly surprised that they kept escalating even when the American people adamantly told pollsters over and over again that they didn't care about Watergate.

What we didn't realise was that various people in the four power blocs were becoming aware of the fact that, incredibly, Nixon had become vulnerable despite his success. And as more information seeped out, they realised they possibly could cripple Nixon and thereby reduce the danger to them of a hostile President backed by a landslide victory. But the odds were all against them at first. The American people had trouble taking the Watergate break-in seriously.

It took bombshell after bombshell (as they were called in those days) to destroy a powerful President. What is fascinating in reconstructing the true story of Watergate is both the *timing* of those bombshells and the surprise twists which made their shocks even more effective. Nixon was never prepared. Time and again after he thought he had stabilised his ship of state, and knew every danger lurking in the waters, another torpedo would explode amidships and Nixon and his crew, including me, would frantically be shoring up bulkheads against a sea of outrage.

The first torpedo emerged from Gray's confirmation

hearings as F.B.I. Director on Capitol Hill. It began the second largest catastrophe of all for Nixon: the transformation of John Dean from the White House point man on Watergate to the leading informer against Nixon.

(The greatest catastrophe was, of course, the exposure of the existence of the tapes.)

5

John Ehrlichman threw a tennis ball high in the air, and lashed at it, his neck cords straining. The ball sped into the corner, bouncing low with a mean twist. I scooped it up and hit a beauty right down the line.

Love fifteen.

Jeanne, John's wife, crossed the court to receive the next service return. (Jeanne would one day call Jo almost in tears after she finally learned of her husband's role in the Ellsberg break-in, 'I can't believe John did that. I can't believe it!')

A double fault made it love thirty.

John served again, and this time I took a mighty backhand swing, more in my usual style. I almost missed the ball entirely. It hit the wood of the racquet and soared into the air in an accidental lob.

Underneath it Ehrlichman circled. The great secret about life as well as tennis, he had always told me, was that 'the man who gets the ball over the net the last time wins'. He waited until the ball bounced, then smashed it away. Jo and I watched it – and the point – go.

Fifteen thirty.

This was in early spring at Camp David. Jo and I had just moved to Georgetown, nonplussing reporters who believed all members of the White House staff despised it. But we loved the pre-Revolutionary town with its brick houses, black shutters, gas-burning lamps, and old oaken doors fronted with brass knockers.

We finished the set (the Ehrlichmans won), and went to Laurel for hamburgers. There we sat, two families in the centre of an invisible storm, taking one small break at our wives' insistence from the White House turmoil.

Since February 28, although we didn't know it, we had been in deep trouble. On that day, lantern-jawed Patrick Gray, F.B.I. Director, looked at the panel of Senators at his confirmation hearing and wondered why they appeared so stunned. He had just volunteered information that startled them. He told them John Dean from the White House had sat in on the F.B.I. interrogation of Watergate witnesses and, worse, Gray had given Dean all the F.B.I. files on Watergate.

Most of the Senators (and the press) had never heard of John Dean. When they checked, they found not some high-ranking member of the 'Berlin Wall' but a clean-cut young staffer who looked like a college student.

On March 7, Gray volunteered more information. He had given Dean no less than 82 F.B.I. reports. And he revealed that Dean had cleared out Howard Hunt's White House safe.

Still reeling from that, the Senators heard on March 13 that Gray had met with Dean thirty-three times between June and September, 1972. It was apparent that every move the F.B.I. had made in the Watergate investigation had been monitored – if not controlled – by John Dean. The next day the Judiciary Committee asked Dean to testify. Dean put in a claim of executive privilege.

Even though the claim was upheld, the world had changed for young John Dean. For the first time he became aware that he was no longer a quiet, eager beaver building up brownie points for promotion in the White House. Suddenly he was the target of national headlines and suspicions. If there had been no Gray confirmation hearings spotlighting John Dean, he probably would not have panicked later on. And the chances are that the public and the press would never have heard of him.

So, one power bloc, the Congress, was utilising one of its unique prerogatives, the congressional hearing, to strike a blow that would have far greater repercussions than they could have dreamed.

'Hey Bob,' said Jo, 'Want some more iced tea?' I poured another glass from the pitcher.

And the next day John Dean told me about a certain cancer.

6

Some days before, John Dean had come into my office lugging a heavy law book. Once there, he took his horn-rimmed glasses off and wiped his brow.

I looked at him. The crisp confident Dean had disappeared. In his place, in front of me, was a frightened young man, nervous and fidgety. His long thin finger stabbed at a legal phrase in the pages of the law book: the law pertaining to obstruction of justice.

I was startled. 'You mean I've done something . . . criminal?'

'That's what it says.'

'I approved raising money for people who worked for us who were in jail, they pleaded guilty, and that's obstruction of justice?'

Dean closed the book and sighed. 'It is if it kept them from talking.'

Dean felt, however, that we would hold the line on what he still viewed as a legal technicality.

He left and I shifted some paperwork on my desk. Everything was crumbling so suddenly I was overwhelmed. As I pondered this disturbing new information, I was filled with a sense of ironic bewilderment. Here was the 'company lawyer', White House Counsel John Dean, announcing to me for the first time that there were possible criminal problems in the payments to the defendants months after he, himself, had come to me for approval of raising the money for these payments. My assumption of their legality and propriety had been based on the fact that the original proposal had come from the White House Counsel. Considering this source, there was no reason even to think about the question of illegality. I stepped out of my office on to the patio. King Timahoe, the President's Irish setter, loped across the south lawn pursued by his handler, who was shouting. A cool breeze swept up from the Potomac. I stood there thinking. What could we do? What *could* we do?

The tight world of the White House was bursting wide open. In the ruins inside was the collapsed wall which I had once built around the President.

I decided the first thing I had better do was to write down every item of my own possible involvement in Watergate.

The first note I wrote was on Donald Segretti.

1974. The District Court House, Washington, D.C. I spotted a slightly rotund man with a jovial smile sitting in the press section at the Watergate cover-up trial. He waved. I smiled. The friendly courtroom spectator was Dick Tuck, the Democratic Party trickster who had bedevilled Nixon in so many campaigns. Because of Tuck, I had agreed with Dwight Chapin's suggestion to hire a trickster for the 1972 campaign, Don Segretti, in a vain hope of duplicating Tuck's magic. As an old campaigner, I rather appreciated Tuck even though he was on the other side.

Dick once donned a motorman's uniform and started a train. It was no coincidence that Nixon was addressing a crowd from the rear platform. Nixon, in midsentence, found his audience disappearing into the distance.

His most famous trick had Watergate echoes. At a Chinatown rally in San Francisco, Nixon was delighted to find smiling Chinese-Americans with signs in their native language surrounding him. Only after the pictures were published did Nixon discover that the signs over his head read in Chinese: 'What about the Hughes loan?'

Now, seeing Tuck, I remembered several newspaper columns reporting a conversation between us in which I said to Tuck, 'You're the one who started all this.' Tuck supposedly answered, 'Yes, Bob, but you guys ran it into the ground.'

After the courtroom session he greeted me. I said, 'Dick, you know that conversation never took place.'

Tuck smiled, 'I know, but you wouldn't want me to change the story, would you? *Playboy* paid me $1,000 for it.'

But Tuck and I both knew that Segretti went too far, and that fact caused me trouble.

I have never met Donald Segretti, but my approval of his hiring was certainly one of my major mistakes. For one thing, it gave one of the power blocs, the press, an early start, if a false one, in their attack. Woodward and Bernstein stumbled on to Segretti's trail early in the game – and made a fundamental error. They wrote that Segretti was the kingpin of a 'massive campaign of political spying and sabotage on behalf of President Nixon's re-election'.

In fact, there was no 'massive campaign'. Segretti visited only a few primary states and never rounded up more than a few volunteers in any state.

Most of the tricks they did were sophomoric: sending 200 pizzas to a small Democratic dinner; dropping white mice at a Muskie press conference with ribbons on their tails reading 'Muskie is a rat fink'. But the exceptions made me angry when I heard about them. Pre-eminently the so-called 'sex-letters'.

Three days before the Florida primary, letters on 'Citizens for Muskie' stationery accused Senator Henry Jackson of fathering an illegitimate child in 1929. And, conversely, of having been arrested on homosexual charges in 1955 and 1957. The two accusations seemed to cancel each other out, but no matter.

In the same letter, Senator Hubert Humphrey was alleged to have been arrested for drunken driving in

Washington on December 3, 1967. None of these charges was true. I publicly apologised for them at the Ervin hearings. But it is also true that none of the charges had any bearing on the Florida primary. Governor George Wallace easily swamped all of the contenders.

I listed all of my other possible involvements in the Watergate mess. I had approved the choice of Herb Kalmbach to raise money for the defendants, and later assumed the use of part of the $350,000 I had transferred to C.R.P. In addition, Dean claimed Stratchan had been receiving the Watergate wiretap transcripts (I didn't know this was not true. To be fair, Dean didn't either).

Perhaps because of all the publicity, the hiring of Segretti bothered me more than anything. Ironically, it later turned out to be so inconsequential it was not even part of the Watergate case indictment.

When John Dean had come to my office to tell me of the possibility of legal problems he had felt we still could hold the line on what he viewed as a legal technicality. But on March 20, late in the day, he said he felt he had to fill the President in on all the problems which he knew nothing about – and which could become a 'cancer on the Presidency'. I completely agreed – and John set up the meeting that night on the phone with the President.

The March 21 'Cancer on the Presidency' meeting of the President and Dean, which I joined later, is by now well known to everyone who has an interest in Watergate. But there was an inner dynamism to that meeting that has been little noticed. The other two participants in the conversation were too absorbed in their own goals to recognise it.

What were their goals? Nixon's was this: To make certain Hunt didn't talk of his activities that touched indirectly on Nixon, ranging from surveillance of Teddy Kennedy to Ellsberg. It was obvious neither Dean nor I feared them as much as Nixon did because he absolutely shocked both of us when he practically jumped out of his chair, insisting on raising the money for Hunt.

Because of this, the dynamism of this fateful meeting was a sort of black comedy. Nixon's reaction to Hunt's blackmail demand wasn't at all what Dean wanted. Dean had not entered that meeting to raise money for Hunt but to try to get immunity for himself. Dean intended to use the Hunt blackmail demand and the other selective tidbits he gave Nixon only as the 'shocker' that would awaken Nixon to the danger – and lead him to grant Dean, the man who knew the most about Watergate, immunity.

What Dean didn't know was how much Nixon had to hide; how frightened Nixon was by a Hunt blackmail threat; his obsession with the need to 'buy time' to figure out what to do. And what Nixon didn't know was how much Dean was *not* telling him. This 'complete' report from the White House was lacking in completeness, especially in those areas of Dean's own peril – his coaching of perjury; directing the investigation, involvement in payments to the defendants, etc.

So the comedy began. Whenever Dean tried to angle the conversation towards his own dangers, Nixon would counter with a shout of 'Get the money for Hunt'. But when Nixon turned to the question of clemency, which Dean had never even mentioned, the crafty young lawyer saw the light. Nixon was only worried about Number One: the President. Whether Dean was or was not to get immunity was a future problem. Right now Hunt must not talk; he must not blow those 'seamy things' that could be tracked to the Oval Office. Some of them truly seamy, and some truly national security in the President's mind. But all of them potentially seamy as far as the public was concerned. And clemency might have to be offered, too, if that was necessary.

Dean reminded him that he couldn't do that before the 1974 Congressional elections and Nixon reluctantly admitted that would be wrong.

In the latter part of the meeting, when I was present, Nixon turned from his obsession with making the Hunt payment in order to buy time and keep him from blowing at the sentencing due in a few days. He came up with a different way of accomplishing this: delay the sentencing itself by getting Kleindienst, the Attorney General, to ask Judge Sirica for a postponement on the basis of new information. He also had the idea, I think picked up earlier from John Ehrlichman, of bringing in a new Grand Jury. This had the benefit not only of delaying Hunt's sentencing and thus his threat to blow, but also of moving the investigative focus away from the televised Ervin hearings and the attendant circus, and into the secret and legally protected Grand Jury room. This proposal appealed to me since it met my objective of trying to get all the facts together in one place *before* any of them were made public. I was deeply concerned about piecemeal release and the resultant press uproar on each item before it was confirmed, corroborated or disproved. My concern certainly was proven by future events to have been fully justified.

The net result of the meeting was that I would telephone Mitchell and ask him to come to Washington to discuss the whole problem with Dean, Ehrlichman, and me – and give the President our recommendations.

That meeting was a crushing disappointment to Dean. Not only did he not get a promise of immunity, but he felt Nixon didn't understand the entire picture.

I think Nixon did understand far more than Dean knew.

Larry Higby remembers the worried expression on my face when I came out of that March 21 meeting. Higby, a sandy-haired young man with a usually cheerful voice, said, 'What's the problem, Bob?'

No doubt, in the context of those times, he was expecting me to tell him another artillery shell had landed in the Oval Office. I sat down in my chair, placed my hands behind my head, and pondered the ceiling before answering. 'Nothing new – except the old man himself. I've never seen him this way.'

Higby urged me on, 'What do you mean?'

'He's acting *strangely.* Dean told him that Hunt was demanding money and he kept coming back to that point, saying, "Get it now. We've got to buy time." Something is really bugging him – even though Hunt's threat is directed at Ehrlichman and it doesn't seem to bother John.'

At 5.20 that afternoon another figure made his first important appearance in the March 21 deliberations. He also had a goal of his own.

John Ehrlichman bore the weight of the Ellsberg break-in as an albatross around his stout neck. The last thing he wanted was witnesses like Dean testifying with immunity. If one of them – such as Dean – revealed the Ellsberg break-in, Ehrlichman was finished. And with immunity, they might talk. But, of course, John didn't put the matter quite so crudely. As the hopeful Dean, yearning desperately for immunity, listened impassively, Ehrlichman said, 'I just don't think that the immunity thing will wash . . . no, I wouldn't spend too much time with that.' He suggested instead a report by Dean, which the President could use as a basis for saying this was as much as he knew about the matter and the White House was not involved.

That report would say, according to our domestic counsellor, 'Mr President, you asked me about these things. Here's my review of the facts . . . I think you could get out a fairly credible document that would stand up, and that will have the effect of trimming the scoop . . .'

Ehrlichman then touched gingerly on his own concern: the Ellsberg break-in. 'The big danger in the Ervin hearings, as I see it, is that they will run into areas that it would be better not to have them get into.'

Nixon knew the way to solve Ellsberg, and other problems: 'The bridge you have to cross, I understand quite soon, is what can you do about [Hunt's] present demand? Now what about that?'

Nixon believes this little-noted comment shows that, despite the fireworks in his morning meetings, he hadn't definitely made up his mind about paying Hunt's demands. I agree. No decision had been made, but his concern was very clear.

Dean topped all perfidy by striking back with a sheer lie. He said, referring to the possibility that Mitchell or LaRue would help raise the money, 'I have not talked with either of them.' Actually he had talked to both of them – *before* he had even raised the subject with the President.

The upshot of this meeting was that Dean reluctantly said that he would write a report which, as Nixon said, 'is very general, understand? [Laughs]. I don't want to get all that Goddamned specific.'

That evening, Fred LaRue of C.R.P. placed $75,000 in a plain envelope and gave it to a courier who delivered it to Hunt's lawyer, Bittman. LaRue would later testify that on Dean's instructions he had telephoned Mitchell that morning or the day before for approval of the payment.

Another superb irony! Nixon's concern about whether or not to meet Hunt's demand was academic by the time of the March 21 meeting where he first learned of the threat. Dean had called La Rue before the meeting and told him of Hunt's demand, saying that he, Dean, was out of the money business, and that LaRue should check with John Mitchell as to what to do.

LaRue called Mitchell in New York, told him Hunt was demanding more money to get his affairs settled before the sentencing due the end of the week. Mitchell asked what had been done about these demands earlier, and LaRue said that payments had been made for legal fees. Mitchell said this one should be too.

Acting on these instructions from Mitchell, LaRue decided to make a payment to Hunt; but he cut the amount from $122,000 to $75,000 to cover only the legal fees portion of Hunt's demand. But, unfortunately for the President, he didn't get around to delivering the money to Hunt's lawyer until late evening of the 21st. And this raised great scepticism concerning Nixon's claim that the payment was not at his direction. He was absolutely right on that point, at least.

Nixon would therefore state on television in 1977 that despite his repeated comments to Dean about paying the money, he cannot be implicated in the pay-off because the money transfer had already been authorised by Dean and

Mitchell, prior to Dean's meeting the President. The chain was: Bittman tells Dean, Dean tells LaRue, LaRue checks with Mitchell, then pays the money.

7

By noon on March 22, another sensation on Capitol Hill had ignited in Gray's confirmation hearing. Gray testified that Dean 'probably lied' to F.B.I. agents investigating the Watergate incident when he said, on June 22, 1972, that he did not know Hunt had an office in the White House.

That afternoon we met again in the Oval Office, joined by Mitchell, who had come to Washington and met with Ehrlichman, Dean, and me in the morning in response to Nixon's request. Mitchell had already indicated to us that the Hunt problem was being taken care of, so the afternoon meeting covered the other concerns – the problems of executive privilege or immunity versus going to the Grand Jury. It was in that meeting that the President told Dean to go to Camp David and write a report. Dean, sweating in the spotlight of Gray, didn't smile when I opened the proceedings by needling him with a remark to Nixon: 'Gray's the symbol of wisdom today. He accused your counsel of being a liar.'

Dean said, 'He may be dead 'cause I may shoot him.'

This meeting is memorable for another reason. In the White House transcript, sixteen pages were omitted, including this passage of Nixon's at the end of the meeting when all of us had left except Mitchell:

> Now let me make this clear. I thought it was a very cruel thing as it turned out – what happened to [Sherman] Adams. I don't want it to happen with Watergate, the Watergate matter. I think he made a mistake, but he shouldn't have been sacked . . . and,

> uh, for that reason I am perfectly willing to – I don't give a shit what happens, [unintelligible] stonewall it, let them plead the Fifth Amendment, cover-up or anything else, if it'll save it – save it for them. That's the whole point.
>
> On the other hand, uh, uh, . . . I would prefer, as I said to you, that you do it the other way. And I would particularly prefer to do it that other way if it's going to come out that way anyway. And that, my view, that, uh, with the number of jackass people that they've got that they can call, they're going to . . . The story they got out through leaks, charges, and so forth, and innuendos will be a hell of a lot worse than the story they're going to get out by just letting it out there.

Mitchell replied, 'Well, the important thing is to get you up and above it for this first operation. And then to see where the chips fall.'

The press jumped on this omission in the transcript, but generally with an omission of their own. They gleefully reported the first paragraph – using a faulty transcript that made it appear even more damaging that it does here. But they left out the second paragraph, which, in context, substantially changes the impression of the President's intent.

The meeting ended with its participants unaware that elsewhere in Washington a judge named John Sirica was studying once again a letter he had received from one of the defendants, James McCord. When he released that letter the next day at the sentencing, one day after the Gray revelations, the Watergate crisis would never be the same.

McCord's letter read:

> In the interest of restoring faith in the criminal justice system, which faith has been severely damaged in this case, I will state the following to you at this time, which I hope may be of help to you in meting out justice in this case:

> There was political pressure applied to the defendants to plead guilty, and remain silent.
>
> Perjury occurred during the trial matters highly material to the very structure, orientation, and impact of the Government's case, and to the motivation and intent of the defendants.
>
> Others involved in the Watergate operation were not identified during the trial, when they could have been by those testifying.
>
> The Watergate operation was not a C.I.A. operation. The Cubans may have been misled by others into believing that it was a C.I.A. operation. I know for a fact that it was not.

McCord then went on to say he 'feared retaliatory measures would be taken against me and my family'.

The letter was released March 23 and a public uproar ensued. Newspapers, which had been deriding the Watergate story, joined the hue and cry. Nixon knew he had to act fast.

John Dean had been dispatched to Camp David to write a report. Dean has later tried to represent the demand for a report as a ploy by Nixon. He contends that the report was to be a phony 'whitewash' that would just say everyone is innocent; satisfy the world that Nixon had thoroughly investigated the Watergate problem and found nothing wrong.

But as the first man ever to hear the report (Dean read it to me on the telephone from Camp David) I can say his contention was groundless. The report he wrote, which was never completed, became a tighter and tighter noose around John's own neck with each successive page. As he saw what he was producing, it became more and more clear to him that this report should never see the light of day. It was obviously nothing like what he later claimed he was told to prepare.

Up in those mountains of Camp David, Dean was undergoing a personal crisis. He would later say he took a romantic walk in the woods, and there, among the rustling trees, realised it was all over; he had to go to the prosecutors. He was aided in this mounting panic on Sunday when he learned that McCord would be reported in the next morning's *Los Angeles Times* as saying that he, Dean, had had advance knowledge of the break-in.

Even though Dean's report still omitted many details of his own involvement while enmeshing others, and the McCord charge was false, he saw that there was no way to escape.

Nixon didn't want to give him immunity. In several of our Key Biscayne-to-Camp David telephone conversations over that long weekend, Dean made a major case to me for his immunity: it would solve everything, he said. He said he could then go to the prosecutors, tell the full story – and cause no trouble for the White House. But this action was not forthcoming from the Key Biscayne White House. After learning about the *L.A. Times* story, John told me he was getting a lawyer, and putting the *Times* on notice for libel. He argued that his acquiring legal counsel would also be a great help for the White House in dealing with the complexities of the case that were rapidly developing. It later turned out that this was a cover for our consumption to avoid any possible concern that Dean might be striking out on his own, which was exactly what he was doing.

John had another worry at about that time. He was finding that Jeb Magruder was beginning to show signs of not continuing to go along with their agreed story. A Magruder break would be a major disaster for John; it worried him greatly.

It is at this general point that Dean shifted roles from one of the protectors of the President to the protector of himself – a shift of enormous historical consequence.

Nixon's concern over this weekend, as it was throughout, was the same as Dean's had become – to protect himself. The difference was, one was the President, the other a junior member of the staff. All of us, other than Dean, were engaged in the effort to protect the President, and fully expected that he would be too.

On Friday, Nixon flew to Key Biscayne for the weekend to try to sort out all the things he was beginning to learn – along with what he already knew or suspected. Meanwhile, the potentially most dangerous man in the White House, John Dean, was starting to see an alarming prospect for himself: jail.

Having failed in his effort to acquire a Presidential grant of immunity, Dean eventually decided to go to the Justice Department with as much of his information as was necessary to gain himself immunity – and no one had more.

On Saturday, I joined the President at Key Biscayne hoping it would be a quiet weekend with the President holed up at his own house. No sooner had I arrived at my villa across the island from the Presidential compound than the telephone rang summoning me to report for work. I found the President of the United States deep in his easy chair in the study. The omni-present well-worked yellow legal pad was in his hand, and several others scattered on the floor beside him. He was so deeply engrossed in whatever was on the yellow pad he barely noticed or acknowledged my arrival. Accustomed to the procedure, I sat down quietly and waited to see what was going to keep us inside working on this beautiful tropical day. I watched the boats out on the bay – just outside the safety perimeter established by the Secret Service around the Presidential territory – and thought how nice it would be to take a Sunfish out for a sail, or go for a long swim.

Finally the hunched figure grunted, shouted to Manolo for some more coffee, and turned back to the first part of his yellow pad. It was obviously loaded with copious Nixonian notes. That was always bad news because it inevitably meant work for me. There goes the sail.

Resigned to my fate, I opened my own pad, took out my pen, and got ready for the barrage. But this time it wasn't a long list of instructions to be noted down now and carried out later. This time he was ready for immediate action.

'I want you to go in the other room and call Colson and check out two things. First, find out exactly what he discussed with Hunt's lawyer when he met with him in

January. Specifically, I want to know whether he mentioned the President in any way when he talked about clemency for Hunt. And I want to know precisely how Colson raised the point and what he said.' Since I didn't know that Colson had discussed clemency with Hunt's lawyer in January, this order came as a bit of surprise, but I was used to that. It was Nixon's habit to assume that I knew what he was talking about, or that I would somehow find out. He didn't often waste much time explaining to me.

Then running his pen down the page of notes, he said, 'I also want you to ask Chuck what the circumstances were of his phone call to Magruder when Hunt and Liddy came to his office before the break-in – and exactly what he said to Magruder. Don't let him give you the runaround on this one. I have to get the truth.' This was not much of a surprise, because I was aware there had been such a telephone call before the break-in.

I waited for further instructions. Nixon had returned to his intensive concentration on the pad in front of him. Then he looked up and said, 'Go ahead, get hold of Chuck and see what he says.'

I went into the adjacent living room, picked up the always available White House telephone and asked the operator to get me Colson. In a couple of seconds, Chuck was on the line. I asked the questions.

He seemed to be expecting them. He indicated no particular surprise, and had the answers at the tip of his tongue. He had, indeed, discussed clemency with Bittman in January, but only in the most circumspect and cleverly contrived way. He said that Dean and Ehrlichman had told him to see Bittman and assure him that Hunt would be given clemency by the President. But he was too clever to fall into this trap. He just told Bittman that Hunt had no need to be concerned about a long prison term. Christmas was the customary time for Presidential mercy. He let Bittman draw his own conclusions. Not too difficult an exercise.

As to the Magruder telephone call. That was just a quick

call by Chuck to Jeb to tell him to make some decision one way or the other about the Liddy intelligence recommendations. There were no specifics discussed and Chuck neither recommended nor disapproved the plans in any way.

Thus assured by Colson that these two points posed no real problems, at least in his version of them, I returned to the study to report my findings. Waiting again for the President to look up from his studying, I gave him my report. He made some notes on his pad, flipped a few pages, ran his pen down the pad, and then gave me instructions for another fact-finding telephone call.

This procedure was to occupy a good part of the day. I made such calls for information, or recommendations, or both to many people including – in addition to Colson – John Connally, Bill Rogers, Dick Moore, and John Dean. In his customary disciplined lawyer-like fashion, Richard Nixon had prepared a complete summary of the questions and problems that faced him, and then proceeded to hack his way through them, one by one.

The only trouble was that this time the problems did not clear up, they became more profound. The whole thing just didn't come together. He would have to wait for whatever light Dean could shine on the subject in the report he was working on at Camp David.

From this time on, Nixon became more and more deeply involved in the day-to-day attempts to unravel and cope with the Watergate mess. And day by day, the mess became worse and worse.

Nixon spent that weekend working through his check list trying to cover the entire scope of the Watergate case (and keep everyone in line). I kept making notes of the information we gleaned.

Two days later, alone in my villa, I read all those notes, including those from Dean's report. The time was early morning. I sipped hot coffee, and studied the confusing facts. Then for some reason the notes blurred and I found myself thinking, of all things, of John Ehrlichman in Paris in 1969, clutching three long loaves of French bread he was taking back to Jeanne. Nixon included us on his trip to Paris for a visit to General Charles DeGaulle, a man whose 'presence' no words can fully describe. Nixon was fascinated by the tall, hook-nosed French leader who epitomised toughness both in victory and defeat. (He was tougher giving up Algeria than his predecessors were fighting for it.)

Our last day in Paris John and I took a few hours off and went sight-seeing. Ehrlichman insisted that he take some French bread, which he loved, home to his wife – cross-Atlantic delivery. But we couldn't find a bakery open on Sunday. And when we finally did find one near Montmartre, Ehrlichman was so pleased he almost gave a not-so-puritanical pat to the girl who waited on us.

I shook my head. The words on my notes unblurred. Why had I been thinking of Ehrlichman? My eyes fell on one word of one note. Ehrlichman's problem: Ellsberg.

That name haunted me. I hadn't heard of that break-in until a few weeks ago. *Two* break-ins by that crazy Hunt's crew, not one? You might, somehow, even in the tidal wave of press hysteria, explain one break-in. But two?

On the following weekend, a trip was planned to San Clemente for the purpose of meetings with President Thieu of South Vietnam.

On Air Force One, Nixon called Ehrlichman and me up to his cabin for another of the interminable Watergate discussions. By this time John Dean had served notice that he was unable to write the report expected of him. (The report that we later found was partially written, but never delivered.) And Nixon had had no contact with Dean since the meeting on March 22, more than a week earlier, except for a couple of telephone calls from Key Biscayne to Camp David over that weekend.

Nixon had decided, he said, to put Ehrlichman in charge of an all out effort to find out exactly what the facts were about Watergate – and to make a damage assessment so that the problem could be handled once and for all. John was not excited by this prospect. As he thought about it, he recognised that it would put him in a potentially dangerous situation legally. The threat of criminal prosecution had begun to raise its ugly head in connection with the 'aftermath'. His lawyer's antennae told him that he might well find himself in possession of potential evidence in a criminal prosecution and with no right, or desire, to turn that evidence over to the prosecutors.

To avoid this situation, he had a brief memo typed up for the President's signature, ordering him to conduct this fact-finding project for the President. It seemed to me he was going a bit far in his caution – but I was sure wrong on that!

While in San Clemente I was banner-headline news again for what must have been the fifth time in the past six months. As always, the revelation was that I was the arch spymaster of Watergate. Only the identity of the accuser was changed. This time it was Lowell Weicker, Junior Senator from Connecticut, starting off the Ervin Committee proceedings with a bang by announcing that H. R. Haldeman should resign. Apparently, James McCord had told Senate investigators that Haldeman 'had to be aware' of plans to wiretap the D.N.C. Headquarters. (The old 'had to' phrase that followed me throughout the Watergate crisis. Because of my position as Chief-of-Staff, witnesses would always testify that I 'had to' have known something.)

The fact that the most vocal Senator on the Ervin Committee has begun the proceedings by singling me out was dolorous news.

As we boarded the chopper later in the day, Henry nudged me and said gloomily in a deliberately exaggerated accent, 'Dis is de day ve all go down mit Haldeman.'

I laughed, as Henry intended me to. Throughout this period, until its very end, he would be a real friend, supporting and advising me (and once saying he would resign if I were forced to leave).

I didn't take his offer to resign seriously, but I did appreciate his moral support.

8

The next day while I was still in California Senator Ervin apologised, saying there was no evidence to back up Weicker's charges. Soon thereafter I made a startling suggestion to Nixon. I wanted to make a clean breast, once and for all, of my own role in Watergate.

He almost winced. 'What do you mean?'

'I want to step forward publicly and admit responsibility for Segretti, and my part in raising money for the defendants.'

Nixon said nothing, but he looked wary as I continued. 'I've already prepared a statement. It covers every bit of my involvement. I've even thought of the best way to release it for the most impact. I'll give it to Dan Rather at C.B.S., and let him interview me on television for an hour . . . '

But Nixon was holding up his hand. 'No. Bob. Put *that* out of your mind.'

He was no doubt thinking of the one time the White House had 'unleashed' Haldeman on television. In 1970, I was almost totally unknown. This anonymity was seen by some press commentators as 'sinister', so someone suggested that Haldeman should make a public appearance. Arrangements were made with Barbara Walters of N.B.C.'s *Today* Show.

Earlier Nixon had called me into his office. He was in a fighting mood. Two Senators, one of them named Muskie, had recently issued bitter statements against his Vietnam War policy. Nixon said someone has to make the point that when Senators make those speeches, they're aiding and abetting the enemy. And they've got to put it in just those words. What the Senators did not know at the time was that Nixon had Kissinger running a series of completely secret talks with the North Vietnamese. The Senators were saying that if we would just talk, the North Vietnamese were ready to make a deal. In Henry's long series of secret talks, we made substantially more generous offers than the Senators were suggesting. So their statements were creating a very real problem.

Now we were sitting in my office, the room jammed with lights, cameras, and technicians, the fire crackling cheerfully in the fireplace, as filming began.

In the middle of a less-than-cosmic interview, Barbara pursed her lips, unpursed them, and asked me what I thought of the Senators who had attacked Nixon on the war. I snapped to and said, 'Those Senators are consciously aiding and abetting the enemy.'

Quick-minded Barbara jumped on it as soon as she recovered from the shock.

'*Consciously*? You really mean to say *that*?'

I gladly confirmed that I did. They certainly couldn't be accused of doing it unconsciously. 'That's right,' I said. I was told later that the groans in the White House were loud.

Now Nixon must have imagined outspoken Haldeman going on television again. What would I say, if pressed? I suppose Nixon visualised the scene:

Q. 'Do you believe, Mr Haldeman, that the President knew about Watergate?'

A. 'Absolutely. The President is *supposed* to know everything and he *does*. That's why he's a great President.'

Q. 'Absolutely?'

A. (After a pause) 'That's right.'

So Nixon vetoed my idea of a public Watergate statement. I still have it – a long document that spells out every detail of my role in Watergate. What would have happened if I had defied Nixon and insisted on releasing it to the press? I'll never know. But I do know it would have taken the edge off the complaints of 'cover-up', at least as far as I was concerned.

But Nixon was concerned about himself – not me. And even if I were successful in purging myself, I wouldn't do him any good in the process and might well do great harm. As the President of the United States, he was perfectly correct in his concern for self-preservation over any interest in assistance to his staff. He should have worried only about himself – at least foremost about himself. I had absolutely no quarrel with this concept at the time, nor do I now. I firmly believed then, and believe now, that the staff is expendable; the President is not.

I thought about this at the time of the Carter-Lance affair, and cringed when President Carter put his own neck on the line in defending Lance. It was a noble personal gesture, and highly commendable and understandable in those terms. But it was the wrong move for a President of the United States to make.

One piece of very good advice I gave Nixon during Watergate was to urge in the strongest possible terms that he not make any statement of confidence in any individual. Let the facts come out wherever they came out, and let whoever had to take the blame, but don't put your prestige on the line by vouching for anyone – especially when you don't know all the facts and possibilities.

Book VIII

THE BEGINNING OF THE END

1

By mid-April, our efforts were coming to a head and were being brought there by the news received from John Dean on Friday, April 13, (even the calendar had joined the attack), that Hunt was about to blow the whole thing, and would be meeting with the prosecutors on Monday. (A bit of totally false information apparently fed to Dean by the prosecutors.)

The concept on our part at that point was that it was essential that the President take some action openly before the whole case was blown open by the prosecution with all the uncontrollable publicity that would entail. We were trying to develop some form of action or some announcement that the President could make no later than Monday that would put him out in front. In retrospect, this seems a rather petty and unworthy motive, but it was of enormous importance at the time.

This was what was behind the effort to bring Ehrlichman's investigations to a head on Saturday, and especially to try to get either Magruder or Mitchell or both to drop whatever reservations they may have had in telling the true story – thinking they were protecting President Nixon.

This puts a different light on the many interpretations of what was said on the tapes of the meetings of that weekend.

The prosecutors at this time were playing a successful game with Dean. They knew he wanted immunity. But once he had it he might not talk. Their game was to make him believe others were talking: that they didn't need his information enough to grant immunity. He would then have to produce even more evidence to convince them.

Dean's quest for immunity was in vain. Step after step the prosecutors double-crossed him. He first offered up

Haldeman and Ehrlichman. Immunity, which he had been expecting, didn't materialise. In desperation, he then implicated the President – and found, to his dismay, that even then the prosecutors would not grant him immunity.

Congress later proffered a limited immunity for his testimony before the Ervin Committee, but that did not save him from the prosecutors. Dean had been shafted.

All along the prosecutors tricked him. For example, in the early stages they lied and told him that Gordon Liddy was talking. Later, they said that Hunt was about to blow. Then they called Dean's lawyer on April 15 with even worse news: Magruder was talking. And this was true. (Another of the power blocs, the bureaucracy, was moving in hard and fast, trying to get out in front of the Congressional hearings. In fact, throughout this stage, the Congress, press, and bureaucracy, far from conspiring together to overthrow the President, were avidly competing with each other for the lead in the chase.)

Dean admits he panicked. He knew he had to raise the stakes if he was ever to earn immunity. So he raced to his lawyer's office, and plunked a copy of the Huston Report on his desk. The report was labelled: TOP SECRET.

It looked very impressive. It *was* very impressive. But Dean had more. Impulsively, he told his lawyer about the Ellsberg break-in.

Bullseye! The lawyer reeled. After he regained his equilibrium, he reached for the telephone to call the prosecutors.

On April 14, Henry Petersen heard for the first time from the prosecutors on his staff about Dean's earlier revelations. (Once again Dean had been shafted. He had obtained a pledge of secrecy from the prosecutors as far as Petersen was concerned because he feared Nixon would learn that he was talking.)

Petersen moved swiftly that very night. At one a.m. he met with Attorney General Kleindienst and conferred until 5 a.m. They decided they had to confront the President immediately with the information they had received from Dean and Magruder. And they agreed that they had to recommend that the President remove Haldeman and Ehrlichman from his staff because the indications were that, at best, we would be an extreme embarrassment to the President when the facts came out and, at worst, we might even be indicted.

From Petersen's viewpoint, as the prosecutor, it would be much easier to extend the investigation to Haldeman and Ehrlichman if they were no longer under the shadow of the President – and especially so if they had been dismissed from the White House staff. He didn't have any solid basis for making criminal charges against us at this point, but he did have Dean's allegations. His problem now was to try to develop corroboration.

On Sunday, April 15, Petersen told Nixon that even though he couldn't guarantee that criminal indictments would be brought against Haldeman and Ehrlichman, he *could* guarantee that 'these people are going to be a source of vast embarrassment to the Presidency'.

To Petersen's surprise, Nixon ' . . . exhibited a lack of shock. Here I was recommending that two people whom he had known and worked with for years be dismissed. I would have been cussing and fuming. But the President was calm and collected.'

(A note for Watergate buffs. It's not generally known that Kleindienst and Petersen intended to start a private law firm together – if Watergate hadn't happened. What bearing this did or did not have on Petersen's actions I don't know. But I will say that while it is the conventional wisdom to blast Petersen for his co-operation with Nixon – and indeed there was co-operation – he never has been looked upon as a friend by anyone below Nixon on the White House staff, except that he was very close to John Dean throughout. In fact, his major suggestion at the Sunday Oval Office conference was that Haldeman and Ehrlichman should be fired, and John Dean retained.)

Petersen was on target when he noticed Nixon was calm at the mention of the firing of his two top aides. What *did* shock Nixon at that meeting was the revelation that Dean was apparently not holding back anything from the prosecutors – and that could include evidence of Dean's meetings with Nixon. From then until the day he resigned, Nixon would be devoted solely to his own survival – and he acted to that end.

After the alarming meeting with Petersen, Nixon joined his old friend, Bebe Rebozo, for a relaxing supper cruise down the Potomac on the Presidential yacht, *Sequoia.* When he returned he met with Ehrlichman and me in the E.O.B. office at 7.00 Sunday evening.

'Well,' he said, 'Petersen wants you both out. Says the evidence that Dean and Magruder are giving the prosecutors implicates you both so much you're an embarrassment to the President.'

I was startled. Petersen felt we should leave? On the basis of what Dean and Magruder had told him? And Petersen was the chief criminal prosecutor at the Justice Department.

Ehrlichman asked what evidence Petersen had. Two thoughts flashed through my mind at that moment: one, somehow the President must survive this tragic chain of events.

Two, on a more personal and less noble basis, I had already faced the fact that the problems arising out of Watergate might make it necessary for me to leave the White House. I had told the President very sincerely that I was fully prepared to leave at anytime he felt it was in his interest for me to do so. But I must confess that I did not think that would really ever become the case. I had not faced up to the idea that I actually might be forced out; that I wouldn't be a part of the second term for which I had held such great hopes.

Now I was confronted with that very real possibility. And it hurt. It was almost impossible to imagine going back to the dull routine of private life – even under the best of circumstances – and certainly not under these circumstances.

I could hardly concentrate on the conversation. But gradually my mind shifted into clear focus. My job was political and therefore it entailed political risk. If I had to sacrifice myself to save the man who had brought me here, I would do it.

Nixon said, 'I told them I'm not going to do anything so drastic until I have some real proof. I will accept Petersen's legal advice, but not his political or P.R. judgement – and so far this is just a political P.R. matter. He says you're an embarrassment, but not necessarily criminally liable.'

'Mr President,' I said, 'if you think it over and agree with Petersen, I'll resign.'

But Ehrlichman said, 'Well, now, hold it. What about brother Dean?'

'What do you mean?'

'He's staying right here on the job, grabbing every document in sight by day, and talking to the prosecutors by night. The first thing to do is to get him out of here – not us.'

But, strangely, Nixon didn't agree. 'Uh, now on that, uh . . . ' he paused. 'I can't fire Dean. I can't risk his going after the President.'

Ehrlichman said, vehemently, 'Well, you certainly can't risk his bouncing around here, playing his little game, tiptoeing through the files gathering ammunition. You've got to persuade him to resign or take a leave of absence – or else fire him – or at least suspend him from his regular duties and order him to work at home and stay out of the office. That will at least close off some access to files and people. Lord only knows what he's doing in here now.'

John saw he wasn't getting very far with this line – except that there was a glimmer of reaction at the thought of the necessity for keeping Dean away from the files.

Ehrlichman said, 'Maybe he'll resign voluntarily. Why don't I try my hand at a little resignation note and see whether he'll apply a pen to it.'

Then we all started to go over, once more, the details of Watergate, this tragedy that was overwhelming us so swiftly. Nixon asked Ehrlichman what had been found in Hunt's safe after the break-in. Ehrlichman said, 'We turned all the material over to Gray.' He explained Dean's strategy of handing the evidence to F.B.I. Director Gray so that if anyone asked they could always say they gave the evidence to the F.B.I.

But Nixon pressed him. 'What did Gray do with it?'

Ehrlichman said, 'Let me call him and see.'

Even with all that had happened, Ehrlichman was still jaunty when he made that phone call. I heard him ask Gray what he had done with the material from Hunt's safe. Then, to my amazement, he said nothing at all when he received the answer. Instead, almost as if dazed, he hung up the telephone, then stood staring at the wall.

'What did he say?' I asked.

Ehrlichman turned to us. 'Gray told me not to tell anyone we had turned over the Hunt papers to him.'

'Why not?'

'He burned them. In his backyard.'

Silence in the room. Nixon and I looked at each other. The significance of the news didn't escape us. The spectacle of the F.B.I. Director destroying Watergate evidence would be a bombshell (as it later proved to be). But for the moment we were more concerned about Ehrlichman. He looked so shattered that we spent the next minutes trying to buoy his morale. After all, he hadn't told the F.B.I. Director to destroy the evidence – Gray had done that on his own. And, besides, the whole idea was Dean's, not Ehrlichman's. But Ehrlichman couldn't be placated. 'It was done in my office. I'm implicated.' He paused. 'Let me call him again.'

Maybe he telephoned Gray again hoping he would hear that it was a joke. I don't know. But no facts changed on that call. Gray had still burned the papers. This time when Ehrlichman hung up, he left his hand on the phone as he looked at us, and said, 'That does it. I'm dead.'

The next morning Dean predictably refused to sign the letter of resignation unless Ehrlichman and Haldeman resigned at the same time, and he told Nixon, delicately yet ominously, that he should not leave unless we left also.

Nixon: 'You don't want to go if they stay?'

Dean: 'There is a problem for you of the scapegoat theory.'

From that moment on, Nixon knew that Dean was a supremely dangerous enemy because of those Oval Office meetings in which Nixon himself – not Haldeman, Ehrlichman, or Mitchell – had made cover-up statements about money and clemency.

Nixon has referred to the next fourteen days as the pivotal time in Watergate. He later implied on television that if he had fired Ehrlichman and me right away he would have come out of Watergate clean. ('I couldn't be a butcher.') Even to put these words on paper exposes the unreality of his concept. What two weeks' difference in time would have meant is zero. Firing us two weeks earlier than he did would have done nothing to alter his culpability in the slightest.

The President was on more solid ground when he stated, in private remarks he made to me years later, that the real turning point of Watergate was his refusal to grant Dean immunity on April 17.

In his April 17 statement, Nixon announced that after 'serious charges' were brought to his attention on March 21, he had ordered a new investigation that 'has produced major developments . . . in finding the truth' about the break-in. He stated that White House personnel would appear before the Ervin Committee, but with the right to assert executive privilege. Present or former high Administration officials could not be granted immunity. This caused Dean to escalate his earlier gentle private reference about scapegoats to a direct public challenge.

That decision on immunity can certainly be viewed, as it is by Nixon, as his major tactical error. If Dean had been granted immunity, he wouldn't have had to reach so high to try to obtain it, and Nixon would never have been dragged in.

What Nixon told me privately, at the time, was that there was a *reason* for not granting Dean immunity. Nixon felt that without immunity Dean would fear the power of the President, because the President was the only man who could grant him clemency. And while the prosecutors were playing their little cat-and-mouse game with Dean, they did not want him granted immunity – since that would give away their main bait.

Earlier I said that two trials and two hearings would all have twist-endings that would strike with devastating timing at Nixon. Of the two trials, the first, the Watergate trial, had already produced its surprise: McCord's letter. Now the Ellsberg trial was brewing another twist. And the Gray hearing, which had temporarily ended, would produce an aftershock based on the testimony. Shock and aftershock would strike in dramatic succession as Nixon fought out his course in the embattled White House, torn between his growing conviction that he had to toss his two lieutenants overboard and his knowledge that he needed us as a buffer.

Later that day, April 17, Petersen's recommendation was supported by Bill Rogers, who was acting as an informal counsel to the President. He felt that we should resign – or take a leave of absence. And from then on the question was not *whether* we should leave, but by which of these means, and when. That was the day Ehrlichman and I retained joint legal counsel to help us with our upcoming Grand Jury and Ervin Committee appearances, which we believed would clear us.

According to Nixon, Kleindienst also had told him, 'Just the fact that both of these clowns [Dean and Magruder] had implicated them, they ought to resign. They haven't served you well, Mr President,' and that sort of thing. Both Petersen and Kleindienst said, 'Make them resign, resign, resign.' (When the time came, Kleindienst was required to resign also.)

Ehrlichman said, 'I think that if we turned up in this crazy information – junk – even though we are not charged with a crime in the ultimate sense – I could write you a letter and say that due to these charges that, obviously, I don't want to impair your situation and I am going to take a leave.'

Ehrlichman added wistfully, 'One concession that I would ask is that people on leave be considered for use of Camp David occasionally.'

The President, confronted with an awkward personal situation, started to gild the lily. According to him, there would be work for us in the Nixon Foundation. 'The Foundation is going to be a hell of a big thing, It's bound to be. These first four years are terribly important and so forth. After all, you understand, looking down the road . . . if you are indicted and tried and found innocent, it washes away.' But Ehrlichman saw something gloomier down the road: the loss of his licence to practise law. I soothed him with, 'You can always handle traffic cases.'

He didn't smile. 'Well, I'm not too pleased with the traffic cases.'

2

By April 19 the situation had worsened. Nixon said, 'It just irritates me when people like Garment [Leonard Garment, a Presidential adviser] and others come in here and say, the hell with people, the Presidency is bigger, and so forth.' Then he moved smoothly to, 'Though looking at it coldly from a P.R. standpoint, from your standpoint . . . let's not just let the day come that, uh, when, uh, the Grand Jury . . . gives us twelve hours' notice.'

What he meant was that if he kept us on, the Grand Jury might indict us, which would look worse for him, of course, than if he had cleaned house himself. The same approach he had taken earlier with respect to Colson.

Then Nixon went on about the Ellsberg case.

PRESIDENT: Well, I can get hold of Petersen. I think the least I could do is to get him in and lay out this whole business . . . I'm gonna level about the National Security study. What I'm going to say is, you know the Bureau. You know that Edgar [Hoover] had very, very close ties with the Marx people. [He] didn't want to investigate the Ellsberg thing. Under the circumstances we had no choice but to go ahead and do it in the White House. We did our best and finally Hoover did take over the case by Mitchell's direct orders.

EHRLICHMAN: You will find in the file an admonition to Hoover from here, and I don't know if it was from you personally or me or Krogh . . . that this was to be handled as a principal case. [Hoover] had laid back for months and months and now refused to let his agents get into it.

PRESIDENT: That's right, so we couldn't use the agents . . .

EHRLICHMAN: Well, he was very tender about how agents would be used in this case . . . And so, certain rather routine investigatory efforts were conducted from here.

I like that, 'certain rather routine investigatory efforts . . . ' But Nixon didn't pause to admire Ehrlichman's phrase-making artistry. 'That's right, because it involved national security . . . ' But Ehrlichman halted the enthusiasm, 'This one was apparently in excess.' But he modified that by saying that nevertheless, 'in the context of how the Bureau works, they might have done the same damn thing.'

Nixon talked about Petersen's advice that Haldeman and Ehrlichman must go. He suggested a leave of absence, not a resignation.

EHRLICHMAN: Sure. I would hope that we can let [our lawyers] have a run at this idea today.

PRESIDENT: Oh, I didn't mean to do it [resign] today, this morning. I'm saying that I don't want it to catch up with us, maybe like tomorrow night, or something.

HALDEMAN: Henry [Kissinger] called this morning to make his point to me, what his view was. He makes basically the same point that if we are on a path where we are going to be nibbled to death, or in one stroke . . . we ultimately are on a path of destruction – just what you're saying.

PRESIDENT: Yeah.

HALDEMAN: Henry said you're getting to the point where you have to go anyway, that we should move ahead of that on a positive basis and fight it externally. But then he said, 'Don't take that step until you're totally convinced that the other result is inevitable. As long as there is still a chance that you can still stay ahead of the other, the White House is gonna be badly hurt.' I think this is true, although, maybe I'm not being objective. I think the President is going to be badly hurt by our stepping out.

And it's then I uttered a statement which, considering it came from me at that time and place, I believe is a classic. 'But the point is, all through all of that, I did not know, and you did not know, and I don't know today, and I don't believe you do really, *what happened* in the Watergate case.'

Nixon and Ehrlichman both agreed, but Nixon said nothing when I added a possible clue: 'I still don't know where Colson is yet. I think that remains to be seen.'

Both of us could see the pressure was getting to Nixon – he looked wan. Ehrlichman suggested to Nixon that maybe he should spend a week in Florida and not take calls, just delegate Shultz or Kissinger, 'take the lid off and don't read the . . . '

PRESIDENT: Don't worry, I don't read the papers.

EHRLICHMAN: Well, I mean . . . Bebe will say the Watergate did this and that today . . .

Nixon, always edgy when Bebe was mentioned by his

associates, quickly cut in, 'Bebe doesn't do that.' Only to be floored by Ehrlichman's famed sarcasm, 'O.K., *great guy*.'

Nixon came back to our resignations. He sensed a problem I hadn't detailed yet. Who could he get to replace us? 'There ain't anybody around here to do this son-of-a-bitching thing. It's hard to find anybody that wasn't involved. They even asked Rose about getting money for these people.'

This was news, then and now. Dean never mentioned any involvement of Rose Mary Woods in the fund raising.

The President flew off to Florida without me for one of the few times since I had been Chief-of-Staff. He had offered Ehrlichman and me the use of Camp David for the Easter weekend since we had to use the time in research for our lawyers.

As was often the case our aides and their wives joined us. We were blessed with beautiful weather that weekend. There was a determined effort to enjoy the holiday as if no great events – such as our precipitous ejections – were on the horizon. Except we spent all our time going through files.

John Ehrlichman was still certain that somehow or other he would weather the storm and stay on. I had graver doubts about myself. The press had built me up to such an extent that because of the public image alone I had become a burden to Nixon. Further, of course, my involvement in Watergate matters appeared then to be much more direct than Ehrlichman's.

I spent some of that weekend telephoning senior advisers I trusted: Henry Kissinger, John Connally, Bill Rogers. Their message was that on the one hand it would be good for the President's 'public relations' if I left, but on the other hand, the President would be losing a 'buffer'. I did not sense any clear, strong or unanimous view that I should leave – just deep concern.

When I called my attorneys to discuss the problem, they said that if I did go, I should *not* resign. 'That's a confession of guilt. Take an indefinite leave of absence because that implies you're merely removing yourself from active affairs while your case is investigated. It also implies that you expect to be adjudged innocent and return to service.' I did expect to be found innocent, but by this time I was starting to realise I would probably never return to the White House.

In the midst of these depressing telephone calls, our families enjoyed the sun at Camp David. Ehrlichman and I stood in front of the very tulips Nixon would point to a week later as he told us we had to resign, rather than letting us take the leave of absence we desired. I have a picture of Ehrlichman and myself on that weekend. Symbolically, we were standing with our backs to the terrace from which Nixon spoke.

On Easter Sunday, Larry Higby aware of the heavy burden of the weekend had moved heaven and earth to furnish us with a special treat: stone crabs, one of my favourite dishes. We gathered around the dining table on our last day together in that rustic retreat in the Catoctin Mountains. As I dipped a chunk of crab into the melted butter, Higby reminded me of something. 'The last time we had a stone crab dinner was June 17, 1972, remember? We had just heard of the break-in.'

I remembered.

3

One of my functions as chief assistant to the President was to bring in all opposing views on the problem *in toto.* When we returned to the White House Monday, I presented one such view in detail to Nixon. It was inimical to me.

John Connally, whose advice Nixon valued highly (Nixon felt Connally was the only politician as tough as himself) had said that I shouldn't look at my option of resigning from a legal standpoint, but as a P.R. problem and, from a P.R. viewpoint, I should go.

Connally warned me of catastrophic damage to myself. As he put it, 'If you resign, an assumption will be immediately made by the public that you're guilty.' (He was right.) He also said that on the short-term basis, 'There's an enormous increase in vulnerability for you if you get out, especially against the deliberate lying.'

The President said that he had talked to the prosecutors again and they believed that 'for the sake of the Presidency, uh, uh, you should step out . . . ' And then Ehrlichman nailed him with a right cross. 'Now let me just spin something out for you . . . I think it's entirely conceivable that if Dean is totally out of control, and if matters are not handled adroitly, that you could get a resolution of *impeachment*.'

The President looked absolutely stunned. This was the first time the grim word impeachment had ever entered our conversations. Ehrlichman pounded ahead, 'I don't know if you've thought of this or not, but I got to thinking about it last night. On the ground that you've committed a crime . . . and that there is no other legal process available to the United States people other than impeachment. Otherwise, you have immunity from prosecution.'

I can say that Nixon never recovered from this statement. Everything he did and said during the last days we were with him harked back to Ehrlichman's prophetic remark about impeachment. He would refer to it over and over again. The unthinkable had been uttered.

And so saying, Ehrlichman unleashed another sensation in the E.O.B. office. Nixon should use the top secret White House tapes as a defence. I was startled. At that point, I thought Ehrlichman didn't even know about the tapes. This is how Ehrlichman's historic suggestion that we use the tapes evolved:

> I don't know what you may have talked about with Dean in those ten or twelve hours you spent there in

> the months of February and March . . . but you get down to a point where you've got John Dean prancing in there and saying 'The President said this, and the President said that', and having someone on your behalf come back and say, 'No, the President didn't say that,' and that's ridiculous. So you get a kind of credibility thing nonetheless . . . Dean's very busy dredging up corroborating evidence and looking for documentation, taking statements from people . . . based on . . . those conversations. And I think, really, the only way that I know to make a judgement on this is for *you to listen to your tapes* and see what actually was said then, or maybe for Bob to do it, or somebody. See what was said there. And then analyse how big a threat that is.

Nixon was intrigued but worried about what was on that March 21 tape. 'We've got the problem when Dean made his cancer on the Presidency speech, he could have discussed the problem of these defendants and, you know what I mean, whether I said anything which would have led him to believe that he could pay them off.'

I said, 'Let's not worry about it. It's either there or it isn't. Let's listen to it.'

Nixon said, worriedly, 'And if it *is* there. Then we have to play it in terms of, I was having to find out what its implications were.' But he was warming to the idea of using the tapes. 'It's certainly important that you go back and get the tapes of everything we had with Dean – and see what the hell has been discussed. Before I meet with Petersen tonight I want to know what the damn tapes are. Now the earlier tapes I am sure dealt almost exclusively with executive privilege.'

A little later Nixon blurted out his real worry about the March 21 tape: 'You remember my saying to Dean, well look, for Christ's sake, "take care of him." Be sure the son-of-a-bitch won't talk.'

Ehrlichman said Dean had approached him and me to raise money for the defendants months before.

Nixon said, 'Dean wanted the money for hush here again?'

But Ehrlichman said that wasn't so. 'Not that early. I think they [the defendants] had monumental attorney problems and were legitimately concerned about how to hire counsel for these guys.'

'For example,' I said, 'after they got counsel, counsel was walking off. Some lawyer . . . it was one of theirs, Hunt's lawyer, somebody, ran into our attorney on the street and said "the son-of-a-bitch still owes me $100,000".'

And Ehrlichman said, 'He's been promised cash payment in full and only received $2500.'

But again Nixon zeroed in on March 21 and the problem of his own guilt. 'What would you fellows answer for example if Dean testifies that there *was* a discussion in which I said Hunt's lawyers had to get paid off.'

Ehrlichman (getting exasperated), 'Hey, before you make trouble on that, let's see what the tapes do.'

We finally moved Nixon off his central concern and got him to talk about something else for a change – us.

Ehrlichman said, 'Well, I come down to the fact that Bob was different from me. And that's a self-serving kind of a suggestion but it keeps coming back to me that this treatment of Haldeman and Ehrlichman is not really taking into account the different press pictures in which we find ourselves at the moment.'

He meant that Haldeman was pictured over and over again as the number one Watergate mastermind. Ehrlichman was not, yet we were being treated as a unit. I said, 'I agree.'

Ehrlichman pressed on, 'I stand at the moment with all kinds of press calling my office saying, "Gee, why does he even have a lawyer?"'

But Nixon pointed out another problem if Ehrlichman wanted to be treated separately from me. We both had the same lawyer. We had felt it was a good idea because we could share legal fees if necessary; and we both wanted John Wilson, one of the great lawyers in Washington. (In the early days, Wilson and his partner, Frank Strickler, worked for no fee at all.) But Ehrlichman shook off that problem. 'As far as the perception of my situation, they don't really know that Dean has *anything* on me, and as a matter of fact the leaks out of the prosecutors' office have downplayed my involvement.'

He didn't know at that time that Dean had revealed Hunt's and Liddy's roles in the Ellsberg break-in to the prosecutors.

He concluded, 'I'm stuck with this dilemma. If Bob and I both take a leave of absence Monday, Tuesday morning, I gotta start answering questions. What do I say? "Well, there's this fellow [Dean] and he says this and that about me and this is true . . ." '

Nixon still didn't get the drift. 'Let me ask you this, then. You suggest *nobody* take a leave then.'

Ehrlichman laid it on the line with a bang. 'I suggest you fire Dean and that Bob take a leave and that I be . . . *prepared to* take a leave the minute the charges surface.'

Ehrlichman later asked what would happen if he had to resign? 'Then I have to get a job. I have to go to work . . . practising law . . . I know immediately where I can go to a relatively good paying job. You wouldn't be terribly happy with it, and I wouldn't be terribly happy with it. But it would be a kinda any-port-in-a-storm situation at that point.'

And it was then Nixon made his mysterious money offer. 'Let me ask you this, to be quite candid. Is there any way you can use *cash*?'

Ehrlichman and I looked at each other. Here we were being drummed out of office for supposed hanky-panky concerning cash paid to the defendants and now the President was offering *us* cash.

We both said, 'I don't think so.'

But Nixon pressed on with the suggestion. 'There's a few, not much. As much I think as 200 [thousand dollars] available in '74 campaign funds already.'

I said, 'That compounds the problem. That really does.'

4

I listened to the March 21 tape on Wednesday, April 25. The first man ever to hear the secret tapes which would one day fascinate the nation. It was agonising work. Nixon's voice was muffled, especially when he sat back in his chair and placed his feet on the desk. The placing of the feet sounded like thunder.

At 4.40 p.m. I was back in the Oval Office to report on the March 21 tape. 'Well, that is hard work. Good God! It's amazing. It works awfully well . . . '

PRESIDENT: Good.

HALDEMAN: . . . in picking up the guest. It doesn't pick you up well. The mike must be set on the side of the desk or something.

PRESIDENT: Could you get them [the guests] both?

HALDEMAN: Yes, on either side of your desk.

PRESIDENT: Very good.

HALDEMAN: And, uh, it's hard as hell to hear you, so you gotta keep looking back and reworking.

PRESIDENT: It's pretty frustrating but uh . . .

HALDEMAN: It's, it's in there. This is the meeting in the morning of March 21.

I then recounted from my notes what had been said at the March 21 meeting. In the notes were these words: 'Then you said, "Suppose you got the money and had a way to handle it. It would seem to me that would be worthwhile but we'd still have the problem of Hunt's clemency." And you said. "Not before the '74 election for sure." Dean said, "It may further involve you in this," and you said, "Yes – and it's wrong." '

The recitation took more than thirty minutes. Afterwards Nixon looked disturbed. I tried to cheer him up.

'O.K. You're drawing Dean out on what he's talking about and the conclusion in fact was, don't do it. You can't do it.'

But Nixon was gloomy, 'It's not a good story . . . I said a million dollars. With a million dollars you could handle it . . . That's an incriminating thing.' Then the President expressed the first note of worry about the possibility of Dean having been 'wired' when he entered the Oval Office that day. 'I hope to God he didn't have a recorder in his pocket.'

He asked me to go over the key parts again and I did, repeating the words about clemency ' " not before the '74 election for sure". Dean said, "It may further involve you in this." You said, "Yes – and it's wrong." '

Nixon clung to that word 'wrong' like a drowning man in a hurricane. 'That's not bad.'

At this time I had listened to about three-fourths of the tape. Nixon said, 'I may have said to Dean *later* . . . "do what you can do on it".'

'Well, you maybe did. I don't think you did.'

Then I told Nixon something that concerned me. 'Let me tell you one bothersome thing in that. I checked the log, when the four of us met in here with you [on March 22] . . . Dean and Mitchell were in for five minutes *longer* than Ehrlichman and I were.'

Nixon caught the drift instantly. 'I discussed money with Mitchell? Never.'

'O.K.,' I replied.

The President (sharply), 'Don't worry about that log.'

But I persisted, ' . . . I can't imagine that you didn't *do* something to follow up on the money. Because you wouldn't just let something like that drop. You'd have satisfied yourself in some way that something was happening on that.'

But Nixon obviously wanted me off that delicate subject. He came back to the key passages in the March 21 tape – that tape which Dean could use to nail him – and it was apparent he was becoming confused himself.

PRESIDENT: At this point we discussed raising the money . . . I said, 'That's wrong,' didn't I? Oh, or wrong on clemency.

(By then he had me confused.)

HALDEMAN: No, you said getting the money was wrong. You wouldn't have said clemency was wrong. I think you felt you had some justification for Hunt.

PRESIDENT: Right.

HALDEMAN: Because of his family, and Hunt . . . and all of the people [the Watergate burglars]. They are all being screwed on an equity basis.

PRESIDENT: At least we didn't *furnish* any money, thank God.

HALDEMAN: Right.

PRESIDENT: Remember I told you later that I could get $100,000.

HALDEMAN: That rings a bell . . . You talked about Rose having some money or something. I remember that.

I don't remember now exactly what I meant about Rose having some money. Nixon had mentioned $200,000 for Ehrlichman and me if we resigned, but Rose's name wasn't mentioned then. Nixon must have told me about it at another time. A few months later when Haig was going over the evidence, one of the main things he worried about was, as he told me, 'the mention of Rose and some assets on the tapes.'

The more Nixon thought about that March 21 conversation, the gloomier he became. What preyed on his mind was Ehrlichman's bold statement about potential impeachment. I tried to buck him up again. I said, 'Agnew for . . . President. Even your worst enemies don't want to do that . . . John is only raising that [impeachment] as an outside possibility . . . that's something he just spun out last night. I hadn't heard his story on that.'

The President said, 'Well I gotta look at it as a possibility.' I told him that Ehrlichman and I were prepared to go out . . . Nixon said, ' . . . on the sword,' and I replied 'If it's the right thing to do.'

Nixon responded: 'Let me say, it's going to be you or Ehrlichman . . . I have got to put the wagons up around the President on this particular conversation [March 21].' He brooded, 'I just wonder if that son-of-a-bitch had a recorder on him. I didn't notice any, but I wasn't looking.'

I told him it was 'almost inconceivable that the guy would try that. After all, he was only coming in to tell you that there was a problem.' Then I mentioned another thing that had bothered me in that March 21 conversation. The way Nixon had jumped on the money angle with such ferocity and relentlessness that both Dean and I were amazed. 'Dean wasn't expecting you to solve it that way. I think you probably surprised him enormously by even raising this point.'

Nixon looked startled. His Chief-of-Staff was being unusually prickly today. He said, 'What?'

HALDEMAN: You know, when you said, 'We could get the money,' I think that's the *last* thing he expected you to say.

PRESIDENT [Angrily:] What did he expect me to say. We *can't* do it?

I explained that Dean was merely spelling out all of the problems of every kind on a general list . . . the 'soft spots'. And raising money for Hunt was just *one* of the problems. I would have gone on to say that both Dean and I saw something damned *peculiar* in Nixon's emphasis on the money, but at that point Nixon was informed that 'Mr Petersen's across the street. Did you want to see him here or over at the Oval Office.'

Nixon said the Oval Office.

5

I left to go home, and had just walked into the kitchen when I found the day was far from over. At 6.57 the telephone rang. It was the President. The fuse to more dynamite was burning. Nixon had just discovered that Dean had told the prosecutors about the Ellsberg break-in. And Kleindienst had insisted on sending a statement to the Ellsberg judge revealing that the break-in had taken place. It could mean a mistrial, and more black newspaper coverage, if the judge released that statement publicly.

Nixon said, 'They have sent that out to the prosecutor . . . If they didn't put it out they'd say why did you *withhold* it from the Ellsberg case? It will not blow the Ellsberg case in Petersen's opinion. I think that was gonna come out anyway, don't you feel so?'

'Probably.' Then I added, thinking of the way the newspapers would play the Ellsberg break-in on top of the Watergate affair, 'It adds confusion to the whole thing.' Nixon responded, 'Yeah, the Watergate buggers try to knock over Ellsberg's psychiatrist.'

Nixon asked me to call Ehrlichman and tell him the unhappy news. He tried to soften it, 'What else could I tell Kleindienst? Forget it? Get my point? I just couldn't do that.'

Then Nixon revealed he was already building up the fortifications on his other problem, the March 21 conversation. 'I levelled with Petersen on all the conversations that we had, and I said, "Now I want you to know this . . . and we'll not be blackmailed on it. We didn't do anything about raising money for Hunt's last demand. On March 21 I started my own investigation." And that's our line there, I think.' He paused. 'Incidentally I think that should be just between you and me.'

He then told me he didn't even want Ehrlichman to

know the 'contents' of that March 21 tape that I had heard. Nixon said, 'As far as that conversation goes, it's one that I had and that you had.'

'Did it bother Petersen?'

Nixon laughed. 'Everything bothers him. But he told me that Dean has always indicated he won't lie for that Goddamn Ehrlichman, but he will, of course, defend the President, da da da da, and I said, well, we'll see. But let me say I made damn clear to Petersen that if I have these fellows [Ehrlichman and Haldeman] resign, I'm in effect saying, "I judge them guilty." I said, "If I do that, I have the right to do it with Dean, too." '

Then he said, 'My own belief at this point is that, for your and John's information, we just gotta stand God-damn firm today, tomorrow, Friday, the weekend. You know what I mean?'

A short-term reprieve; Haldeman survives until Monday. Nixon said that if the Ellsberg thing blew, that was all right because it was 'gonna come out anyway. Whatever John Dean knows is gonna come out, Bob.'

'That's right,' I said.

And now Nixon made a comment which, in the history of the tapes, is of significance. A couple of weeks ago, he had thought about destroying the tapes. Now he said, 'But, incidentally, you know, I always wondered about that taping equipment, but *I'm damn glad we have it, aren't you*?'

I had heard that Dean had a 'big bomb' he was going to explode for the prosecutors. 'Wasn't Petersen supposed to get some big threat from Dean or something?' I asked.

Nixon said, 'I think it's this March 21 conversation, don't you? What else could it be?' He stopped, then added, 'The only problem is to handle Dean in such a way that he doesn't become a totally implacable enemy. I've treated him decently, more decently than he deserves.'

But Nixon's self-satisfaction didn't last long. 'On the other hand, he may become totally intractable. And if he does, you're gonna have one hell of a pissing contest.' In the same dour mood he returned again to Ehrlichman's thunderbolt about impeachment. 'I was just thinking a little bit more about the impeachment thing. I don't see the Senate or any Senators starting an impeachment of the President based on the word of John Dean . . . Except he could have recorded his conversation, you know . . . I can't believe that he could have walked in there with a tape recorder that day because – I'm not trying to do wishful thinking – but on that particular day, he wasn't really out to get the President.'

I attempted to get him off the subject, but no luck. Nixon said, 'Unless he tape-records every . . . does he [he was pleading for reassurance], does he tape-record *everything*?'

'No. No.'

'Does he, you're sure of that?'

'No, I'm not *sure* of it,' I replied, 'but I just never had any reason to believe that he did.'

Nixon now bucked himself up. 'Let me say that this is April 25. We can figure that this day is the day we start up. Seriously, I don't think I'm being Pollyanna-ish about it . . . ' (That was a line I was to hear frequently over the next year.) And he got back to the questioning of our resignation vs. leave of absence. We wanted the leave of absence. 'You know, when you really stop to think of it, in terms of this whole thing, the line of everybody, Connally, Rogers, *et al.* I mean the resignation line, that is so terribly *attractive* in terms of a couple of days [laughs].'

'That's right.'

'You know what I mean . . . now the President's finally started off with a new team. But then for Christ's sake, something else blows, hah?'

'That's right,' I said.

Nixon said, however, that if we stayed on and went down to the Grand Jury, he had a problem. The press would say, 'Rather than the President cleaning house, the Grand Jury did.'

One minute later Nixon called Ehrlichman and informed him that the 'piece of paper' on the Ellsberg case had been sent to Judge Matthew Byrne. Ehrlichman must have heard this out, glumly. It was the worst possible news for him.

No rest for John. It must have seemed to Ehrlichman that Nixon had hardly hung up before he telephoned again. He had talked to Kleindienst in the interim. Nixon said he had put pressure on Kleindienst to 'do everything you can to see that this is not something that comes out publicly.'

Knowing Ehrlichman's sarcasm and his confidence in Kleindienst, I can imagine the tone of his one word answer, 'Great!'

'I don't know whether it'll work or not,' Nixon said. He told Ehrlichman he wanted him to think about the leave of absence business. 'The point is the leave of absence doesn't convict anybody.'

Ehrlichman saw he was in trouble, but blamed it on me, not Ellsberg. 'I tell you, I made a mistake in joining with Bob in retaining counsel . . . '

'I think you're right. Yeah, because your case is different from his. You better change pretty fast,' Nixon advised.

'If I could, figure out some way of getting a little separation, I think it's wise to do so.'

Nixon couldn't agree more. 'You've got to do it, you've gotta do it. Because John, as you know I love you both but boy, uh, staying together, you're in a hell of a lot more trouble than if you go separately. I know your situation, and of course Bob's is more difficult.'

Ehrlichman said that his participation in the cover-up was 'very perfunctory' in the whole chain of circumstances. He had given his approval for Kalmback to raise funds, period. But Nixon reminded him of the Ellsberg problem, which was Ehrlichman all the way. Nixon once again apologised to Ehrlichman for 'sending the paper out to Byrne. I didn't have any choice. Kleindienst came in and said, "I've got to do this, Mr President. I'm sitting on this thing and it's volcanic." '

'I could have said, "Dick, that's National Security. Don't pass it on.' But if I do it, Dean's got another hammer at our heads.'

Then Nixon got a nasty surprise. While talking about the Ellsberg break-in he told Ehrlichman that 'Dean probably will say "I was working on the Ellsberg break-in under Ehrlichman's direction." Right? Is that what he'll say?'

Ehrlichman said, 'I don't think Dean can say that. Dean was not directly involved.'

The President was startled, 'He wasn't?'

'No.'

'Then how the hell does he *know* about this? This is hearsay?'

'Snooping over the fence,' Ehrlichman replied.

Nixon now realised that he had been trapped by Dean. He could have denied the Ellsberg break-in, told Petersen it was just hearsay – but it was now too late. He had been trapped by the circumstance that Dean's information was relayed to him secondhand by Petersen. But Dean had earlier laid the ground-work, telling Nixon that the C.I.A. knew about the break-in and would undoubtedly eventually tell the F.B.I.

A few minutes later, Nixon was again on the telephone to me. Subject: Did Dean have a tape recorder when he entered the Oval Office March 21? He had become compulsively and incessantly worried about Dean's mythical tape recorder. Now he asked, rather pathetically, 'Is there any way that, uh, either surreptitiously or discreetly or otherwise, that you could *determine* whether Dean might have walked in there with a recorder on him?'

Frankly, I was sick of hearing about Dean's recorder. By now it was almost definite I would leave the White House in disgrace, and the President was going on worrying that Dean might nail him with the same device he hoped would protect him: a tape recorder. But Nixon wouldn't stop. 'The point is that that's a real bomb isn't it?'

'Yes.'

'Sure is. That's what may be his bomb. In other words, he puts that tape recorder on the desk of Henry Petersen and says, "I got a recording of the President of the United States and here's what he said." '

I told him it was impossible, inconceivable. I said all the right words to Nixon, but he wasn't listening. His mind was clamped on a nightmare vision of Dean with a slight bulge under his coat. Could it be?

He ploughed ahead: 'One thing about those things, you think that you know when a fellow walks into me, and I didn't look at him that closely, but you were there, Goddamnit, I mean. I'd think that . . . even the smallest ones are bulky enough . . . with a fellow like Dean you'd sort of see that, wouldn't you? Where do you carry them?' he asked irritably. 'In your hip pocket or your breast pocket?'

I told him I had heard it was on a strap under your arm. 'I really think it's so remote as to be almost beyond the realm of possibility.'

'In this matter, nothing is beyond the realm of possibility.'

Nixon then worried for a while that Dean had made a memorandum of the conversation if not a tape recording, but then dropped that worry because 'it would be Dean's word against the President's.'

Then he grew angry, saying, 'The point is now that if he's going to have this pissing contest, all right, bring it out, and fight it out, and it'll be a bloody Goddamn thing.' Then he turned philosophical. 'You know, in a strange kind of way, that's life, isn't it? But even though it will be rough as a cob we'll survive and some people you'll even find . . . in Mississippi, you'll find a half dozen people that will be for the President.'

I laughed. At least he was off the Dean tape recorder. But my laugh hadn't finished before he was back on his obsessive fear about it. 'Anyway, I thought that maybe you could *check* that thing.'

I said that I couldn't.

Pleading. 'There's no way you can check it?'

'There isn't *anything* to check.'

Still no good. 'You've never heard that, uh, that he'd ever done that before?'

I toyed with the idea of saying yes, Dean always tape-records every conversation. In fact, unknown to you, Mr President, *I* am his secret transcriber feeding the prosecutors. Instead I said, 'Never, never.'

To which Nixon laughed nervously. 'Well, if worse comes to worse and he does have one, well, we've got one, too.'

6

April 26, 1973, time running out. I met with Nixon in the White House. 'I don't think it should ever get out that we taped this office, Bob. If it does, the answer is, we only taped the National Security information. All other information is scrapped, never transcribed. Get the point? That's what I want you to remember. You never want to be in a position to say the President taped somebody.'

And he went on, 'I just don't want you to disclose that tape [March 21] to Ehrlichman or anybody.'

I was amazed. Was Nixon losing his grip? Ehrlichman was the one who had *suggested* I listen to the March 21 tape. 'I've already . . . he *knows* that I went over it, of course.'

This conversation led to Ehrlichman's mention of impeachment. Nixon said, 'I slept a little on that and it's good for John to look at it that way, but, my God, what the hell have we done to be impeached?'

I told him that John didn't believe he was going to be impeached but that he thought it was the 'game Dean is trying to play.'

Then Nixon rattled off the facts of his innocence. 'I didn't know about Kalmbach; I didn't know about the 350 [the $350,000]; I didn't know an effort was even being made to pay legal fees. My point is, and I'm not trying to be selfish, but the point is the story is very true that I didn't know a thing. Now there's only one weakness in that . . . the Pappas thing. Dean said Pappas was helping.'

Thomas Pappas was a Greek-American millionaire who was a prominent Nixon backer. I consulted my notes on the March 21 tape. In that conversation, Dean had said to Nixon, 'Mitchell has talked to Pappas.'

But Nixon explained that this still didn't show he had any knowledge of the money-raising because 'Pappas never mentioned that here in this office. Never mentioned that . . . All he said was, "I'm helping John's special projects," and I said, "Well, thank you very much. I appreciate it very much." He didn't tell me what it was about.'

Then, to my distress, Nixon was off again on his concern about Dean's tape recorder. 'I just can't believe that even John Dean would come into this office with a tape recorder.' Finally he expressed his real concern straight out, 'Let's leave out Ehrlichman and Haldeman – how's Dean gonna take on the President?'

We discussed what Dean would say about Nixon, but neither of us knew for sure even what Dean had done. I told Nixon that when Dean was working on his report at Camp David I had called him and he said, 'Send me to the Grand Jury and give me immunity, and we have no problem. Because I'm the only one in the White House who has any real problem on this. And it would stop at me, and if I'm immune it doesn't matter.'

Ehrlichman and I had suggested to Nixon that if we had to go, it was essential Dean should go too. But Nixon was so concerned about his own survival that he was afraid to take the step of firing the very man who was informing against him. He said, 'John's theory that the President should fire Dean's ass out of here has to be examined in terms of: does that unnecessarily give Dean a motive where he'll go wild against not only Ehrlichman and Haldeman, but *the President*? We can't let that happen.'

This turned out to be a shrewdly prophetic fear – since that's exactly what did happen.

What also held Nixon back from firing Dean was something the clever young lawyer had told Petersen: 'I [Dean] am never gonna be able to express anything but the greatest respect for, *and even affection for*, the President.' But Dean had also told Petersen 'Don't let him get involved in an obstruction of justice' and that worried Nixon. 'What do you think he meant by that?'

I told him I didn't know. Nixon seemed to me to be desperately reaching everywhere. Now he said he *had* to know what Dean was saying about him. 'I'm gonna ask you – Moore has been very close to Dean. Is there anything out of the way, I mean . . . see, there's *nobody* who can talk to Dean. How about if Moore [Richard Moore, Presidential adviser] just has a talk with Dean? See what the hell he has in mind?'

Nixon confided why he wanted Moore to see Dean: as a bearer of a threat. He said that if Dean didn't get immunity and he was convicted, 'there's only one place where he will ever get any possibility of clemency.'

I said, 'I sure wouldn't say *that* to him.'

'Oh, no, no, no. But, I mean, after that [conversation] that's gonna be in the back of his head. Absolutely.'

That afternoon I met Nixon in the White House for the last time as a staff member, although I didn't know it. Both Ehrlichman and I believed we were going to take a leave of absence, and there was at least a slim chance we would return.

It was at this very last meeting that two explosions occurred – the surprise ending of the Ellsberg trial and the aftershock of the Gray hearings – that would drive Nixon to the edge of the wall. First, a call from Kleindienst about Ellsberg. The judge was making Nixon's statement public and asking for an investigation which could lead to a mistrial.

Nixon hung up the telephone, ashen-faced, 'Hotter than hell. It was now or after the jury. What the hell, comes down to bust the Ellsberg case.'

I said, 'I can't figure that Ellsberg break-in. Some of this stuff is just . . . '

'Bizarre.'

I said, 'Completely beyond belief.'

Nixon: 'Trying to discredit Ellsberg.' Then he referred to the wiretapping of Joe Kraft in 1969 (which he *now* admits he *personally* ordered). 'Yeah, and something in Georgetown . . . I think Ehrlichman told me that,' all in a tone of wonder about the 'bizarre' happenings.

But worse news was to come when the telephone rang again, two minutes after Kleindienst's shocker about the Ellsberg case. The *New York Times* had gotten on to the story that Pat Gray had *burned* the document from Hunt's safe and was going to publish it tomorrow. First Ellsberg, then Nixon's F.B.I. director destroying evidence on the same day. Nixon called Kleindienst immediately. 'About this report from the *Times*. This involved Pat Gray – Dean giving them the contents from Hunt's safe . . . and that Gray destroyed it, you know . . . don't you think Gray ought to resign? What do you think? How do we handle it? What can we do? I know this is, uh, an awful thing . . . oh, sure, sure, it's going to come out in the paper. But Dick, Dick, for crying out loud, Goddamnit, these damn things happen.'

He hung up. Then called Petersen. While waiting for Petersen, he said bitterly to me, 'John [Ehrlichman] shouldn't ask for a week. Look, he knew, he knew . . . look, the point is, he knew . . . '

Nixon was so upset he had difficulty hiding it from Petersen. He wanted Gray to resign.

> Would you mind discussing it with Kleindienst? I think, uh, let's not put it in a context where I, uh, I love him too. I love *all* of you, but you know what I mean. I want him to be out of the way so that he doesn't look like an ass . . . Why the hell did we start the damn thing? I'll be damned if I know . . . What did Dean tell you? Yeah, Dean says that Ehrlichman told Dean to destroy them – that other, so-called,

> 'deep-six' them? Right. Well, I don't know. I'm not going to try to tell anybody to change the story and so forth. Because I want, I understand we want the truth, but I, I, I, just can't, uh, believe, I just can't believe that anybody's *gonna* believe that the Director of the F.B.I. was handed some documents and told to destroy 'em. Ha! You wanna see? My God, yes, and that he did it, I mean destroyed them! Bet J. Edgar Hoover's got every doodle that anybody ever had around right there in his files.

Now, more than ever, Nixon was worried about Dean. He told Petersen:

> You've gotta decide on Dean, you know what I mean? Let me just say one thing, the decision is *yours.* He comes to you but, but, don't be concerned that he holds uh, a trump card or blackjack and so forth. There's not going to be any blackmail here and, uh, don't you agree . . . uh, it's not the President, you can be sure of that. The President's family all know that they may try a little of that and they may say, 'Well, they all knew about the cover-up and so forth,' all right, fine, fine, but, uh, don't let 'em *blackmail* you. Don't you be a bit concerned. I mean Dean, let me say that Dean now has about as much credibility as Magruder has, which ain't much.

When Nixon hung up on that call, he had aged. He said angrily, 'Here is the problem. The thing that of course is the loose cannon out there is again the son-of-a-bitch Dean.'

Nixon called Ziegler into the office to discuss how to handle the *Times* story on Gray which would break in the morning. It was decided Ehrlichman would have to 'react' to the news story. Ehrlichman drafted a statement, came in to check it with Nixon, then left.

Silence.

I said, 'It's been hard, when every afternoon you just sit

here knowing some other story's gonna turn up. You don't know what it's gonna be. But you know Goddamn well, the phone's gonna ring and Ziegler's gonna say, "Yes, what's the matter with this or that," or thirty other things. I get it every night at home.'

I paused thinking of the chaos and pressure of the last two weeks, and said that sometimes the thought of a leave of absence was tempting.

The President said, 'Okay, let me spin it out the way I would feel. The way I would say it is this: because of the charges that have been made and will continue to be made, I cannot conduct the office. Therefore I feel under the circumstances that the proper course of action is for me to take a leave until I have an opportunity to clear myself of charges.

'I really feel at this point, Bob, it's better for you. You can fight the Goddamn thing better from the outside.'

I told him I agreed. 'I'd feel better and it'd work better and everything else.'

'And once this thing is clear that at least carries you through the trial. (I think he meant the Ervin hearings.) That's what I want – through the Goddamn trial, and after that, you may want to resign.'

'That's right,' I said.

It turned out that the Gray revelation about burning documents was the straw that broke Ehrlichman's back. After discussing my leave, Nixon said, 'I think John's case prompted this thing. The shit has hit the fan with this one for him . . . you know what I mean? Whatever Gray says . . . it looked like Ehrlichman was trying to destroy evidence . . . I've got to clear the Goddamn air. How do you do it? At least you get a couple of targets who move from one place to another. It's true they'll target in more on me. But then I'll assume the responsibility and I will say I am responsible. I regret and I do not pass the buck to anybody else . . . I don't wanna make a Checkers speech for the sake of the press.'

The last moments I remember in my final official conference with Nixon were pure nostalgia, beginning with the reference to the Checkers speech, then moving smoothly into that set piece – the 1,091st suggestion that I read his book, *Six Crises*. 'That statement in *Six Crises* – nothing about the chapters, but the introduction which I took almost a month to write . . . the point is . . . the very worst time is to try and make the Goddamn decision. Once you've decided, then you feel fine.'

Then on to a mention of that other old favourite, the firing of Sherman Adams. 'Len Hall said that Adams might have cheated Eisenhower. Eisenhower said, "I want to keep him," so it was really compounded. That's why Adams hated my guts ever thereafter.'

And finally, believe it or not, one last vindictive order: 'We've got to get out the Goddamn story, Bob. People have forgotten the violent years involved. They have forgotten . . . I mean, "Fuck you, Mr President. Fuck you Tricia," and all that shit, not just words, but what violence, the destruction, the teargassing, the commotion. What in the name of God . . . And the fucking Secret Service can do one thing. I want those threats collected. I told you that before . . . '

And the man who had once created a team of private investigators called the Plumbers, which spawned Hunt and Liddy and thereby triggered his own disaster, said, 'I mean, we don't have any *investigators*, that's our *problem*, see?'

I saw. But what was there to say? I went home and started writing my request for a leave of absence.

7

Sunday morning, April 29, 1973. I was having coffee with my wife in the kitchen of our Georgetown townhouse. Our 14-year-old daughter, Ann, was still asleep. Jo said, 'It's funny you haven't heard.' She was referring to discussions that were going on at Camp David between Nixon and Rogers as to the disposition and final execution of her husband. I said, 'I think it will be a leave of absence, not a resignation.' The telephone rang. A nervous Nixon was on the phone.

'Uh, Bob, we have to make a decision on this, and I've thought it through all the way. It's got to be a resignation.'

My lawyer's voice in my mind telling me, 'Not resignation. Not resignation. That's a clearcut statement to the public that says "Guilty". Fight for the leave of absence, at least.'

I said, 'You know my views on it. But if that's your decision, I'll go with it.'

I had adopted the invariable practice, in the Nixon decision-making process, of expressing my views as strongly and effectively as possible during the time the decision was being formulated in Nixon's mind. I also made sure all other viewpoints were at least as strongly represented. If it was something in which I was directly concerned or on which I felt strongly, I would fight hard for my position. But, without exception, once the decision was finally made – whether for or against my recommendation – I then made every possible effort to see that it was carried out as effectively as possible. I developed a pretty good ability to sense when the decision was still pending or when, in Nixon's mind, it had been made. That was the case now.

Nixon said fine, he knew I would say that, but then he turned to a more troublesome character: John Ehrlichman. 'Uh, I'd like you and John to come up to Camp David *together*.' That bothered me. Even at this moment he was worrying about his own discomfort. He knew Ehrlichman would be angry and he thought that the way to ease the problem was to have both of us there in one room together while he swung the axe. I, the good soldier, would hold Ehrlichman still, I suppose.

'Mr President, I strongly feel that you should talk to us *separately*. We can come up together – but you ought to talk to each of us alone.' I didn't feel it would be fair to Ehrlichman for me to be there when Nixon told him he would have to resign. I knew what I would say, but I didn't know what Ehrlichman might argue, and I figured that was Nixon's problem, not mine. That was an unusual attitude for me because my normal approach for years was: how can I help ease the President's problem? But in this case I felt it was his problem and I wasn't going to help him.

Nixon said, 'O.K.,' he would see us separately, but 'talk to John on the way up and explain to him what the situation is.'

In my lap again, and really no way to avoid it. Jo was looking at me, worriedly. 'What did he say, Bob?'

I didn't want to tell her it was resignation until I had spoken to the President and it was definite. I said 'I'll know for sure after I see him. But either way, I'm leaving the White House.'

I don't know for certain how Jo felt because she shares an attribute of her husband's about emotions: she doesn't display them. But I knew one thing that was bothering her. We had only moved into Georgetown a few months ago but she *loved* the place.

Our daughter, Ann, came pounding down the stairs on her way out to the park, unaware of anything that was happening. I said, 'Have a good time.' Then went up to my room and got ready for the trip.

Our other children were scattered all over the country. Susie and Peter were in Minnesota and Hank was in Los Angeles. I wanted to tell them I was leaving the White House before the news came out. There's a press pool at Camp David where the reporters stand in a little shack by the helipad and observe arrivals and departures and they would have the story on the wires in a minute. So after I came down, Jo started getting the kids on the telephone. We left it in doubt as to whether it was a resignation or a leave of absence because I still wasn't certain.

I called Ehrlichman. 'Voice of doom,' I said. 'We go to Camp David today.'

'What's the word from the mountain top?' Ehrlichman asked.

I said I'd tell him on the way up there. I ordered a helicopter to pick us up at the Pentagon helipad and soon a White House driver in a blue blazer with a White House seal on his lapel was at the door to take me to the Pentagon.

A Presidential chopper was sitting on the helipad waiting for us. I wouldn't be seeing that again. I waited in the sun for John Ehrlichman. It was midday. Inside the Pentagon, even on a Sunday, security clerks were at work, messages spilling out of chattering teletypewriters; on other floors military personnel would be on duty, coffee on desks, monitoring communications throughout the world. The Pentagon. Vietnam War, May 8, 1972. Sitting in the Oval Office debating with Henry Kissinger on a military move to end that war. Past. Gone.

Ehrlichman's car drew up and the tall, healthy looking Ehrlichman came over to me. He was in a grim mood. I said, 'We'll talk on the chopper.'

The doors closed and the chopper rose swiftly into the sky and started up the Potomac River towards Georgetown. I knew I needed to talk to Ehrlichman but for a few moments I just enjoyed that spectacular view as the chopper swung low over the River. I saw the Capitol and the White House, and then, there was Georgetown below us, all little brick houses. I could actually pick out the house we lived in. The chopper flew north towards Maryland where Larry Higby lived. I had alerted Larry by telephone; and he told me later that he stood on his lawn and watched that helicopter sweep north towards Camp David and political exile. By then I was in deep conversation with Ehrlichman.

Thank God you have to talk very loud in a helicopter – a fact that made it easier for me under the circumstances. I leaned over to John and said, 'It's resignation, John, not leave of absence.'

Ehrlichman swore angrily. '*Both* of us?'

'That's right.'

Ehrlichman said nothing for a while and I knew what was going through his mind. He felt he was barely implicated in the Watergate cover-up. If he had any real problems, it was in Ellsberg, which was a different matter as far as he was concerned. The press didn't see it as a different matter, of course. John didn't argue with me, either because of the loud helicopter engines, or because anything he had to say to me was no longer important. I was not the Chief-of-Staff. His arguments, if any, would have to be carried directly to the Commander-in-Chief. But he did say, 'Well, Goddamnit, he's not going to tie us in one bag with Dean.'

I agreed. It was bad enough that we could be forced to resign, but to be associated with Dean *in the same statement* made it triply bad. If that happened, the President would be saying to America, 'I've investigated and I've solved it. These three people, alone, did it – and I'm firing them together.'

We were now over the Maryland farm country of rolling hills with fences. Then the Catoctin Mountains were in the distance. As we approached, the helicopter had to go up very high, and from there we could see wooded forests climbing up the mountains, and then Camp David, a little settlement on the top of one mountain in a small clearing among the trees.

As usual a naval officer was waiting for us. 'You're to go over to Laurel Lodge.' When we arrived, Ron Ziegler was standing outside wearing the dark blue Camp David jacket and tie. Ron was looking tired and emotional. He had been spending long hours 'hand-holding' with the President – preparing for this moment.

I had been through that often in the past and I knew it was hard work. When Nixon was going through an emotional problem, you had to share it with him, try to help him to a decision that was difficult. Sometimes you wouldn't know yourself what was the right decision, so you couldn't be sure exactly how to aim your advice. This was the kind of problem that he worried about over and over again and you just had to sit there and discuss it over and over again. It was draining. Ron looked fatigued.

For Ziegler this moment was especially difficult – he owed his career at the White House to me. I had hired him and I had always been the strong reed upon which he leaned for help.

Laurel Lodge is a large cabin. There is a spacious living room with early American sofas and easy chairs. A huge fireplace dominates one side of the room. Wall-sized windows look out over the trees. Ehrlichman – still angry – nodding to Ziegler, went into the living room, opened his briefcase and took out a yellow pad. I suppose he was preparing notes for his argument to Nixon. Ziegler touched my arm. 'The President will see you first. Let's take a walk.'

I strolled through the forest with the tall press aide I had once hired. The one I used to enjoy kidding by calling him 'Whaleboat'. Ron expressed his own anguish: 'It's been a horrible experience. I'm so damn sorry.'

All was silent.

He said, 'The President's taking it so hard. He's just totally broken, Bob.'

I thanked Ron for his concern, which was real. People have asked me: How did Ehrlichman and I feel at that moment? I think Ehrlichman felt that the forced resignation was unjust. And he was reacting in anger to the unjustness of it. I agreed it was unjust. But I was not reacting to it. I just don't react to unjustness. That doesn't mean I didn't care. I was sad; but I wasn't angry. If something is inevitable, I move on.

Aspen Lodge, where Nixon resided, was several hundred yards away from Laurel. We used bicycles and golf carts to get around Camp David. I chose a bike to pedal over to meet the President, which is, I suppose, rather an unusual way to ride to political doom.

I parked the bike and went through the main door into the large living room. Looking out through the huge plate-glass windows on the other side of the room, I saw the Maryland mountain countryside.

The President was waiting for me. He came over, patted my shoulder and said, 'Let's go out on the terrace.'

We walked out on to the terrace. I could see this was

a deeply emotional moment for him. It was hard for him to start. He said, 'This is so beautiful; these lovely tulips down here.'

Beneath the terrace the mountain slopes sharply. Banks of tulips are planted in rock gardens all the way to the bottom. A picturesque flagstone terrace is bordered by a low stone wall. Nixon's eyes seemed misty. He looked out over the view and gestured with his arm as if to encompass all of the beauty of Camp David: 'It will always be available to you, Bob.'

A well-intentioned but meaningless gesture, because obviously there was no way I would ever be invited to Camp David again. (And I never was.) Nixon was trying to ease himself into what was obviously a very difficult situation.

We were standing on the terrace next to the telescope. We both stood with one foot on the wall, and talked as we looked out over the valley.

Nixon said with a hushed voice, 'You know, Bob, there's something I've never told anybody before, not even you. Every night since I've been President, every single night before I've gone to bed, I've knelt down on my knees beside my bed and prayed to God for guidance and help in this job.'

I was deeply touched by this. He went on: 'Last night before I went to bed, I knelt down and this time I prayed that I wouldn't wake up in the morning. I just couldn't face going on.'

'Mr President,' I said, 'you can't indulge yourself in that kind of feeling. You've got to go on. If there are other problems, they have to be dealt with, that's all.'

He patted me on the shoulder as if my words were what he expected from me. We went back into the living room. He told me he had gone through this problem over and over. He had come to the conclusion that the only way to deal with it – given where we were and what the problems were – was for us to resign, not take a leave of absence. I told him again that I disagreed with his decision because I didn't think it would do him any good. The press wouldn't stop going after him, the Congressional hearings wouldn't stop just because he had gotten rid of us. And he would lose his buffer. But if that was his final decision. I would operate as I always had done as his Chief-of-Staff. 'Once the decision is made, I'll abide by it and do the best I can to carry it out.'

Nixon still looked shaken. 'I'm not going to put anyone in your job, I'm going to change the whole system and just deal with department heads in the White House.' I told him the one thing our lawyers requested was that our resignations and Dean's be treated separately. In other words, do it at least on different days so we weren't connected as a general house-cleaning of villains. To my surprise, Nixon vetoed that idea. 'No, I've thought this all through and I've got to do it all at once. I can't drag it out.'

And right then I sensed his real attitude. Despite his very real anguish, the general house-cleaning was the approach he felt was best in his own interest.

This brings me to a personal point that really bothered me when Nixon went on television in 1977 to recreate the resignation scene. He ascribed to his meeting with Ehrlichman exactly the same words about his 'praying not to wake up' as he had said to me. Ehrlichman has confirmed that Nixon did speak the same words to him.

This hurt me. Through the years since then I had believed that what Nixon said to me was a personal emotional baring of his soul to me alone of the sort he was not often wont to do. I had been moved, and felt a kinship to him. Now I see that this was just a conversational ploy – a debater's way of slipping into a difficult subject – used on both of us.

As I was leaving, Nixon said 'This is all going to come out O.K.' This was his standard line throughout all of this period. And he raised the point again that there were funds available to help us with our legal fees. I said, 'No, we'll work that out some other way.'

I stepped out of the front door and pedalled back to

Laurel Lodge to tell Ehrlichman not to waste his breath on argument. But John must have gone to Aspen by another route because he wasn't there when I arrived. I went out on the terrace, lugging my briefcase and sat in a deck chair in the sun. I telephoned Jo and told her to call the family and tell them that I was going to resign. We would be moving back to California.

Even though the sun was beating down I felt ice-cold. I guess I was in a state of shock, but my mind was clicking as rapidly on details as ever. I called John Wilson, my lawyer, and told him about the resignation. He was furious. He said, 'He's throwing you out cold? I can't believe it.' I calmed him down and we talked about the need for me to prepare a resignation letter to submit to the President. All of this would become public the next day, but we had to go through the ritual of submitting a letter of resignation and Nixon writing an acceptance in reply.

I sat and waited for Ehrlichman. Two marines walked by, rifles slung, talking quietly. When Ehrlichman reappeared he was more grim than ever. Everything Ehrlichman had feared had come true, only worse. He had fought to be separated from me, and now he was not only in the same 'bag' with me, but with John Dean, also. John was angry. He called Wilson and his wife. We then talked about the letters of resignation and their timing. Together we went back to see the President for the last time.

Bill Rogers, who was acting as Nixon's adviser during these last days, came in. Bill was a warm human being, a very decent guy. He and I had been close. He said that he was sorry, 'What we're doing is the right thing for the President. And I know ultimately it will turn out to be the right thing for you.'

I sensed that Ehrlichman was going to give an Italian salute to this suggestion, but I merely intervened by saying, 'We don't agree, but at this point it doesn't make any difference.' It became clear that Rogers was going to stay on for dinner with the President, and we were no longer wanted. So we took our leave and helicoptered back to

Washington, leaving the rustic pleasures of Camp David behind forever.

Jo was waiting. She said the only person she hadn't told yet was Ann, our fourteen-year-old, who was still out at the park shooting baskets. So when Ann came home, I told her myself which really hurt me because she was crushed and ran to her room, crying.

Ann had blossomed as a result of our move to Georgetown. She was enjoying life there. She had acquired some good friends at the National Cathedral School. And she saw this crisis as, 'Does this mean that we have to leave Washington?' and I said, 'It probably does.' She was too young to be emotionally affected by my leaving the government, but she hated to leave *Washington*. And I felt in some way that I had let her down. I was very concerned about how all the children understood my situation because I knew how hard it would be for them. But Ann's concern was for something I couldn't do anything about. I knew I had to leave Washington.

The next day I went into the White House on the same basis I always had. I called my immediate staff into the office and told them 'I'm resigning'; and they would have to maintain the continuity of the operation of the White House.

The day following the announcement of my resignation, all was different. Television crews camped in front of our house before dawn and waited patiently. They lounged on portable folding chairs set up on the sidewalk or tossed a Frisbee in the street.

When I arrived at my office that day there was an F.B.I. guard posted outside of it. I asked him if it was all right to go in. He said, 'yes, but you'll have to leave your briefcase outside because you can't remove anything.' I went into my office and straightened things out as best I could. I knew I would have to consult my files when the time came for me to be called before the Grand Jury and the Ervin Committee. I was so absorbed I didn't hear Nixon come down the hall. He saw the F.B.I. guard standing there and, in an outburst of anger, shoved him roughly against the wall.

Nixon went on to his Cabinet meeting and made an emotional statement about our resignations. Then he returned and apologised to the guard.

A little later, I was gone.

Book IX

PERSONAL DIARY OF THE FINAL DAYS

1

General Alexander Haig whom I recommended as my replacement as White House Chief-of-Staff was, fortunately for him, ignorant of most Watergate matters. Consequently both he and the President had to keep in touch with me from time to time on Watergate problems, as the breakdown of the Nixon Administration escalated into a complete collapse.

Those were hectic days for me. I was called before Grand Juries; House and Senate hearings; the Ervin Committee; and finally, preparations for my own trial on a criminal indictment for conspiracy, obstruction of justice and perjury.

On May 2, the first day after I left the White House, President Nixon called and asked me to see him in his office at 5 p.m. The first note I listed in preparation for the meeting was: 'General Haig.'

Nixon had said he didn't want another Chief-of-Staff. At this meeting I told him that he *needed* an executive head now more than ever – and General Haig was the logical man for the job.

Ramrod straight, crisp mannered, diplomatic enough to have served under Henry Kissinger and survived (in his shop Henry was as feared as I had been in mine), Haig had worked smoothly with the President in the White House. Because Kissinger was abroad so often Haig had had many opportunities to confer with Nixon on various problems.

Nixon agreed to the idea and told me to work it out with Haig. I telephoned Haig, Vice Chief-of-Staff of the Army who was in Atlanta on a military matter, and told him he had a new assignment – replacing me – and the

President wanted to see him the next morning. And that's how Haig got the job.

Nixon's first great battle ahead would be the televised Ervin Committee hearings, scheduled to begin in June – and, specifically, John Dean's testimony.

In the following days Nixon and Haig both called me to discuss their strategy in which I, as it turned out, would later play a major role. They expected Dean to testify to Nixon's March 21 statements about raising money to pay off Howard Hunt. I said that, because I had been at that same Oval Office meeting, I would testify that the overall thrust of the meeting was Nixon's intention to 'probe' Dean to find out what really happened. As to raising money for Hunt, I felt Nixon had at one point said that would be wrong.

At that time no one had any idea that the White House tapes would be revealed, so there would be no testimony that I had listened to the March 21 tape. I would just testify to my memory of the meeting, refreshed by a review of my notes (which, of course, included the detailed notes made while listening to the tape).

Nixon's initial grand strategy was to preempt Dean, himself, by making a speech on May 22, 1973, in which he would come as close as he dared to admitting everything he had done – and thereby vitiate the thrust of Dean's testimony. But there Nixon unknowingly made an error so vast that it helped sink him in the end.

I share the blame because he talked with me in preparation for the May 22 speech. He told me he was admitting everything in the speech. 'I'll say I ordered the Plumbers. I had the Huston Plan. I told Haldeman and Ehrlichman to meet with the C.I.A.' And everything he did had been for national security reasons. In his words, 'I'm going to put an N.S.C. cover on the whole thing.'

This is where I should have warned him about the June 23, 1972, conversation, which would eventually emerge as the 'smoking gun' tape. But nearly a year – and many tumultuous events – later, I couldn't remember all the details of that one meeting.

The real genesis of the meeting with C.I.A. officials, of course, was pure politics. Dean had asked me to stop the F.B.I.'s investigation of the Mexican bank connection through which the Watergate burglary money had been laundered because that investigation could hurt the campaign finance committee and the donors.

I didn't object at that crucial point when Nixon said he was going to put an N.S.C. cover on our meeting with the C.I.A. because that's the way I remembered it, too. In his May 22 speech Nixon claimed that the request to the C.I.A. for help was not political. When the June 23 tape was revealed fifteen months later, with dialogue between Nixon and me showing the political motive, the press was quick to look back to that speech and pinpoint it as an occasion when Nixon had lied.

Americans seemed to react more violently to the belief that their President had lied to them than that he had actually participated in a cover-up. Both he and I thought at the time that he was telling the truth. We were wrong.

All the while that Nixon planned his strategy and made his moves to thwart John Dean, I was absorbed in a private problem. Unsure whether I would eventually be brought to trial, and scheduled for testimony in various agencies and courts, I couldn't even begin to look for a job.

Ehrlichman and I had rejected Nixon's offer of financial support. Then the offer of a job on the Nixon Foundation was withdrawn because of 'the problem that you may be indicted'. Meanwhile, legal fees were clearly going to start mounting. I wrote Nixon a note. A friend had suggested that through Nixon's close friend, Hobe Lewis, the editor, *Reader's Digest* might pay Ehrlichman and me $50,000 as an advance for exclusive rights for first publication of anything we might write in the next four years regarding the first Nixon term. I told the President that it would insure that our work would be in the hands of a friendly publisher where it would receive proper treatment, and would certainly help our financial situation.

Nixon called the next day and said the idea of our

writing books was excellent. As usual, he had a twist on the deal. Instead of our writing our own books, we would work on *his* book. 'Talk to Hobe on a confidential basis and tell him that the President intends to write his memoirs, and I want you two to begin the job of preparing the basic documents to cover the first four years.' He said it should be totally confidential. 'If Hobe thinks that is workable, tell him to call me.'

The next day Nixon called me again on the Hobe Lewis idea, and made me an offer that would have certainly solved all my financial problems. The trouble was, neither of us was fully aware of the significance of his offer at the time. In May 1973, the existence of the White House tapes was still Nixon's deepest secret. Nixon said, 'I've decided today that I will give you all of the White House tapes, from the time we installed the system until April 30 of this year. You can tell Hobe Lewis, on a strictly confidential basis, that you own them. That ought to interest him in retaining you to do the Nixon research.'

I didn't follow up on that. Probably because this was the kind of suggestion Nixon often would throw out and then later forget or retract. Perhaps the thought of going through two years of White House tapes was too daunting. People forget that it takes two years to listen to two years of tapes. Or perhaps other crises quickly exploded and the offer just passed from my mind. But I remembered, after the existence of the tapes became known, that there was a time when Nixon offered to *give* them to me. As it turned out, they were priceless. You couldn't put a value on them. (One routine letter of Nixon's was recently auctioned off at the Hamilton Gallery in New York for over $5,000.)

The drama continued to build as Dean's public testimony neared. On June 3, Senator Ervin rejected the special prosecutor's request for a postponement of the Committee's televised hearings to avoid interference with the criminal process, saying, in effect, 'It's far more important for the American people to know the facts than for a few men to go to jail.' And the *New York Times* reported that

Dean had met with Nixon thirty-five or forty times between late January and April to discuss Watergate – a story obviously leaked from Dean's secret testimony in staff conferences on Watergate.

Nixon now felt that Dean not only would appear on nationwide television to make his devastating charges, but he also would exaggerate his closeness to the President. Dean had met with Nixon about ten times in all and only from February 26 to March 22. On June 3, Nixon called me and said, 'I'm up at Camp David and I'm trying to straighten out the facts here. Buzhardt's analysis is that this isn't the time to take Dean on personally [in reference to the *Times*' story about Dean's thirty-five or forty meetings with Nixon].' Then he said, 'Kleindienst told me that he was surprised that I wasn't seeing Dean *daily*. All these weeks Dean's been giving the Justice Department the idea that he was in *daily* communication with me from the time Watergate happened.' He added, 'That's why Justice let Dean sit in on the F.B.I. interviews right after Watergate.'

Later that day he called again to say 'We're trying to work out a game plan for the week when Dean testifies'. That game plan included Nixon, himself, listening to all the tapes of his meetings with Dean.

The following day, June 4 (as I have recounted), he called me after going over a number of the significant tapes himself in preparation for Dean's testimony, and laid on my shoulders the burden of explaining the most damning tape of all, the March 21 conversation. This was after he had said to his personal aide Steve Bull, who was setting up the tapes for him, 'It's that damn conversation of March 21 . . . Bob can handle it. He'll go up there and say "I was there and the President said," etc.' But Dean's testimony wasn't scheduled until June 25, and I wouldn't be appearing on television screens to refute him until late July.

The pressure on our family in Washington by the press was enormous. Every Watergate development brought a horde of newsmen who would camp out front waiting for the exiled Chief-of-Staff to comment. We made arrangements to return to California.

On June 15, 1973, we left Washington for good.

Larry Higby had arranged for one last White House car in which he would drive Jo and me to the airport.

Moving four children with assorted birds, dogs, fish, etc., across the country isn't an easy chore, but Jo had managed it beautifully and they were all gone. All that was left was our own departure. Buried among suitcases, we drove towards the Memorial Bridge where Abe Lincoln sits in white marble majesty. I had passed that monument many times in Presidential motorcades; motorcycles roaring ahead, white-gloved M.P.'s directing traffic, Henry Kissinger beside me making jokes, people along the route, waving.

'We're a little close on the time,' Higby said, snapping me out of my dreams of past glory. We were to catch a morning flight to Minneapolis where our daughter Susan was graduating from college. Then we would fly to Los Angeles.

We arrived at Washington's National Airport with only minutes to spare. While I checked the bags with the porter outside the terminal, Jo rushed inside to check in. A few moments later she came back out with such forlorn expression that I said, 'What in the world's wrong?'

In an almost imperceptible whisper, she answered, 'I forgot something.'

I assumed she was referring to something she had forgotten to pack, which was still back at the house. But Jo had forgotten something more important than that.

'The reservations,' she whispered, 'I forgot to make our plane reservations, and the flight is full – not even standby.'

By then, Higby had gone and we were stranded at Washington National Airport. The master of precision in the White House, as I had been known, was now established as not so precise a master in his own family. To make matters even worse, throughout our walks back and forth through the airline terminal lugging all sorts of bags, we were constantly faced with people reading the *Washington Star*, which had an unpleasant banner headline about me.

We learned that the next plane to Minneapolis was four or five hours later. We took a cab back to our empty house and killed the remaining hours until the afternoon flight. A few days later we flew to Los Angeles from Minneapolis to be greeted with an editorial page cartoon in the *Los Angeles Times* depicting me as Frankensein. The caption read: 'Nixonstein.'

2

John Dean testified before the Watergate Committee on June 25. And Nixon had a surprise. For three months, Nixon had been obsessed by his March 21 conversation with Dean in which he had told Dean he could raise a million dollars, if necessary, to pay off Hunt. But what obsessed the Committee was the earlier September 15, 1972, conversation with Dean. Because Dean testified that his impression at that meeting was that Nixon was well aware of Dean's cover-up activities.

This testimony was explosive because Nixon had stated over and over again that he knew nothing about the cover-up until March 21, 1973, when Dean told him about a certain cancer. Dean's testimony created turmoil in the Committee room, Senator Edward Gurney thundering, 'In other words, your whole thesis in saying that the President of the United States knew about Watergate on September 15, is purely an impression; there isn't a shred of evidence that came out of the meeting?'

I believe it was then that Senator Howard Baker originated the phrase which was to become the most famous in the hearing, 'What did the President know, and when did he know it?'

Noting the Senators' interest in that September 15 conversation, I knew what to expect. When I returned to Washington preparatory to testifying, Nixon called and asked me if I could review the September 15 tape, too, which I did on July 10.

And then Alex Butterfield, hesitant, soft-voiced, told the world that Mr Nixon had White House tapes that recorded *all* the meetings testified to by John Dean. The great debate – was John Dean a liar? – could be solved by evidence preserved by the President himself!

A nation reeled. I'm sure Nixon did, too. I kept my balance because I'd been expecting it all along. Higby had warned me that any of us might be asked about the tapes. And I had told Haig that, if asked, we would have to answer truthfully. But I don't believe Nixon felt that the question would ever arise.

All signals off. I had been prepared to testify to the March 21, 1973, and September 15, 1972, meetings as a *participant*. Now Nixon agreed I had to reveal that I had *listened* to the tapes, as well. It would make my testimony even more effective.

In spite of my 'Nazi' image, I appeared before the Watergate Committee in my normal mien, causing many reporters to cry, 'Fraud.' I still managed to create havoc when I told the stunned Senators that I had actually listened to those secret tapes.

Questions boomed; outrage sputtered. 'The United States Senate can't have those tapes but you, a private citizen, can?'

Finally I was allowed to give my version of the tapes. It earned me a perjury charge and conviction. My position was based on the rationalisation that my notes were impounded, and I had not been able to reconstruct a completely precise recap of them while sitting in an attic room of the E.O.B. with a Secret Service guard impatiently tapping his foot while I read through them. I was not permitted to make any copies or notes; I had to work with my recollection, as I stated. But there is no doubt that I was trying my best to protect the President with my testimony. As I read those notes, I looked for the best possible construction for the President's interest – just as he had expected me to do.

Ironically, the one overriding concern that I had in preparing for testimony and my opening statement – which I had carefully written and rewritten under the scrutiny of my attorneys – was to avoid any possibility of a charge of perjury. I recognised that as a major danger in this kind of reconstruction by memory and was determined to avoid it. But I didn't.

The result of my testimony was to add to the furor to obtain the White House tapes, culminating in 'The Saturday Night Massacre' in which Special Prosecutor Archibald Cox was fired and Attorney General Elliot Richardson and his assistant quit in protest.

Actually Nixon intended an action even more drastic: abolishing the Special Prosecutor's office completely; firing every one of its hungry attorneys; and not reinstating the office, no matter what the howls of outrage. By coincidence I was in Washington that Saturday preparing for an appearance before a Grand Jury. General Haig called me and we discussed the President's intentions. I agreed on one principle: by that time, only incredibly drastic action could possibly save Nixon. He was being chewed to death from every side.

In this case, as in the past, Nixon did just enough – by firing Cox – to infuriate the nation, but not enough to save himself. Instead, he was soon appointing another Special Prosecutor, giving up the first batch of tapes, and resuming his slide into a very special niche in history – somewhere below the waterline.

Nixon, the man of *Six Crises*, believed in miracles, which meant he believed in himself. From Checkers to the Vietnam War, he had always, miraculously, survived.

But now the power blocs were in full command – and no miracle was to appear. Congress was warming up for its most drastic move: impeachment. The bureaucracy had an added ally, created by Nixon, himself: the Special

Prosecutor's Office. The press was breathlessly escalating every new development into the most lurid headlines and dire analyses. And the intelligence community, as usual, lurked in the unseen background, its damage already done.

3

I had a deeply frustrating, useless feeling as the wolves started to close in on the President's heels and as he continued to follow the strategy of throwing an occasional baby to them to try to stop the chase. Unfortunately, each baby, right from the beginning, had only whetted the wolves' appetites and convinced them more strongly that they were on the right track. It was obvious, from the outside, that this was happening, and that in any event he would soon be the last baby left.

But I was on the outside, a victim of one of the early attempts to appease the wolves that had done no good at all. I could only hope that something would eventually break in our favour. I did occasionally touch base with the President, or Al Haig in response to some request of theirs, or in my own attempt to try to be of some help. Not having yet had the opportunity to review the tapes that later became available, and not yet knowing much of what had earlier transpired outside my own knowledge, I still had no realisation of the probable reasons for many of Nixon's actions and reactions.

In several lengthy letters, I tried to urge him to change his basic approach from one of reaction and apparent desperation to one of strength and initiative. I made the point that all of his successes had come from his acting strongly and courageously in the face of great opposition – never from backing down or giving in, in spite of much advice to that effect.

Sometime after the 'Massacre' I received a call from General Haig who said that the President was listening to more tapes. He told Haig that the tapes involving Colson were 'the *last* ones he wanted to hear.' Haig laughed when he said this. He went on to complain about problems he was experiencing trying to run the White House during that chaotic winter of 1973. 'Rose Mary Woods and Ziegler are problems because they're insecure,' he said. 'I have to keep bucking them up.' And he was getting absolutely no help on Watergate from the new counsellors Nixon had brought in. 'Harlow, Laird, and Armstrong refuse to do anything on Watergate,' he told me. 'They'll help on the ongoing government problems, but they won't touch the Watergate business.'

Haig told me the press was about to 'cut loose on Larry Higby (who was still at the White House) on the grounds that he's nothing but an extension of Haldeman in the White House and nothing more than Haldeman's eyes and ears stashed away in the White House.'

Haig said he had learned this from an editor of *Parade* magazine who was a friend of his, and from two others.

Larry had told me he was making every effort to be helpful to Haig. But he believed Haig should not have made himself the chief spear carrier on Watergate, for which he was unsuited, but instead should have concentrated on running the White House. I completely agreed. Haig now returned Higby's criticism in fine style. He said Higby had joined the 'pussy fire group,' referring to groups of Vietnamese who shot from behind bushes and wouldn't stand and fight. In this Haig was somewhat correct. After numerous attempts to reach Haig and others who were handling the Watergate defence, Higby along with several of the young White House aides were going public in an attempt to reach Nixon and others to prevent the death of the President through a thousand cuts. Haig said the pussy fires were a group of young White House aides who met every day – and gave Haig trouble every hour. And then Haig added a P.S.: the *Parade* magazine editor had a next-door neighbour who 'went to college with you –

she's a tennis player, and she has a fixation about your "rigid Nazi-type activities," unquote.'

Haig then warned me: 'They have an uncanny intelligence operation in the Jewish community that is out to get you – and the *Parade* editor is a part of it. They're determined to do you in, and this ties back to your "Nazi" activities and all that stuff, you know.' Haig talked about the Jewish community as if it had a big sinister plot against me. I told him to forget it because I couldn't believe it was true.

On January 27, 1974, Nixon called to tell me the battle for the tapes was raging. 'Dick Moore is urging an accommodating line on the tapes. The problem is we might lose. If the court doesn't agree, then you're really stuck.' He then told me what he considered the key to his downfall. 'The turning point was April 17 when I didn't give Dean immunity.'

How Nixon wished now he had granted Dean that immunity!

4

Nixon's next stand was in the Supreme Court. There the battle for the White House tapes would be fought. He had already surrendered a number of tapes to the Special Prosecutors, but they and the Impeachment Committee were hungry for more.

By July 6, 1974, the Supreme Court was hearing arguments on the case of the White House tapes. Nixon called me later to say, 'Regarding the Court, if they leave any "air" we can handle it.'

This is a simple sentence with enormous implications. What Nixon was threatening was potentially one of the greatest Constitutional crises of this century. By 'air', he meant anything other than a unanimous decision would not be obeyed. If the U.S. Supreme Court had handed down a majority decision, Nixon would have defied the Court and refused its order to turn over the tapes.

When the Court, on July 8, 1974, ruled 8–0 against Nixon, it unknowingly averted what might have been a supremely critical confrontation between the Executive and Judiciary powers. But Nixon had to bow to that unanimous decision of the Court, many of whose members had been appointed by him.

5

And then, with the Supreme Court ruling, it was all over. Nixon's lawyers and Congressional supporters were listening to the June 23 'smoking gun' tapes, and turning faint. The next sound Nixon heard was running feet as the lawyers bolted for the side doors.

Then he was all alone, with only family. Julie said, 'Stay in there and battle.' Give Julie credit. She was a fighter. I like her.

Nixon would later tell me he had been 'finished' long before he released the June 23 tape. In his words, his fight for survival was 'eight months of pure hell and agony – for nothing.' A Senator, while the battle was still going on, had informed Nixon that the Southern Democrats, his last hope, wouldn't 'hold' if it came down to an impeachment vote.

But, on August 6, one day after he released the June 23 tape, creating a national uproar – as much because of his accompanying statement as the tape itself – he appeared in a Cabinet meeting and said he wouldn't resign, no matter what. He was still holding the line, even to his inside 'official family'. On that day he was torn by conflicting advice from his staff and family, and by his own belief that he was an effective President being driven out of office for a freakish event. Sometime during that day or night of Tuesday, August 6, however, he apparently finally faced the inevitable. At least that's what he told me in an unforgettable telephone call on the morning of August 7.

Wednesday morning, August 7, 1974. Jo and I were having an early breakfast at her family's beach house in Newport Beach. The telephone rang and I answered. The White House operator was on the line and said the President was calling.

The usually strong, resonant voice was subdued, tired, defeated.

'Bob, I want you to know that I have decided I must resign.'

The telephone felt cold in my hand. After all the thundering editorial demands for resignation and unceasing Congressional calls for impeachment – to hear President Nixon himself say in a quiet voice that he was resigning was a shock.

I had been half-expecting this news in some form ever since the release of the 'smoking gun' tapes and the resultant uproar. I had called Ron Ziegler on Tuesday and said, 'Ron, I have one final demand to make on you, and I don't want you to let me down. When it comes to the point that the President decides to resign, and I'm afraid it will, I want you to let me know *before* any announcement or final action is taken, because I want to talk to him once before it is too late.'

Ron agreed that he would do this if it was at all possible. He had no idea what the outcome was going to be, but shared my pessimistic view.

I assumed this call from the President was in response to my request to Ron, but I have never been able to verify this.

I asked, 'Is this a final decision, and are you sure you are doing the right thing?'

Nixon replied that it was final. 'There's no use fighting it any more. I just don't have the political support in Congress that I need to continue to function as President. And I can't let the country be torn apart and our foreign policy destroyed by six months or more of an impeachment trial.'

There was obviously no point in my trying to argue. The tone of finality was complete. (But most inside reports now indicate that, in fact, he had not yet made the final decision at the time of the call to me, and that it was not made until late that night or early next day.)

I had a horrible sinking feeling. All the great things – the China break-through, the détente with the Soviets, the progress towards reorganising the government so it would work – all lost. The man I had seen at the pinnacle of power, exercising with such great skill that power given him so resoundingly by the American people was now at the other end of the telephone line quietly telling me of his humiliating decision.

But I had had a reason for my request to Ziegler. And despite my sadness and compassion for this now-broken man, I felt there was still one thing I should raise with him.

'If this is your final decision, then, as always, I'll do anything I can to help in carrying it out, although I personally oppose it.

'There is one point I would like to raise, which I would never mention unless I was sure that you were totally committed to the resignation. I firmly believe that before you leave office you should exercise your Constitutional authority and grant pardons to all those who have been or may be charged with any crimes in connection with Watergate. I think it's imperative that you bring Watergate to an end before you leave – for the sake of the country and especially for your successor.

'I realise this is a minor point in contrast to what you are now facing, but I think it is very important.'

Silence. Then Nixon said, 'I haven't had a chance to

give that any thought, but I assure you I will. I just don't know what should be done.'

I suggested that I prepare some written recommendations and get them to him. I asked, 'When do you plan to make an announcement?'

Nixon sighed and said, 'I'm just not sure, Bob. Not before tonight, and probably not until tomorrow.' I could see that I wouldn't have much time to prepare anything. I wanted to say one word, or a few, to the President that would encompass my feelings at this moment that our grand adventure together was ending so sadly. But the moment was too awesome; my emotions too mixed. I said, 'Whatever happens, I wish you the best, Mr President. I wish I could do something to help.'

He said, 'I'm afraid there's not much anyone can do to help now,' and the historic conversation ended.

I called Haig a little later in the morning to tell him of my conversation with the President. Al seemed quite surprised and said that things were in a very delicate balance, and that he did not know what the outcome would be. He did not feel the decision was yet final, but that the President was slowly moving in that direction. He was obviously completely absorbed in the resignation question, not the least interested in my pardon idea. He told me to get the material to Presidential Counsel James St Clair.

Through my lawyers in Washington, I did send in a complete recommendation for a blanket pardon to all Watergate offenders, past and future. I also recommended a pardon to all Vietnam draft evaders on the grounds that these two acts would eliminate the remnants of the two major traumas of the Nixon Presidency, and enable President Ford to start with a clean slate. I strongly felt this was a sound recommendation, but I pointed out that I obviously had a personal interest, since I would be among the beneficiaries.

My wife felt this pardon effort was a mistake and that my advice to the President was not sound. I am now sure she was right, at least in my personal interest. I still think, while it would have hurt Nixon's position a little more, there wasn't very much farther down for him to go. And it would certainly have helped President Ford begin his Administration without the burdens of Vietnam and Watergate.

The next thing I remember is chaos. A message from a Mr Joyce, F.B.I., Los Angeles. I called Joyce, who said, 'We've had word from our Boston office that there's a threat on your life. Someone called in and said you're going to be killed tonight. We have to arrange protection for you.'

I said that was ridiculous. The threat was received in Boston, and I was in Newport Beach, 3,000 miles away. Nevertheless, Joyce said, 'It's serious.' The next thing I knew the Newport Beach police arrived at the house on Bay Island where we were staying. It's a little island that you can't drive on to. You have to park your car on the peninsula, and walk across a bridge.

And there I was, talking to a Newport police sergeant, who said, 'We have a Coast Guard launch that will be moored right off shore. A helicopter will be above your house, and our men will surround the island and secure everything.' I thought, now of all times. I could just see the pictures of Haldeman in a besieged fortress, a man so terrible someone wanted to kill him.

I pleaded with the sergeant. I didn't want protection. He finally agreed to have the Coast Guard launch and helicopter standby someplace else and, instead of a troop of policemen, he would station two plainclothesmen, one at the bridge, the other by our house.

All of this time, telephone calls went back and forth between Ehrlichman, myself, and others of the President's men. What was happening in the White House? Was any thought being given to the pardons?

The hour was too late – and the President too broken. On August 8 Richard Nixon announced he would resign. A month later, on September 8, he was pardoned for all crimes arising out of Watergate. Twenty of the President's men who had thought they were acting in his behalf were convicted.

But there are all kinds of convictions and all kinds of prisons and I suspect the lonely man in San Clemente is in the worst one of all.

CONCLUSION

Where does all this leave us? What is our conclusion? First, we must conclude that we do not yet know the whole Watergate story, and recognise that we may never know it. Many mysteries remain. Contrary to the almost unanimous public opinion at this time, the case has not been settled; it is not as simple as we might wish; and it may never be fully solved.

But at the risk of enormous oversimplification of a vastly complex case, we can try to draw some general conclusions from what we do know:

1. The Watergate break-in itself came about as a result of President Nixon telling Charles Colson to get some information regarding Larry O'Brien; of Colson assigning the job to Howard Hunt; of Hunt using Gordon Liddy and the C.R.P. capability and resources to repeat the pattern of their earlier Ellsberg break-in.

2. The break-in effort collapsed because the Democratic Party was ready for it. They knew it was going to happen, and let it. And the C.I.A. monitored the burglars throughout. Finally, the break-in was probably deliberately sabotaged.

3. The subsequent cover-up came about as a result of a variety of motives and concerns in the minds of a number of people.

President Nixon feared a Colson role in the break-in and suspected that John Mitchell might also be involved. He wanted to protect them. In addition, he feared the revelation of what he called 'other things,' including both national security matters and Colson political projects.

As Chief-of-Staff I followed the general path of events with no personal motivation other than the presumed wish of the President and the protection of the re-election campaign.

Ehrlichman had a special concern of his own because of the Ellsberg break-in.

Dean, anxious to promote his own career by proving he could handle anything, took advantage of this golden opportunity; although he also may have had some concern regarding his pre-knowledge of Liddy's intelligence plans.

Colson tried to withdraw completely from the whole cover-up chain (a very unusual posture for him to take in a matter of this kind), but became involved anyway, in the message of clemency for Hunt.

Magruder tried to save first himself, and then the campaign. He knew exactly what the real dangers were right from the start.

Mitchell remained very much in the background after the early days, and was apparently as much, or more worried about the 'other things' as he was about Watergate.

The C.I.A.'s real role and motivations remain a mystery – but they were there.

The many others involved did what they were told – or what they thought was expected of them.

4. The cover-up collapsed because it was doomed from the start. Morally and legally it was the wrong thing to do – so it should have failed. Tactically, too many people knew too much. Too many foolish risks were taken. Too little judgement was used at every stage to evaluate the potential risk vs. the gains. And when the crunch came, too many people decided to save their own skins at whatever cost to the President or anyone else. Especially John Dean.

And all the while, the four major power blocs were waiting in the wings to take the fullest advantage of the sword that was being so surprisingly handed to them. The press, the bureaucracy, the Congress, and the intelligence community, all had their own reasons for seeing that the sword was wielded most effectively.

Thus, there were many players in the Watergate drama –

and behind them all lurks the ever-present shadow of the President of the United States.

At least at the beginning of each phase of the Watergate cover-up, all those involved thought they were acting on behalf of the President, and for his best interest. Yet none of them had any direct instructions from the President to do any of the things they did. And most of them were capable, intelligent, dedicated, law-abiding citizens believing they were serving their country.

And the ultimate irony is that the Watergate break-in stands as the only major political scandal in history in which not one of those who brought it about was personally benefited by it in any way – and no one other than those who brought it about was personally hurt by it in any way.

It is all too easy to conclude that the Watergate disaster is clear evidence of the failure of the Nixon White House staff system. Actually, it is just the opposite. It is the exception that proves the rule.

Had Watergate been handled through the usual White House staff system, and been managed by Nixon in his usual fashion, it would never have happened in the first place. And even if it had happened, it would have been handled in such a way as to avoid the disaster it eventually became.

The problem was not the White House staff system – which functioned so superbly through all of the other demanding events of the Nixon years – but the failure to handle this particular problem in the usual way. Why was this one dealt with differently? Partly because the D.N.C. Headquarters break-in was completely a political problem, coming under the responsibility of C.R.P. instead of the White House (the whole reason for setting up C.R.P. was to handle political operations outside of the White House).

This particular problem was also handled differently because either the President did not know, or did not choose to tell us, what it was really all about and what he wanted done about it.

One of the reasons for my lack of concern after the Watergate break-in was my complete confidence that President Nixon had always told me everything of any importance, and that I therefore always had all the information I needed to assess the relative dangers at any time. But if my theory of the break-in is correct, then it is obvious to me now that this confidence was, at least, in this case, misplaced.

Colson and Nixon had been operating in an area to which I paid little attention, but one which I should have realised could potentially cause a problem. John Ehrlichman warned me several times about Colson's dangers; and I had had to jump on Colson a few times myself.

Yet I preferred running the risk of Colson's getting out of control to losing his value to me in filling Nixon's need for lengthy discussion and planning in many political areas which I would have had to handle if Colson hadn't been there. Even though I knew he was a potentially troublesome person and represented a real possibility for damage, I let him go ahead rather than doing something about it. I felt that his benefits outweighed his risks – and that I could keep a close enough rein on the risks to avoid any major disasters.

So perhaps arrogantly, I went on my way, confident that Watergate was a 'third-rate burglary' fouled up by some of the people at C.R.P. and that any political attempt to tie it to the White House would fail.

I dealt with what came before me, leaving the rest to others, and not really worrying about the whole thing. This was admittedly an unusual approach for me to take, but I had plenty of other things to worry about, and there were many other staffers such as Dean who could handle Watergate. At least that's what I believed then, to the extent that I thought about it at all.

This was perhaps Nixon's most important mistake. For if he had concluded that the break-in resulted from Colson's implementation of a presidential desire to link Larry O'Brien to Howard Hughes, it must have been obvious to him that the bulkheads we had assumed would contain the break-in to C.R.P. would never hold.

A plan can be developed to handle almost any problem (and we had coped with many) as long as that problem is known. Many people have wondered why Watergate was not handled better. It's a fair question. The answer may be that we did not know what we were dealing with until it was too late. We thought we knew at the time, but a key part of the puzzle was withheld from us. Most of us would have been willing to sacrifice ourselves, if necessary, to save the Presidency that we believed in. But we couldn't even do that because we didn't know the real situation. And because we didn't know, many of us weren't even concerned at first – especially as the President gave us no hint.

This claim of lack of concern throughout the White House seems to be hard for most people to swallow. They just can't believe that virtually all of our time and energies weren't consumed with the unending Watergate battle. I can certainly understand this disbelief – especially now that Watergate has produced such earthshaking results and has been so thoroughly analysed and rehashed. But in the days when it was happening, it was only a very small blip on the overall radar screen of White House activity, interest, and concern.

For example, all the tapes that were thought to be useful in finding out what actually had gone on in the Watergate cover-up were subpoenaed. They covered a few meetings on a few days in June, one in September, a few in January. It was not until the end of February that there was any real White House concentration on Watergate and by then the cover-up was practically over.

I remember a stiflingly muggy Washington summer day in 1973, in the fifth floor attic room of the E.O.B. with its corrugated tin roof and almost unbearable heat. Even the little window air conditioner had given up and was just dripping water on the floor as the ice which jammed it melted in the heat. I had been locked in there for more than two hours and despite the urgency of my work on my files, which had been stacked there after being confiscated from my office and the offices of my staff, I was about to give up.

The ever-present Secret Service agent was obviously not enjoying his task any more than I was mine. But all he had to do was sit there and watch me, jotting down in his little book the identification of each set of papers I looked at in the files. He had to make sure that I didn't take any of them, or make any notes from them. Even the small television camera on the wall that reported any movement in the room to the command post in the basement seemed to be moving a little slower.

I finally finished sorting the huge stack of yellow sheets that were my notes of all my meetings with the President for the Watergate period – from June 1972 until my resignation in April 1973. I had pulled out every single page that had anything on it that might have any bearing on Watergate – usually just a line or two amid a heavily filled page of notes on all kinds of other topics.

Despite his clear lack of interest in the whole affair, I couldn't resist pointing out to the Secret Service agent the difference between the two piles of paper in front of me. The pile of pages that had any mention of Watergate on them was less than a half-inch high. The pile of all the other non-Watergate pages was over a foot high. Clear indication of the relative importance of Watergate when it was happening.

Looking back, with the advantage of hindsight and a lot of knowledge I didn't have at the time, I can see that my loyalty to President Nixon and my assumption that I knew all that I needed to know led me to some serious errors of judgement. This was compounded by the fact that I was not a lawyer.

I was blinded to the realisation that, in the cover-up – or containment as I considered it – crimes were being committed. What I thought then was a natural effort to avoid any unnecessary political damage from Watergate I now can see was an illegal programme of obstruction of justice.

My part in the early stages of this programme – the

diversion of the F.B.I. by the C.I.A., the authorisation of fund-raising for the defendants, the later use of part of my $350,000 fund by C.R.P. for the defendants – was wrong.

And my part in the later stages – the efforts by Nixon to deal with the problems of which he became increasingly aware starting in March 1973 – was also wrong.

I am deeply sorry for every act of mine that furthered this effort. I especially regret my failure to recognise what was really happening and to take whatever steps I could to stop it.

Tactically, as well as morally, there were many mistakes. They can be summed up in that we totally failed to get out ahead of the curve at any point. We were always one step behind, reacting instead of initiating, always backing and filling. For example, my proposal that I go on TV and present the facts regarding my involvement and then answer questions was a good idea. My error was in not pursuing it more diligently.

Given the total picture after the break-in, I have to conclude that the cover-up, in some form, was inevitable. It was not planned ahead as a great conspiracy – it just grew one step at a time as people, believing they were acting in the best interest of the President, took steps to meet each problem as it arose. My most profound personal remorse today comes from the realisation that my errors contributed to that growth.

What was the effect of Watergate?

This question probably has been more thoroughly answered, at least in quantity, than any question in recent history. But it is always discussed in the context of what happened as a result of Watergate. I think I have nothing to add in that direction. I do think it is worth a moment of exploration to look into what I feel is a more meaningful direction. What would have happened if there had been no Watergate?

Others may disagree but, if there had been no Watergate, I believe that:

Richard Nixon would have served two full terms as President of the United States. In his second term he would have brought to fruition the major initiatives launched in the first. With the overwhelming popular mandate he received in the 1972 election, the effective coalition of the New American Majority, the end of the trauma of Vietnam, and his reorganisation of the Executive Branch of the government, he would have been able to move ahead with far more success than in the first term, despite the continuing problem of an opposition Congress.

A few specifics. I believe that:

The Soviet détente and the opening to China would have been pursued vigorously and effectively with many positive results. The Middle East initiative would have been maintained and stable peace established in that area. The domestic economy would have been stabilised in a sound balance between full employment and control of inflation.

John Connally would have been appointed Vice-President after Spiro Agnew's resignation and would have been nominated by the Republican Party for President in 1976. He would have been elected by a strong majority – on a pledge to continue and expand upon the policies and programmes of President Nixon. Henry Kissinger would have never become Secretary of State, but would have continued his remarkable partnership with Nixon, and then departed from government when the Nixon Presidency ended.

The United States would have celebrated its Bicentennial with joy, enthusiasm, renewed patriotism and dedication, and most importantly, with a fully justified optimism for the future. A solid structure for world peace would have been established, along with a sound internal economy. President Nixon would have achieved his oft-stated objective of a full generation of peace in the world and prosperity without inflation at home.

Watergate was the immediate activating cause of President Nixon's downfall. But in a larger sense, the root cause was far more substantial than this 'third-rate burglary' and its aftermath. Watergate, properly handled, could probably have been survived. Instead, Nixon, as he has said, gave his enemies a sword which they plunged in and twisted, to bring about his collapse.

Just as he who lives by the sword must die by the sword, so he whose image or public perception is based on an inaccurate overbalancing of his good qualities must be brought down by the revelation of flows in that imbalanced portrayal.

Because his opposition was so fierce and effective and dedicated, or so he believed, and with good reason, President Nixon felt that we just had to be fiercer, more effective, and more dedicated. Because a far more than adequate job was being done consistently to bring out all of Nixon's deficiencies, real or imagined, our mission was to do an even better job of bringing out all his merits. As with any human being there were both deficiencies and merits to be found. And the merits far outweighed the flaws in actuality – but not in presentation. Or at least that's what we thought – and that's what motivated our efforts to correct the imbalance.

But inevitably, this effort became unbalanced itself. We pushed too hard and overplayed our hand. Part of this was due to our ineptitude compared to the skill of the opposition, and part was owed to our reaction to the constant prodding from our leader, and his unceasing dissatisfaction with the results.

By presenting Nixon, or attempting to, as 100 per cent pure and good, we were setting him up for a disastrous fall when it was demonstrated that he fell short of that absolute – as all humans must. Had he been more accurately portrayed as he really was, complete with flaws, there is no doubt in my mind that he would have succeeded mightily because his reality, the total balance of light and dark, was more than enough to place him in the topmost echelons of great American presidents. The problem was that there was no way to present an objective portrayal of Nixon as he really was. There was only the adversary process of the opposition portrayal of absolute bad and our portrayal of absolute good. Neither was on the mark. We were much closer to right, but the opposition had more resources than we did in getting their story across.

I am still in occasional communication with President Nixon. Our conversations now are a bit stilted – not the free give-and-take of the old days. And we disagree on some of the elements and interpretations of what happened at Watergate and why. But I know he feels very deeply distressed by the outcome of my years of service to him and its effect on my life. And I feel very deeply saddened by the spectacle of this potentially great leader sitting useless and alone in San Clemente. I continue to have the utmost respect for the President that Richard Nixon could have been, and usually was; and utmost sorrow for the tragedy that brought him to his present state, thereby depriving this nation and the world of the continuing leadership of the man I believe uniquely fitted the overwhelming demands of the times. I am confident that the perspective of history will greatly change the attitudes and views of those who evaluate the Nixon Presidency from the current continuing obsession with all that was bad – and there was some – to a real appreciation of all that was truly great and good – and there was an enormous amount.

In the frequently used words of the man with whom I worked so closely for so long. 'Let me make one thing perfectly clear.' I am today enormously proud of my service in the White House and very grateful to Richard Nixon for making it possible. I have paid a terrible price for that privilege, but I have had plenty of time to reflect on the question of whether it was worth it. There is absolutely no doubt in my mind today that if I were back at the starting point, faced with the decision of whether to join up, even knowing what the ultimate outcome would be, I would unhesitatingly do it.

Few men in all of history have had the privilege of being raised as high as I was; and few have had the tragedy of being brought as low. And even fewer have experienced both extremes – from the peak of the mountain top to the depth of the valley. It has been an enriching experience in all of its phases – each in its own unique way. I am eternally grateful for all of it and for what it has taught me.

GENERAL NON-FICTION

0352	Star	
301392	Linda Blandford **OIL SHEIKHS**	95p
396121	Anthony Cave Brown **BODYGUARD OF LIES (Large Format)**	£1.95*
301368	John Dean **BLIND AMBITION**	£1.00*
300124	Dr. F. Dodson **HOW TO PARENT**	75p*
301457	**THE FAMILY DICTIONARY OF SYMPTOMS**	95p*
398914	J. Paul Getty **HOW TO BE RICH**	60p*
397829	**HOW TO BE A SUCCESSFUL EXECUTIVE**	60p*
398566	Harry Lorayne & Jerry Lucas **THE MEMORY BOOK**	60p*
39692X	Henry Miller **THE WORLD OF SEX**	60p
395311	Neville Randall & Gary Keane **FOCUS ON FACT:** **THE WORLD OF INVENTION (illus)**	75p
39532X	**THE STORY OF SPORT (illus)**	75p
39529X	**THE PSYCHIC WORLD (illus)**	75p
395303	**THE STORY OF CHRISTMAS (illus)**	75p
395338	**UNSOLVED MYSTERIES (illus)**	75p
397640	David Reuben **HOW TO GET MORE OUT OF SEX**	85p*
398779	Fiona Richmond **FIONA**	50p
396040	Idries Shah **THE SUFIS (Large Format)**	£1.95
395478	Michael Smith **THE DUCHESS OF DUKE STREET ENTERTAINS**	£1.50♦

† For sale in Britain and Ireland only.
* Not for sale in Canada.
♦ Film & T.V. tie-ins.

GENERAL NON-FICTION

0426 Universal/Tandem

	Thomas B. Costain **THE PAGEANT OF ENGLAND:**	
123190	**1135-1216: THE CONQUERING FAMILY**	£1.50
123271	**1216-1272: THE MAGNIFICENT CENTURY**	£1.50
123352	**1272-1377: THE THREE EDWARDS**	£1.50
123433	**1377-1485: THE LAST PLANTAGENETS**	£1.50
184033	Ben Davidson **THE OFFICIAL FONZIE SCRAPBOOK**	70p* ♦
08571X	Hyam Maccoby **REVOLUTION IN JUDAEA**	75p
168623	Xaviera Hollander **THE HAPPY HOOKER**	80p*
163443	**LETTERS TO THE HAPPY HOOKER**	80p*
168038	**XAVIERA GOES WILD**	80p*
166787	**XAVIERA ON THE BEST PART OF A MAN**	80p*
134265	**XAVIERA!**	80p*
17996X	Xaviera Hollander & Marilyn Chambers **XAVIERA MEETS MARILYN CHAMBERS**	80p*
124901	Fridtjof Nansen **FARTHEST NORTH**	£1.00
175158	Sakuzawa Nyoiti **MACROBIOTICS**	50p*
181638	Suze Randall **SUZE**	75p*
180755	Grant Tracy Saxon **THE HAPPY HUSTLER**	70p
134931	La Leche League **THE WOMANLY ART OF BREASTFEEDING**	60p
141970	Erna Wright **THE NEW CHILDBIRTH**	75p
067282	**THE NEW CHILDHOOD**	75p
054938	**PERIODS WITHOUT PAIN**	60p

0426 Hanau Distribution

087232	David Lewis **SEXPIONAGE**	70p
087151	**THE SECRET LIFE OF ADOLPH HITLER**	75p
086864	Linda Lovelace **INSIDE LINDA LOVELACE**	60p
086945	**THE INTIMATE DIARY OF LINDA LOVELACE**	60p
086007	Gerard I. Nierenberg & Henry H. Calero **HOW TO READ A PERSON LIKE A BOOK**	95p

†For sale in Britain and Ireland only.
*Not for sale in Canada.
♦ Film & T.V. tie-ins.

Wyndham Books are obtainable from many booksellers and newsagents. If you have any difficulty please send purchase price plus postage on the scale below to:

Wyndham Cash Sales:
P O Box 11,
Falmouth,
Cornwall.

or

Star Book Service:
G P O Box 29,
Douglas,
Isle of Man,
British Isles.

While every effort is made to keep prices low, it is sometimes necessary to increase prices at short notice. Wyndham Books reserve the right to show new retail prices on covers which may differ from those advertised in the text or elsewhere.

Postage and Packing Rate

UK

22p for the first book plus 10p per copy for each additional book ordered to a maximum charge of 82p.

BFPO and Eire

22p for the first book, plus 10p per copy for the next 6 books and thereafter 4p per book.

Overseas

30p for the first book and 10p per copy for each additional book.

These charges are subject to Post Office charge fluctuations.